A Hunt
FOR
Justice

For Gail Fox

all the best,

Lucinda D Schroeder

November 18, 2009

Montrose, Co

A Hunt
FOR
Justice

The True Story of a Woman Undercover Wildlife Agent

Lucinda Delaney Schroeder

THE LYONS PRESS
Guilford, Connecticut
An imprint of The Globe Pequot Press

The Lyons Press is an imprint of The Globe Pequot Press.

10 9 8 7 6 5 4

Printed in the United States of America

Library of Congress Cataloging-in-Publication Data

Schroeder, Lucinda Delaney.
    A hunt for justice : the true story of a woman undercover wildlife agent / Lucinda Delaney Schroeder.
       p. cm.
    ISBN 13 978-1-59228-882-3
    ISBN 10 1-59228-882-0
    1. Schroeder, Lucinda Delaney. 2. Wildlife crime investigation—Alaska—Case studies. 3. Wildlife crimes—Alaska. 4. Undercover wildlife agents—United States—Biography. I. Title.
    HV8079.W58S34 2006
    364.1'8—dc22

                                                                                        2005028609

To Lonnie and Megan, with love

Contents

*

Preface

AS A FEDERAL WILDLIFE LAW ENFORCEMENT OFFICER, I spent my career enforcing the hunting laws of the United States and of foreign countries. In doing so, I championed ethical and legal hunting. Nothing in this book should be construed as being anti-hunting. My job was to stop illegal hunting and poaching that diminished legal hunting opportunities. I fully acknowledge and respect the tremendous contribution that hunters have made to wildlife conservation worldwide.

Lucinda Delaney Schroeder
Albuquerque, New Mexico
October 2005

Acknowledgments

FIRST I WISH TO THANK MY HUSBAND, LONNIE, for supporting me throughout my career with the United States Fish and Wildlife Service, and for being such a terrific husband and father. Also, thanks to him for going through this manuscript down to the most common denominator: the word.

Thanks to my daughter, Megan, for being the courageous and caring young woman that she is, and for being a role model to me in so many ways. I'm so proud of her I could burst.

Operation Brooks Range would not have been successful had it not been for the professionalism of Special Agent Tim Eicher, to whom I add my thanks and admiration for his tireless contribution to preserving our nation's natural resources. Thanks also to AUSA Steven Cooper for his work on Operation Brooks Range and for his undying support of the U.S. Fish and Wildlife Service's law enforcement operations in Alaska.

Thanks from the bottom of my heart to Willie J. Parker, who believed in me from the beginning and whose support I drew upon when times were rough. Also, thanks to Larry Hood and Bill Zimmerman, who nominated me for the "Ten Top Employees" recognition I received in 1993. I'll never forget that.

There were many who believed that my story was worth writing and helped me by reading chapters and providing feedback. Harriet and Jeanne from Albuquerque stayed with me for four years poring over every word, as only good writers do. My enduring thanks to them both.

Thanks to Monica Faulkner in California who gave me dozens of helpful suggestions that got me off to a roaring start.

Overwhelming thanks to Diane O'Connell with Words into Print in New York, who made my book proposal shine and led me to my wonderful literary agent, Linda Konner.

Total thanks to retired special agents Wally Soroka, Walt Kocal, and Adam O'Hara for the important details they added to this work, and for their years of service to wildlife law enforcement.

Very special thanks to Bill True (bill@debillpictures.com) in Minneapolis who read this manuscript several times and gave it the screenwriter's magic touch that made scenes come alive.

More special thanks to Ivar Husby, Assistant Chief of the Norwegian national police department, who read chapters as he winged his way across the Atlantic to do undercover work in the U.S. His comments were the most unique.

Millions of thanks to Linda Konner, Linda Konner Literary Agency in New York, for her endless patience and professionalism in the way she handled my book and, of course, me. I'll never let her go.

Many, many thanks to Lisa Purcell and Jennifer Taber, my editors at The Lyons Press, who gave their magic touch to the manuscript and made it shine.

I wish all writers could be as blessed as I have been with the wonderful community of friends and associates who supported me and added to this work. Most of all, *A Hunt for Justice*, and stories like it, would not be possible if it weren't for the dedicated special agents, wildlife inspectors, intelligence analysts, and wildlife forensic laboratory scientists of the U.S. Fish and Wildlife Service I've worked with for decades. Together we grew and developed our skills to do good things for the natural world we loved and revered. We considered our job a privilege, and it's my hope that readers will see that spirit as the heart of this story.

Author's Note

The names of all defendants and the informant in Operation Brooks Range have been changed to protect their privacy. Also changed is the name of the chief of law enforcement for the Alaska Department of Fish and Wildlife, and the names of the U.S. Fish and Wildlife Service's special agents in charge for Alaska and Denver, Colorado. The names of the Madrid booking agent and his company have been changed along with the name of the U.S. Embassy Regional Security Officer in Madrid, Spain, and the colonel in the Spanish Guardia Civil.

The name of "The Bear's Den" is fictitious and its location has been changed to protect the identity of the true proprietorship.

The names of my family, the U.S. Fish and Wildlife chief of law enforcement and special agents, the U.S. Embassy employee in Madrid, Spain, the Spanish investigators in Barcelona, Spain, and the Assistant United States Attorney in Fairbanks, Alaska, are real.

It is not the critic who counts: not the man who points out how the strong man stumbles or where the doer of deeds could have done better. The credit belongs to the man who is actually in the arena, whose face is marred by dust and sweat and blood, who strives valiantly, who errs and comes up short again and again, because there is no effort without error or shortcoming, but who knows the great enthusiasms, the great devotions, who spends himself for a worthy cause; who, at the best, knows, in the end, the triumph of high achievement, and who, at the worst, if he fails, at least he fails while daring greatly, so that his place shall never be with those cold and timid souls who knew neither victory nor defeat.

—Theodore Roosevelt

BOOK I

CHAPTER 1

The Bear's Den

"TURN HERE!" I blurted out as Roy cranked the steering wheel of his red Corvette into a gravel parking lot. The car's headlights raked across a shabby wooden sign:

THE BEAR'S DEN—COME IN
GRIZZLY BEAR INSIDE!

Roy Martin squeezed the car into the lot, which was crammed with battered pickup trucks plastered with weathered buck deer decals. As we stepped out into the heat of a late-June evening in Minnesota's north lake country, the mosquitoes attacked from the surrounding tall pines. Batting them away, we hurried across the parking lot to a well-known hunter's hangout that clung to the banks of the St. Croix River marking the border between Minnesota and Wisconsin. The stars were especially bright, for the closest city lights were in Minneapolis, one hundred miles south.

A dim light over the door revealed splintered wood siding that cried out for nails and a new paint job.

"Nice joint," I muttered.

Roy held open the warped wooden door and smirked, "It's even better inside."

A thick haze of cigarette smoke assaulted my eyes as they adjusted to the dim, beer-scented room illuminated only by Bud Lite and Point Beer signs that glowed like beacons in a fog. Cautiously, I slipped through, pausing for a moment at a mounted grizzly bear that stood on three legs with one paw and pearl-dagger claws stretched in an attack stance. I sunk my hand into its shaggy coat and an image of it fishing in freshwater streams, grazing on sedge grass, and digging for tender roots in the vast open wilderness flashed across my mind. The coat of this mighty animal, which once glittered in the warm sun, was now cloaked in dust. His eyes were blind and the paint on his plastic tongue was chipped. I glanced at the tarnished brass plate at his feet that read, "Shot by Leroy R. James, Brooks Range, Alaska, 1990."

Dozens of mounted ducks, geese, deer, and elk heads lined the walls, along with more than a hundred sets of antlers. Across the bar, six men dressed in camouflaged T-shirts and ball caps were perched on bar stools, barely moving, making me wonder how much life they had left in them. Eventually, two of them turned slightly to eyeball me, the only woman in the place.

Roy, who was built like a small bear himself, had bulky shoulders mounted over an ample stomach. His hair was thick and brown and he had a curly dark beard. As if in his natural environment, he slid onto a bar stool and motioned me to sit next to him. After getting seated, I pulled a Swisher Sweet cigarillo from my purse, slowly peeled off its cellophane wrapper, and lit up.

Roy leaned toward me and whispered, "I didn't know you smoked."

"I do tonight. See any of your old buddies?"

"Naw. But I haven't been in here for a couple of years."

I watched the bartender, a half-bald, fortyish man with piercing dark eyes and arching eyebrows. He was a big boy, six feet and roughly 250 pounds. His shirt stretched over a beer belly that even his imposing size couldn't completely accommodate. His hands were rough and chapped, maybe from weather, or maybe from washing hundreds of bar glasses in steaming water.

"That's Moose James," Roy whispered. "He owns the place."

Moose James kept up with several conversations as he slid glasses from the beer tap to the bar, made change, and wiped the already spotless deep-purple counter. His motions were smooth, efficient, and almost robotic.

Finally, he made eye contact with Roy. With genuine surprise he called out, "Hey, Roy, the van-man! Long time no see!"

"Hiya, Moose!" Roy stood up and stretched his arm across the bar for a handshake.

Moose enveloped his hand. "So, how's the van business in Chicago?"

"Great. Just great." Roy turned to me. "This is my girlfriend, Jayne. Jayne, this is my old buddy Moose James. I told ya about him."

I blew a thin stream of smoke and managed a smile.

Moose cracked a wide grin. "No shit! I've never seen you with a real girl. So, what'll it be? The usual?"

"Sure."

"What about you, Jayne?"

Wanting to fit in, I said, "The same as him."

A moment later, Moose set two glasses in front of us filled with Korbel and Coke. I took a cautious sip. Strong, but I had to admit it had a soothing taste.

"Say, Roy," asked Moose, "you still got that black bear you and me hunted the last time you were up here?"

"Sure do. That was a damn good hunt. I still got that bear rug on my living room floor—darn thing trips me up every time I come home drunk."

Moose laughed as if he well understood Roy's hardship.

While Roy and Moose were catching up on old times, I surveyed the rest of the bar. Standard equipment—a worn pool table with a metal lampshade. A single lightbulb dangling above it and a jukebox in the corner stocked with country-western music. What was different about this place was that it was buried in mounted birds, fish, animal heads, and antlers. A black bear displayed in a glass case took up one corner. A fox posed in a frozen crawl on a piece of driftwood, while deer, elk, and moose heads peered down on the bar patrons. Ducks, geese, and ptarmigan were stopped in their tracks along the tops of shelves.

A separate wall featured six, thirty-pound muskies, a prized sport fish in the northern lakes. Daredevil lures dangled from their gaping mouths. Randomly pasted on the walls were numerous photographs featuring hunters with their deer and bear kills from a dozen hunting seasons. As odd as it seemed, I wanted my picture on the wall, too.

The Bear's Den was definitely a hunter's hangout where hunting and fishing were what mattered most and big egos were as plentiful as the mounts on the walls—and its heart and soul was Moose James. Soon I was listening to him entertain his customers with tales of his hunts, which had undoubtedly helped fill the bar. The eighty square feet behind the bar was his stage and we were his audience. He didn't hold back as he expounded on how he sweat buckets in Arizona and froze his ass off in Alaska, and how he nearly starved to death in a desperate attempt to get another trophy animal. Moose carried his bar patrons with him as he climbed impossible mountains, endured uncompromising weather, almost drowned in a raging river, and trudged farther on foot than any other man. He dazzled his fans with spellbinding tales of his fortitude and his brawn, and his description of a majestic bighorn sheep, which he said was the second biggest he had ever shot—bigger than most Boone and Crockett records. Meanwhile, his loyal followers swayed to his spell and craved more.

Moose's magnetic charm as a storyteller had made him the undisputed local hunting icon. And the sight of him, in all his commonness, a tavernkeeper with a Johnny Walker label on his shirt, made his miraculous leap into the world of grit and guts even more appealing.

When Moose was done, a skinny, whiskered guy who took the stool next to mine was soon hunched over a beer like a hawk defending a kill. He was probably only in his late thirties, but he had a ragged look, like he'd spent most of his life in bad weather. His T-shirt featured a picture of a buck with crosshairs strategically placed for a heart-lung shot. Even though it was only early June, I heard him say something about the upcoming deer season in October and decided to strike up a conversation.

"Say, where's the best place to hunt the big Burnette County bucks?"

He seemed surprised that I would even speak to him. "Uh, I mostly hunt north along the St. Croix River."

"Really? Whereabouts?"

"The same place where I got me a near-Wisconsin state record last year." His sly smile revealed yellow teeth that seemed too big for his mouth.

"No kidding? What were you shootin'?"

"I got me a .300 Savage."

"Got a scope on it?" I asked, taking a drag on my dainty cigar. I followed his glance downward, and tugged my denim shorts an inch farther down my thigh.

"You bet."

"What kind of ammo did you use?"

"Hey, I ain't ever heard a woman talk guns so much. You hunt?"

"Sure do."

"Wow, a pretty lady hunter."

"Don't call her a lady," grunted Roy. "She ain't used to it."

I jabbed him in the gut with my elbow. "Knock it off, chum, or you'll be next in my scope."

Yellow-teeth, as I'd quickly named him, howled at my threat.

Moose brought Roy a second Korbel and Coke and then leaned on the counter and cocked his head at me. "Did I hear you say that you hunt?"

"Last year I shot an antelope in Wyoming . . ."

"With thirteen-inch horns," interrupted Roy, beaming proudly.

Yellow-teeth stared at me wide-eyed. "By yourself?"

"Of course by myself." I tossed my hair back and took another drag. "I've also hunted deer and elk, but I'm especially deadly on ducks. Last year I shot over twenty ducks by sound alone."

"What the hell? Couldn't you see 'em?"

"No, it was just after sunset."

"Would you listen to that," howled Yellow-teeth.

Meanwhile Moose was silent as he studied me. I had just made a blatant admission of poaching. Hunting hours ended at sundown.

"No kiddin'," said Moose. "Where were you?"

"Texas. Just north of Corpus."

Moose rubbed his rag on a nonexistent spot on the gleaming bar. "I've heard there's some fantastic duck huntin' in Texas. Never been there though."

I dug into my purse and handed Moose a picture of me wearing hip waders, posed on a boat while hanging onto an over-limit of ducks as indisputable proof of my hunt. Moose studied the picture and smiled with approval.

"Who's the guy in the picture?" he asked.

"My guide. He did a fantastic job."

Yellow-teeth jabbed my arm. "Moose here is a huntin' guide himself, ya know."

"What do you guide?" I asked, tapping my ashes.

Moose broke out in a grin as wide as his face. "Sheep, moose, bear, caribou. Wolves too, if they get in the way."

"You can't be guiding for animals like that around here."

"Nope. Alaska. I work for the best outfitter up there. His name is Bob Bowman."

"Hey, I'm impressed. You do much huntin' yourself?"

"Moose only hunts when he's breathin'," snickered Yellow-teeth. "He's killed most all of these critters here."

"Includin' the big grizzly you were admiring," Roy added.

"Actually my dad shot that bear," corrected Moose. "But I guided him."

"What's your favorite critter to hunt?" I asked.

Moose set one foot on a beer carton and expanded his chest. "I'm mostly a sheep hunter myself. It's the most fantastic huntin' on earth. I've killed all four subspecies in North America, including the Dall sheep in Alaska."

The fact that Moose James was a sheep hunter defined him in a particular way. Sheep hunting is to hunters as the Indianapolis 500 is to race car drivers—the top of their sport. Physically demanding, sometimes dangerous and thrilling, sheep hunters crawl over rocks, along edges of cliffs, and up mountains to outwit an animal that can sense danger from more than a mile away. Most sheep hunters hold a special appreciation for sheep and their genetic predisposition to survive in the harshest environments. I suspected that Moose was of a different breed and liked to kill sheep purely for the bragging rights.

"You know what?" Moose said. "You and Roy should come up to Alaska and hunt with Bowman and me."

"Hey, we'll be there." Roy pushed his empty glass toward Moose. "Just as soon as Jayne here buys me a plane ticket and a bear license."

Moose didn't budge. "Jayne, you oughta hunt Dall sheep in Alaska. It's the most fantastic experience you'll ever have. Guaranteed."

"I'd love to get a Dall," I said. "But I've heard that Dall hunting can be very dangerous. I'm not interested in dying just yet."

"It's tough, all right, but when you hunt with Bob Bowman, it's guaranteed. You hunt a moose, you get a moose. You hunt a bear, you get a bear. And if you want a Dall sheep, I'll make sure you get an easy one." He gave me a conspiratorial wink and added, "If you know what I mean . . ."

I suspected that he meant there would be some cheating going on that would ensure an easy kill. Even though that was the kind of action I was looking for, I wasn't ready to fork over a pile of money to someone I'd just met.

Then Moose added, "How 'bout you, Roy? You wanna hunt sheep, too?"

"Naw. I want a bear. And the biggest one up there. Does Bowman have any openings left for this season?"

"No way. The camp's been booked for months. Next season's open though. Bob's pretty picky about his clients, but I think I can get you two in."

"Wait a minute," I blurted out. "Who says we're even going to Alaska? Roy's got this crazy idea I'm going to pay for *his* hunting."

"Well, is that true?" asked Moose.

"Damn true," Roy shot back. "Her ex was a rich son of a bitch, and he left her with a pile of dough."

"Wait a minute . . ." I stammered.

"Yeah," continued Roy. "And he left her for some big-chested bimbo who can't even shoot."

Yellow-teeth and Moose's guffaws drew the attention of the other patrons. I glared at Roy as if to say *shut your damn mouth.*

"Which is why we're goin' to Alaska." Roy put his arm around me and squeezed. "Ain't that right, sweet Jaynie?" Roy nudged his glass forward again and Moose brought him another drink. Then he said, "Come on, buddy, talk her into it. I'm countin' on you."

"Hang on a minute," said Moose as he disappeared into a back room. He came out with a videotape and held it out to me. "This is Bob guiding hunters in Alaska. Bear, moose, sheep . . . it's incredible. After you see it you'll be beggin' to go up there. Guaranteed."

"Thanks, but . . ."

He shoved the video at me. "Take it. And here's this year's brochure, too. It's got all Bob's prices in it."

"Well, thanks." I set the video aside, scanned the fancy four-page, colored brochure featuring hunters posing with their trophy animals. Then I glanced at the price list. A moose hunt cost six thousand dollars, a sheep seven thousand, and a grizzly bear seven thousand. Combination hunts were as much as eighteen thousand dollars.

"Wow! Pretty hefty prices," I said sliding the brochure and videotape into my oversized black leather purse.

"Not when you consider that everything's guaranteed," Moose replied.

It was midnight when the bar crowd began thinning out. Most of the drinkers had only a few hours to get home and to sleep before reporting to their logging or road-crew jobs by dawn.

"Hey, Roy," I said nudging him. "We should get going."

He nodded, downing the last of his drink.

"Let me know if you want me to save you a spot next season," said Moose.

"I'll give ya a call in a week or two to firm things up," said Roy as he teetered off his stool.

"You'll have a great time," Moose said one last time. "Guaranteed."

Outside, the fresh air, though still muggy and warm, felt like salvation. Roy headed for the driver's side, but I stopped him. "Hey," I said. "You know you shouldn't be driving."

He sighed and tossed me the keys. I pulled out of the parking lot and turned onto Highway 48, a narrow two-lane road that meandered around the hundreds of pristine lakes that were home to loons and had bountiful crops of the wild rice that make the Minnesota North Woods famous.

After settling into the feel of the road, I pulled a tiny cassette tape recorder from out of my bra, and turned if off. "Okay, I got it all." I shot Roy a glance. "How do you think it went?"

"Ha! It was as easy as water off a duck's back. They all fell for us."

"Except you didn't follow our plan—I could have killed you in there."

"You need to loosen up and go with the flow," chuckled Roy.

Roy and I weren't really from Chicago, nor did we own a van business there. That was a cover story we used to conceal our identities. I'm really Lucinda Schroeder, a special agent with the United States Fish and Wildlife Service, and Roy Martin was Roy Hanson, a small-time bear poacher turned paid informant. Our visit to The Bear's Den was the first step in Operation Brooks Range, a major federal investigation into the poaching of wildlife in Alaska.

Roy and I rode for a few minutes in silence before I revealed what was really on my mind.

"Listen. The plan was for you to introduce me to Moose James and let me ask questions, not book hunts right off the bat. You never act anxious to hunt with a crook."

"You said you wanted to go huntin' with Bowman," grunted Roy.

"No I didn't! I said I wanted to get more information about Bowman."

"Jeez, you feds are so damned anal. How you gonna know if he's a violator unless you hunt with him? You're sure not gonna find out nothin' sittin' on your ass in the Dairy State. You should be happy that Moose is practically begging to take us huntin' with Bowman."

"What do you mean us? You were just supposed to get me an introduction and I'll take care of the rest."

Roy shrugged. "Go ahead. But, I'm your best cover. Moose knows I ain't no game warden."

Roy was right. When he wasn't working as a large-equipment operator he did contract undercover work for wildlife conservation agencies as part of his sentence for bear poaching. Roy and Moose had hunted bear together with several locals, and had racked up some minor wildlife violations. The local wardens didn't cite anyone in order to keep Roy's cover intact because they felt that Moose would commit larger violations in the future that would earn him some jail time. At this point Moose was not suspicious of Roy, which made him a valuable informant, but I could tell he was going to be difficult to control.

"And what about that ridiculous story you told about my being dumped by an ex-husband for a bimbo? Now I've got to build my entire cover story around being a divorcée. I can't believe you did that."

Roy laughed. "You needed a better cover, so I made one up for you. You oughta be grateful."

"I have a great cover story, or *had* one."

"Look, everything went great. No one was the least bit suspicious and you snared old Moose like a salmon on a spring run. Which is good, because I want to go to Alaska and shoot the biggest grizzly I can fit in the crosshairs of my scope."

"Don't count on it. Tomorrow I have to report to the case agent in Alaska that you told Moose James that we're ready to go hunting. That wasn't part of the plan. And another thing: you really pounded down the drinks tonight. Do you always drink that much?"

"Only when I'm working."

Roy's glib attitude about drinking bothered me right away. Excessive drinking on an undercover assignment could come back to bite like a Doberman with a grudge. In court I'd seen more than one defense attorney successfully challenge a prosecution witness's memory because the witness had admitted to heavy drinking.

I drove Roy to his rented farmhouse on the outskirts of Stillwater, Minnesota. The rickety house was shedding white paint like snowflakes, but seemed to suit Roy after his nasty divorce. I slid into my Ford Explorer and started it up. Just before leaving I rolled down the window and told Roy that I'd call him in a couple of days, after I'd spoken with the Alaska case agent.

"Yeah, keep me posted," he said. "And let me know when I can start packing."

_____

CHAPTER 2

A Road Less Traveled

AS I SETTLED IN BEHIND THE WHEEL and headed east on I-94 for the four-hour trip to Madison, I fingered the tape recorder out of my black leather bag where I had a Sig Sauer 9mm handgun concealed in the false bottom. I put the tape in the player and listened to the recording I had made inside The Bear's Den. I grinned as I listened to myself brag about what a great hunter I was. The truth was I hunted illegal hunters. That was my job: I'd been on few legal hunts. Outlaw hunters had taught me to stalk, shoot, and field dress deer, antelope, elk, and birds, never knowing that I was only there to catch them violating the law. The picture I'd shown Moose was from one of my old cases. The duck guide in the picture was now sitting in jail. Over the years I had put my share of poachers behind bars.

Even though I had been a special agent for the U.S. Fish and Wildlife Service for eighteen years, in 1991 there were still only nine women agents out of 210 total agents in the agency, and there were still plenty of male agents who thought women were incapable of performing wildlife law enforcement work.

In 1974, I was the third woman agent hired by the U.S. Fish and Wildlife Service, and the first woman to tackle the demands of field work. The other two females were assigned to ports in New York and Hawaii, where they checked cargo and baggage for smuggled endangered species.

I have a degree in criminology, a major that appealed to my passion for delving into mysteries and the criminal mind. I yearned for a life of adventure and as far as I was concerned, the only road I wanted to be on was the one less traveled.

Admittedly, I didn't look like a law enforcement agent. A blue-eyed blond, I stood five feet, three inches tall and weighed 125 pounds. With an affinity for stylish clothes and fingernail polish, I may not have looked like I could catch a fly, much less a law violator. Typically I was fun-loving and compassionate, but when it came to protecting wildlife I dealt with the violators like a pit bull. My inner strength came from my upbringing. My father was a career Air Force officer and my family moved every three years, to places like the Philippines, Spain, and Washington, D.C. To make the best of our situation my mother's mantra was, "bloom where you're planted," and thanks to her, I quickly learned to adapt to my constantly changing world. Flexibility plus perseverance were important keys to my growing up, and they became the same traits that would later see me through undercover work and many difficult cases.

My first itch to solve a case came in June of 1964. I was just twelve years old, living in Spain, when my father took my family on a camping trip high in the French Pyrenees Mountains.

One evening, my father and I followed a path to one end of the campground to a small food store where we purchased a loaf of French bread. I walked smartly behind my father listening to the German, Spanish, and even Swedish that peppered the air. Then, quite unexpectedly, words of American English poked through. My colonel father veered off the path and headed straight toward it. He led the way around tents, cooking fires, and Peugeots until we came to a Ford sedan where we met an American family of four. A U.S. Army captain stationed in Germany introduced us to his perky blond wife and their five-year-old son. The boy's grandmother was sitting in a camp chair wearing a pouty and mean look on her face.

My father and the captain talked about their command posts while the captain's wife asked if I missed my American school, Friday-night football games, and cherry Cokes. I admitted that I did. The grandmother groused that Europe was no place to raise American children.

A few minutes later we said good-bye to our fellow Americans and tramped back to our campsite, marked by our 1957 Pontiac station wagon and a blue Coleman tent. My Alabama-born mother sat in a lawn chair sipping French wine. She had set our camp table with a red-and-white plastic tablecloth and a paper cup full of honeysuckle. My father always said that the highest hair on her head wouldn't make her five feet tall and that her Deep South accent always made him crave black-eyed peas.

After the sun went down the air turned cold, and my father announced that it was time to head for the beds. With only flashlights, we stumbled into our tent, and then into our sleeping bags. The chilly air knocked me out within minutes.

The next morning I woke up to the sound of the American captain's voice outside.

"Colonel," he whispered, "I hate to bother you at this hour of the morning."

"No problem," said my father, "What's up?"

"It's my mother-in-law."

"Is she sick?" asked my father.

"No, she's dead."

My mind snapped alive while I pondered how such a thing could have happened. I had heard my dad talk about the French dissidents. Maybe they killed her. Or, maybe she drank a bottled Coke with a cockroach in it. Then, I started to reason like my mother. It was just pure meanness that killed that woman. She was probably so mean Satan wouldn't take her.

"How the hell did she die?" asked my father.

"I don't have any idea, sir. She was fine last night. What should I do?"

"France is a hell of place for an American to get caught with a dead body. They don't like us here," my father said.

I knew what my father was talking about. I had seen "Yankee go home!" signs painted everywhere.

"But, sir, don't you think I should contact the French authorities?" asked the captain.

"The hell with the French. You'll be in more trouble if you do. If you turn over the body, you'll never get it back, and worse, they might arrest you for murder."

"Colonel, I didn't do anything to her. She just died. We found her this morning. My little boy thinks she's still sleeping and my wife is a wreck."

Then I heard my father's voice turn secretive. "Keep her in the tent. Have your wife take your son into the village for a while. You and I will roll up the body in the tent and then load it into my station wagon. It won't fit in your sedan. Later, you and your family can follow me across the border into Spain, which is less than a hundred kilometers from here. We'll notify the authorities there. We'll tell them she died in Spain, of natural causes of course."

I knew the captain wouldn't argue. After all, he was talking to a colonel.

Then my father and the captain starting walking away, their voices fading until I could no longer hear them. *Nuts*, I thought.

At that moment my mother woke up and went outside to the ice chest to fetch eggs and bacon. I couldn't believe that in the middle of a murder investigation I was going to have to help cook while my two lazy brothers were still laid out as if morning had been canceled.

After nearly an eternity, my father returned and told my mother that the captain's wife and son had gone into the village to shop. He said he'd be gone later that afternoon for a few hours. My mother looked puzzled, but knew better than to ask questions.

Meanwhile my whole body was tingling with curiosity. I had read enough Nancy Drew mysteries to know that this woman didn't just die. Something or someone made her die. The answer was out there somewhere, and I figured it was up to me to find it. Just then, my father gave me the evil eye, which meant he wanted to be alone with my mother.

Happy to escape, I headed straight to the captain's campsite. Slowly, I crept into the area where the captain's family had been. Shivers ran down my spine as I laid eyes on an army-green tent, rolled neatly and innocent looking, but with a body inside. Imagine, a woman I had seen just twenty-four hours earlier, laid out like a mackerel inside all that canvas. Then I picked up a faint hushing sound from around the tent. Just like in the Nancy Drew mystery *The Whispering Statue*, I suspected there was something alive that wasn't supposed to be. I turned and ran.

Lurking around the campground I decided to watch for anyone who looked suspicious. I soon realized that everyone looked a little suspicious — after all, this wasn't Nebraska. But I wasn't going to give up. The girl detective Nancy Drew was my idol. Smart and independent, she had the determination of a hundred galloping horses and I was convinced that figuring out what, or who, killed the woman in the tent was my undeniable destiny.

I prowled around the camp for several more hours until I saw my father driving the Pontiac toward our campground. I strained my eyes to see if he was hauling a tent, but he wasn't. I got to our camp just as he was taking a seat across from my mother at a table already supplied with an open can of beer.

He took a swig. "Dammit," he said. "Someone stole the tent."

My mother's mouth dropped wide open. "Oh my Gawd," she gasped. "What are you goin' to do?"

My father took another swig. "Not a damn thing."

My mother didn't say a word. Not a single word.

Meanwhile my heart was about to jump out of my chest. "Dad," I said desperately. "What happens when whoever stole the tent finds the body?"

My mother shot a daggered glare at my father. "How in the world did she find out about this?" She then turned to glare at me. "Well?"

"I heard Dad talking to the captain about it. I wasn't snooping."

My father stood up and gave me a killer stare, "We're not looking for the tent. In fact we are going to forget all about this right now."

"But, Dad, someone might be getting away with murder. I know I can solve this. I can feel it inside."

"You," said my father in a deep, controlled tone, "are going to forget about this matter entirely. And you will not mention it to anyone, ever. Do you understand?"

The colonel had spoken, and I had no choice but to lower my head and choke out a "Yes, sir." I would never be the heroine who solved the mystery of the body in the missing tent—even though I knew I could have.

I completed my basic special agent training in Washington, D.C., in 1975, and shortly thereafter I flew to Nashville, Tennessee, for an interview with Special Agent in Charge (SAC) Willie J. Parker. Parker, who supervised a four-state region, was revered as one of the best agents in the Service. Before being promoted he'd just completed a stint in Maryland where he'd made hundreds of legendary cases against market hunters in the Chesapeake Bay who were killing canvasback ducks by the thousands over areas baited with corn. He also caught trappers who set out baited traps for live ducks that were bound for the gourmet restaurant market. The canvasback population was plummeting and Parker had made it his personal crusade to stop the slaughter. I held him in complete awe.

The job I was interested in was in Raleigh, North Carolina. Parker put me through a grueling daylong interview, asking me a dozen times if I was tough enough to do a field agent's job. I kept telling him I was, while wondering how superhuman one had to be to do this job.

Then he asked, "Are you a coward?"

"No," I answered emphatically.

"Good. Cause, the good Lord don't like cowards."

Parker was a tough-talking, no-nonsense field man and I was surprised that he'd consider hiring the first woman agent for a field position. But apparently Parker liked to try new things. He hired me that day but said in doing so he'd put his neck on the line with the Service. He told me sharply that he didn't want to be proven wrong. I promised him that I wouldn't let him down, even though agents were already placing bets that I wouldn't last six months.

On a blistering hot day in August, I drove my Toyota loaded with my belongings to Raleigh and met my immediate supervisor, John Mink. He was a big man with blocky shoulders and a face that looked like burled wood. Tobacco stains streaked down his chin and onto his shirt. To me, he looked like a backwoods moonshiner.

He lost no time saying what he thought of me. "You need to know right off the bat that I think this rotten idea of Parker sending me a woman stinks. I wanted a bright, young fellow I could show the ropes to, not some girl I gotta haul around."

Even though my face grew hot and fiery red, I said nothing as the insults flew. My military upbringing taught me to respect authority. I listened as he told me that my new job would require me to work sixteen-hour days, checking duck hunters in the cold and mud, operating boats in dangerous weather, and working with male game wardens who had jealous wives.

"You'll never make it," Mink said firmly.

Later that day he took me to his house and introduced me to his wife who stood at the kitchen sink peeling vegetables.

"Mary, here she is. I just want to tell ya, I ain't gonna try and get in her pants."

His wife turned and looked at me with a dropped jaw as if she was astonished at her husband's crudeness.

My first few months working for Mink were a nightmare. My training didn't include motorboat operation and when Mink told me to take a Boston Whaler out on the intercoastal waterway I had to figure it out on my own. He harshly criticized me on how I ran the boat and loaded it on a trailer. He didn't like the way I interacted with hunters and walked out on a talk I gave to state officers about federal wildlife laws. Nearly everything I did was wrong.

I never said a word, however, because I didn't want to be pegged as a complainer and prove my detractors right.

Determined to make it, I learned to operate boats and I worked long hours in freezing weather where I apprehended waterfowl poachers in the Currituck Sound and throughout North Carolina's intercoastal waterway. I worked with dozens of state officers who discovered I was both competent and professional. Far from being apprehensive, many of their wives became my friends.

In my first undercover case, I posed as an archaeology student who traveled with her "professor," hunting for artifacts along the Black and Cape Fear Rivers. The professor was John Kennedy, a supervisor with the North Carolina Department of Natural Resources who at the time had a visionary idea of undercover work. He reasoned if an undercover team could spend time along the rivers, they'd get to know the local fishermen and would be able to buy illegal game fish from them. The investigation was necessary because the rampant sale of game fish was causing a sharp decline in the fish populations in the rivers of North Carolina.

This case was unique in that Kennedy was well-known to many of the perpetrators as a conservation officer. To conceal his true identity he donned a thick brown wig to cover his all-white hair and wore oversized sunglasses. He wanted a female partner to further confuse his targets. Kennedy was right. Using his plan, we made exactly one hundred cases and significantly curtailed the poaching. After that case, not only was I hooked on undercover work, but I'd also learned firsthand how devastating poaching could be on wildlife.

In October 1976, Willie J. Parker called unexpectedly and ordered me to move over the weekend to Asheville, North Carolina, where I'd report to a new supervisor. I later learned that an Assistant U.S. Attorney had complained to Parker about the degrading and sexist comments Mink was making about me. Parker was outraged and rectified the situation immediately by transferring me. Eventually Mink left North Carolina and finished his career in relative isolation.

Being a waterfowl man, Parker wanted me to learn how to identify ducks practically with my eyes closed. To accomplish this he sent me to the Patuxent Wildlife Research Center in Maryland to participate in a waterfowl identification class. In this training session, Service employees gathered to determine the species, age, and sex of duck wings sent in by cooperating hunters. This was part of a survey to determine the status of the waterfowl population in the United States. During a one-week period, thousands of duck wings were "keyed out," and for a novice like me it was an excellent way to become proficient at identifying waterfowl.

About midweek I was learning my duck wings but I was also developing an interest in Lonnie Schroeder, a young waterfowl biologist who supervised the table where I was working with five other people. Lonnie held a master's degree in wildlife biology from Colorado State University and was energetic and enthusiastic about his work. When he told me he was from North Dakota, I remember thinking that this was such a far-off place, even though I'd been around the world.

With the patience of seven saints, Lonnie taught us neophytes everything there was to know about ducks and then graciously opened his apartment to us for margaritas and Mexican food. I thought he was both intelligent and kind, and I wanted to know him better. I wasn't sure how he'd take me, however—a woman who "chased" men for a living.

Before leaving Patuxent I gave Lonnie my home phone number and to my delight he called me, and we started a long-distance romance. Since I hadn't much time for a social life, Lonnie was a refreshing addition to my life. He was a hunter who loved the outdoors, and he firmly believed in wildlife law enforcement. He was the only man I'd met who didn't trivialize my job and accepted the fact that I was in it for the long run. He also understood that I did undercover work and that sometimes this was the best way to catch crooks. Although he was a little taken aback when I joked that I'd had three previous "husbands."

We spent our courtship alternating between Maryland and North Carolina, and in November 1977, we were married in Silver Springs, Maryland. Nearly everyone at the wedding had some connection with the U.S. Fish and Wildlife Service and an FBI evidence photographer photographed it. My job was now my life.

In order to be together, Lonnie and I applied for two vacant jobs in Utah. Lonnie was offered a position as a wildlife biologist in Salt Lake City. The law enforcement SAC in Denver didn't want a woman agent in Utah and refused to hire me. Clark Bavin, the chief of the Division of Law Enforcement, intervened; I had proven myself and he overruled the SAC's decision. I asked if I could work in Salt Lake City, but the SAC refused my request. The position would be fifty-five miles north in Brigham City. Lonnie and I bought a small home in Brigham City and he commuted the fifty-five miles for the next four years. When I eventually transferred, the Brigham City position was moved to Salt Lake City.

In Utah, I had to gain the confidence of a new supervisor, a U.S. Attorney's office, agent colleagues, and state officers. Consequently, I worked hard making waterfowl poaching cases, catching falcon nest robbers, and arresting eagle shooters. I also worked on my first undercover big-game hunting case in the Black Hills of South Dakota. This case involved a poaching ring of six who sported T-shirts that read "Pringle Hunters Do It Better at Night," attesting to their illegal night-hunting practices.

In 1981, Lonnie and I transferred to Watertown, South Dakota, where we could live and work in the same place. Watertown was a small town in the northeastern part of the state, full of prairie marshlands with plenty of waterfowl for Lonnie and plenty of wildlife poachers for me.

In around 1983, the SAC in Denver retired and was replaced by Ted Moore, who at six feet, four inches and nearly three hundred pounds, could use his size to intimidate people. Typically, he hired big male agents, which led to a running joke in the Service that he hired agents "by the pound."

Moore had just finished a two-year stint in Washington, D.C., and was ready to take charge from his Denver office. He let me know right away that the only reason that a woman agent was in his district was because I had gotten there before he did. Boy, did I ever miss my mentor, Willie J. Parker.

In 1985, after eight years of marriage, Lonnie and I became the proud parents of our daughter, Megan. Her birth filled me like nothing else ever had. Even though I now felt like my world was complete, I suspected that being a mother might create a hitch in my career. I was right. During my six-week maternity leave, Ted Moore's deputy called me three times with the same message. "You're a mother now; things are different. This may be a good time to consider resigning."

I ignored these calls and reported back to work. For the next two years, however, I noticed that my male colleagues were getting sent to Montana on grizzly bear patrols or to Alaska on walrus cases, while I tended to minor local violations. This created a long dry spell in my own experience log and I was going crazy. In spite of this, I still considered my life's purpose to stop those who exploited wildlife for greed or money, and catching them was still the only job I wanted.

On a day that was so cold the snow creaked when you drove over it, SAC Moore arrived at my office to conduct a station inspection. He strolled into my tiny, windowless office equipped with a black, single-line dial telephone, a used electric typewriter, an army-surplus metal desk, and two filing cabinets. The office was built in a heated garage where I kept seized vehicles and freezers full of illegal wildlife. The only decoration was a poster of Annie Oakley with her gun.

He sat down on the other side of my gray desk with his bulky arms folded on his barrel chest. "You're a mother now," he said, getting to the real point of his visit.

Here we go again, I thought, holding back a tired yawn from having been up all night with Megan's nagging cough.

The chair creaked ominously as Moore shifted his weight. "Well, as a mother, your priorities are different. Nothing is more important than that little girl of yours, and I want you to take good care of her."

His condescending tone jangled every nerve in my body. This from the man who two years earlier had come to my home and taken Lonnie aside and given his "permission" for Lonnie and I to start a family. Regardless, I endured Moore's demeanor with stoic patience as I explained that Lonnie and I fully intended to care for our own daughter.

Moore grunted and shifted his weight, causing the chair to protest again. "I just don't think this job is for mothers. There's too much travel and long hours, not to mention the risks. You can't do it all."

"Look," I said, "there are millions of mothers out there working and raising families. I'm no different. I want to work. In fact, I want all the assignments I can get."

His eyes narrowed as he leaned back in his chair. "Oh? Is there a particular assignment you want?"

"Yes. I want to go to Alaska, on a walrus patrol. You keep turning me down."

Moore tightened his beefy arms across his chest. "You don't understand. The assignments up there are dangerous. The Eskimos are liable to get violent over agents telling them how many walrus they can hunt. A little gal like you might rile them up even more. I just don't want you to get hurt, especially now that you're a mother."

I sucked in a long breath. His patronizing speeches were crafted to make him look like he cared. I knew better, but he had a lot of power and could make or break my career. Leaning across my desk I pounded my fist lightly.

"I can't just sit here like some pencil-pushing desk jockey. I'm a field agent and I want to be where the action is. I want to go out there and kick butt— wherever it is."

Stone-faced, he looked down at his yellow pad and scribbled some notes. "Okay," he said. "I'll see what I can do."

He left in a new Ram Charger equipped with the biggest mud/snow studded tires money could buy and headed to his next station visit in Devils Lake, North Dakota. As I sat alone at my desk, I had an ominous feeling that my career had been dealt a backhanded blow.

Three weeks later, Moore called to offer me an assignment in San Diego, California—an immersion course in Spanish. "You'd be right on the border where they speak the stuff."

"I was more interested in a law enforcement assignment, not training."

"This is the best I can do. I recommend you take it."

My response was probably what he hoped for. "How much Spanish am I going to use in South Dakota for God's sake? Besides, my Spanish is already pretty good. I used to live in Spain you know."

"Listen, you'd be perfect for this. You're my first pick. Of course you'll be away from home for six months."

Six months! Moore knew when I asked for assignments I was talking about a week or ten days away from home. I couldn't leave a baby for six months. When I turned down the training, Moore had achieved his objective. Now he could say that he had offered me advanced training and I declined. He would use this against me if I ever filed a complaint claiming that he failed to offer me opportunities to advance my career.

After that phone call, I heard very little from the Denver office. As the next three years dragged on, I watched the better out-of-state cases go to my male colleagues while I spent most of my time in South Dakota tending to routine matters. I ached for more challenges. All I wanted was more. I wanted to be recognized as the good agent I knew I was, I wanted to be a good example for my daughter, and I wanted a case that would truly have an impact on saving wildlife. Meanwhile, I pictured Moore waiting for me to quit out of sheer boredom while his "lads," as he called them, marched on.

In the fall of 1990, I did something highly unorthodox for an agent at my level. I called Larry Hood, the Minneapolis SAC, and asked if I could meet with him. I'd known Larry since the day I was hired and felt I could speak with him candidly. Larry suggested meeting at the Waubay National Refuge in northeastern South Dakota.

On a mid-fall day Larry and I sat outside on a picnic table overlooking Waubay Lake. While the temperature was crisp and cool and the leaves were gorgeous mixtures of gold and red, I was in so much emotional pain that I hardly noticed. As the sun glistened off the lake and a few wild ducks floated by, I poured out my heart.

"My career is going down a rat hole," I explained. "I got a call from an informant about some eagles that were being shot from an airplane in the Black Hills and Moore wouldn't let me go and investigate. He said he didn't have the money. That's just crap! He doesn't want me to have a good case."

"That's a pretty big case to let go like that," said Larry.

"I'm sure he got someone else to work it. Anything good that comes up goes to another agent while I get left with the dregs."

Larry was silent and seemed dismayed as I went on.

"On top of that, a woman I know in personnel told me something I'm not supposed to know about."

Larry's eye's widened. "What's that?"

"Moore has given every agent in his district a special achievement award except me."

Larry ran his hand across his mouth. "Whoa, that's bad. Real bad."

"Do you think I could file a discrimination complaint against Moore?" I asked.

"Sure you could. But you'd only win the battle with Moore and lose the war with the Service. You don't want to be pegged as a troublemaker."

Squinting into the sun, I looked at Larry. "I was afraid you'd say that. But what should I do? My career's almost dead."

"There's no doubt Moore's no good for you. I'm sitting here watching you pop antacids, you've lost weight, and, to be honest, you look terrible. You may be a prickly little thing at times, but you're worth helping out. There's no doubt about it, you need to get away from Moore. I've got a station opening up in Madison, Wisconsin, and I don't have anything against female agents. Would you be interested?"

"Gosh yes! What about Lonnie? Do you think he could get a job there, too?"

"I think so, there's a wetlands office right in Madison and I heard they just lost a biologist. I'd be happy to make a call for him."

I couldn't believe my good luck. The vivid colors of the leaves in the trees suddenly became real as I thanked Larry over and over and rushed home to tell Lonnie.

After I told Lonnie about my meeting with Larry Hood he said he was in complete favor of a change. It would be good for Megan, too. She was in kindergarten and first grade was just around the corner. Before I knew it, we were on our way to Madison. With Larry Hood as my new SAC, I felt like my career finally had new life.

As I drove past the quiet town of Tomah, Wisconsin, I marveled at how quickly things had changed. I had gone from having almost no complex cases, to landing a promising one in Alaska — a very desirable professional destination for Fish and Wildlife agents. Because of the rough terrain and harsh weather conditions in Alaska, you had to be in top-notch physical condition to do field work there. Moore would never let me go to Alaska and now I had my chance to go there and pursue two suspected violators who were reputed to be pillaging Alaska's wildlife. Any good agent would jump at the opportunity.

Everything seemed set for me. I was living in a good place with good neighbors. Lonnie liked his job and Megan was doing well in her new school. Life was so good except for one thing. A haunting voice made me worry that I'd lost my edge and maybe even the guts to work such a complex case like the one in Alaska. Doubts gathered like a storm about whether I could do the very thing I had yearned to do for years. Maybe I needed more time to get my confidence back and could work in Alaska in a few more years. But this case wasn't going to wait — it was staring me in the face. As I pulled in to my driveway at 5:00 A.M., I felt torn between wanting to take on the Alaska case and the fear that I would fail.

———

CHAPTER 3

The Creed of Greed

SIX-THIRTY A.M. I slammed my hand on the alarm clock to shut it off.

Lonnie rolled over and groaned, "What time did you get in last night?"

Ignoring the question, I got out of bed. I didn't want to admit that I'd only been home for a little while.

I dragged myself into Megan's room to find her snuggled beneath a peach comforter that matched the flowered, pure "little girl" wallpaper. As I rubbed her tiny back to waken her, I felt a slight vibration rumble through the house and heard the sound of a city bus screeching around the corner. Then came the stinging odor of diesel fuel. The day after we had moved into the house, we realized we were on a major bus route—a detail not mentioned by the real estate agent.

I carried Megan downstairs to the family room that was adjacent to the kitchen, propped her up in front the TV and turned on some cartoons. In the kitchen I made pancakes for her and poured a bowl of cereal for myself. Even though it was summer, Megan still went to "school," a day camp that began every morning at 7:30 A.M.

Lonnie walked into the kitchen wearing a simple uniform with brown pants and a khaki shirt with a U.S. Fish and Wildlife patch on the sleeve. He was heading out into the field on a wetlands project. He gave me a hug. "How did it go last night?"

"I met the bad guy. He's a fine, upstanding citizen who likes to shoot everything he sees."

"Figures. I woke up at one in the morning and you still weren't in."

"I know. I had to drive to Stillwater to drop off the informant."

I wondered to myself how many mothers hung out in bars with poachers and then drove all night to get home. Probably none. But it was my job.

Lonnie gripped his hand to his hip and looked at me sternly. "I hope you're being careful out there. Megan and I need you."

"I *am* careful." I knew I sounded defensive but didn't have to be. Lonnie understood the secrecy and unpredictable long hours of undercover work better than most husbands. Although I never let on that I sometimes smoked Swisher Sweets to blend in.

Lonnie grabbed his lunch sack, kissed Megan, and then me. "Love you," he said as he went out the door. I worried that he might be torn between supporting me in my job and the effect it could have on our family, especially if something bad happened to me.

After Megan ate her pancakes, I got her dressed and then strapped her into the car seat in our used Audi. The early morning Madison traffic to her summer day camp was unusually light. *Everyone is on vacation . . . except me.*

Holding her little hand, I guided Megan into a school building where six other mothers were mingling and chatting. I knew one of them and stopped momentarily to speak to her.

"Hi Sarah, how's it going?"

The chattering stopped abruptly and Sarah managed a low-volume acknowledgment. I understood. I wasn't part of the Mingling Mothers Club. One of the teachers made it known that I was a federal agent and from then on I had been greeted with stares of suspicion. These mothers, who talked openly about birthday parties and swimming lessons, stopped their conversations whenever I approached, causing pangs of rejection to ripple through me. Even though I yearned for a connection with them, I never got it. *To hell with them, I've got more important things to do.*

I gave Megan a hug and released her to her friends who were down the hallway. I was in a hurry to get back to my house and pick up the Explorer and drive to the office. I was required to have it with me during the workday in case I was called out.

* * *

At my desk I retrieved the videotape Moose had given me the night before and set it aside. Then I scanned the glossy colored brochure. At the top it read, "Alaska Nature Adventures," and advertised hiking, nature trips, photography, fishing, and sport hunting.

The front of the brochure was dominated by a snapshot of a huge grizzly bear lying dead in the snow. Crouched behind the bear was a broad-faced man with a white beard wearing a wide-brimmed hat and sunglasses. He was holding a rifle. The text read: "Grizzly are relatively plentiful, a good-sized interior bear will usually square at eight feet. Cost: $7,000." My eyes searched deep into the picture for clues as to how this animal was killed, but there were none. Pictures like this masked the truth, because the real story behind the hunt took place long before the camera was taken out. In another photo, the profile of the bulky horns of a Dall sheep and a hunter's face beaming with accomplishment were cast against a sharp blue sky while the white carcass of the hunter's trophy shone brilliantly. Under the photo it read: "The Brooks Range is noted for its Dall Sheep. Full curl, 40" plus rams are not uncommon. Cost: $7,000."

This was the kind of trophy that Moose James was so insistent that I get. He wanted me in this picture. I stared at it for a long time, wondering if I'd ever get there.

There were no photographs of people hiking, fishing, or·taking pictures, only pictures of dead bear, caribou, moose, and sheep. This appeared to be purely a hunting operation. It seemed like the dead animals in the pictures were the only reason Bowman was in business.

I stood up from my desk and reached into a metal file cabinet for a case report written by Tim Eicher, a special agent stationed in Fairbanks, Alaska. Eicher was a former New Mexico game warden who learned to fly airplanes and two years later landed in Alaska. Even in Alaska he wore roping boots and a cowboy hat whenever weather permitted.

One of the first pages of the report was a handwritten letter by a game warden who suspected Moose James of poaching wildlife.

REPORT OF VIOLATION—10/05/89

Moose James blasted another big buck off a bait pile last Thursday at 4:00 A.M. He's been showing pictures of it to the dirts who hang out at his bar. He's slaughtering ducks over bait, too, hundreds of them, and there's

rumors that he's back to blasting bear. He's raping wildlife resources and
getting away with it. Let's do something!

The handwritten words had been photocopied so many times that I could barely read them. Moose James was a habitual poacher, who needed desperately to be stopped, but then the letter mentioned someone else.

Every fall Moose flies to the farthest extremity of civilization (Alaska).
The area he hunts is supposedly in the vicinity of a large wildlife refuge.
He guides for a guy named Bob Bowman who uses airplanes to hunt.
They kill everything they can. They are raping the resources in Alaska and
are just the kind of guys we want to get. Many lowlifes idolize them.

The letter reminded me that guys like Moose and Bowman were the very reason I investigated wildlife crime. For me, every animal poached from the wild was stolen from the public who legitimately hunted or watched wildlife. I had spent my life camping and hiking and every time I saw a deer, a grouse, or an eagle I felt a special joy in my heart. Wildlife belonged to everyone, and to me no one had a special privilege to exploit it for monetary gain. There was no question that Moose and Bowman were bad news. The problem was proving it. The information was almost two years old, and the trail was stone cold.

Eicher had sent me the report and had followed up with a phone call. He asked me to make an initial covert contact with Moose James at The Bear's Den and see what kind of information I could pick up about Bowman and his operation.

Eicher had also checked on Bob Bowman's activities in Alaska and discovered that Alaska's wildlife department had been watching Bowman since 1981. Bowman ran a big-game guiding and hunting operation out of a remote fly-in camp on the Ivishak River located along the north slope of the Brooks Range some ninety miles south of Prudhoe Bay. He was flying Piper Super Cubs, two-seater single-engine airplanes that functioned like aerial jeeps in the Alaskan bush. They could take off and land on tundra and were the backbone of most fly-in operations. A 1984 intelligence report from the Alaska Department of Fish and Wildlife stated that Bowman was suspected of over-bagging caribou, bighorn sheep, grizzly bear, timber wolves, and moose.

While it was true that Bowman had the elements of a violator—small airplanes, wealthy clients, and lots of big game—it was also true of a lot of outfitters in Alaska. Every year sixty-four thousand licensed hunters took to the fields and mountains in Alaska to hunt big-game animals for their meat or hides, or for trophies. Hunting regulations were set according to the results of biological surveys used to determine how many animals could be "harvested" while still maintaining a healthy population. Hunting permits were issued based on the statistical probability that only a certain percentage of hunters would be successful. Assuming that Bowman's clients all had obtained permits and licenses, Bowman's operation could be completely legal—in spite of all the bad rumors.

It was hard to know what to do next. Even though Bowman walked and quacked like a duck he might not be one. The question was—would it be worth checking him out?

I looked at my watch and decided that although it was still early in Fairbanks, Eicher might be in the office. I picked up the phone and called him.

"U.S. Fish and Wildlife, Law Enforcement," said Eicher.

"Hi, it's me."

"Hey, I was hoping to hear from you. How did it go at The Bear's Den?"

"Roy introduced me to Moose, and he really wants us to hunt with Bob Bowman."

"Already? You're as good as they say you are."

"There's more. Moose gave me a video of Bowman's hunting operation. I haven't watched it yet. It might be a honey."

"Holy cow, that's great! But I hope you didn't book hunts just yet. I have to get approval from the SAC first."

"The informant verbally committed us to hunts, but I tried to back off. So the answer is yes and no. The problem is Bowman's camp is booked for this fall. We'd have to wait until the '92 season."

"Shit, that's a long way off. But I think we should go for it. Sounds like you're in with Moose and he can get you into the camp. Bowman's not going to change anything in a year. If anything he'll get worse."

"You know, according to your own report, you don't have a shred of information that Bowman's actually doing anything wrong. All you've got is speculation."

"That's all I can write officially. Personally, I think Bowman's shooting the shit out of everything that moves up here."

"How can you be so sure?"

Eicher's voice became deeper and more precise, "You don't understand. Bowman flies clients in and out of camp, all day, *every* day. These are big-paying clients and Bowman is busting his ass to get them trophy animals. They shoot bear, sheep, moose, caribou, and wolves up here and have to file kill reports to the Alaska Department of Fish and Wildlife. I got the reports filed by every hunter who hunted with Bowman during the last five years. Every one of them successfully bagged every critter they went after. We're talking hundreds of animals. You know that ain't possible, unless they violated their asses off."

"If he's so busy, how come you haven't caught him?" I asked with mild sarcasm.

" 'Cause we've got 591,000 square miles of country up here and only five federal agents and about ninety state officers who have a thousand other priorities. Catching someone outright poaching up here is like trying to catch an ant in an ocean."

"Why don't you pull Bowman's hunters before a federal grand jury and grill them about their hunts. Someone will spill their guts eventually."

"You don't understand," Eicher said again. "This is a word-of-mouth operation; most of Bowman's hunters are either his buddies or are foreigners of some kind. His buddies aren't going to rat him out and we can't reach the hunters from Europe. We've got to catch this asshole cold right here in Alaska."

"So why did you call me for this?"

"Because we've got to throw Bowman a whole new look. We've never used a woman undercover agent and he'll never suspect one."

I had to admit that the cover was a good one, but still I remained silent.

"Look," said Eicher, "do you remember Ron Hayes, the notorious airborne hunter who agents Joe Ramos and Adam O'Hara caught up here in the eighties?"

"Sure I do. Joe caught Hayes airborne hunting but Hayes couldn't resist the easy money he was making from flying and killing so he went right back into business. A few years later, Adam O'Hara set him up and caught him again. It was a fantastic case," I said.

"Yeah, well, Bowman idolizes Hayes. He wants to get rich just like Hayes did, and have big-shot clients like Hayes did, except he don't want to get caught and go to jail. Hayes lost seven planes and ended up with a one-hundred-thousand-dollar fine. Bowman knows that and he's being extremely careful with who he lets in his camp."

I thought back to what I knew about the Hayes investigation. Around 1980, Special Agent Joe Ramos, a handsome Latino who speaks fluent Spanish, was handpicked to infiltrate Hayes's camp because two wealthy and politically influential Mexican nationals were booked to hunt there. Joe set his cover up in a border town in Mexico and went to hunt at the Hayes camp. At the camp, the Mexicans, picking up the American "border Spanish" in Joe's dialect, suspected that he might be a U.S. citizen. Joe explained to them that border Spanish was common in the town where he "lived," but the Mexicans weren't convinced. They told Hayes that they thought Joe might be a U.S. *federale*.

Hayes brutally threatened Joe, warning him that if he found out Joe was an agent he'd either drop him off on the tundra and leave him, or kill him outright. For days Joe held tight against the intense scrutiny, concealing an open pocketknife in his clothing to be ready in case he was unexpectedly attacked. Joe insisted that Hayes call his "business" in Mexico to verify his identity. One of the Mexican hunters did just that and, after a lengthy discussion with Joe's "contact," the hunter came away satisfied that Joe was legitimate. Finally, Hayes took Joe on an illegal hunt where he herded a grizzly bear to him with his plane. Joe shot the bear which sealed Hayes's fate in federal court.

While inside the camp, Joe gathered enough evidence against Hayes, the Mexican nationals, and other hunters to have Hayes arrested and shut his hunting and guiding business down. Agents seized Hayes's Cessna 185 and a Piper Super Cub. In court, Hayes was fined, lost his guide's license, but didn't serve jail time.

I remembered talking to Joe about the Hayes case months later. He trembled as he relived his traumatizing ordeal. Could I hold up like Joe did if the same thing happened to me? I wasn't sure.

Even after his arrest, Hayes couldn't resist the lure of the hundreds of thousands of dollars a year he was making, or the prestige he enjoyed as a famous Alaskan big-game guide and outfitter. Without a guide's license he resorted to opening the exclusive Alaska Rainbow Lodge situated on the Kvichak River on the Alaska Peninsula. Soon he had famous clients from the sports and political world, along with a list of wealthy businessmen. Some of Hayes's fishing clients wanted to hunt, so Hayes quickly turned his business into a cast and blast operation. Hayes hired pilot Michael Tessier to spot wildlife and herd grizzly bear to his handpicked clients who had more money than time.

To catch Hayes again, the U.S. Fish and Wildlife Service set up its own undercover big-game booking agency, which was "owned" by Special Agent Adam O'Hara, a big, burly man with red hair and a strong Northeastern accent. Under the guise of checking out hunting operations for his "clients," O'Hara hunted with a number of suspicious hunting operations throughout the country, developing evidence against them in the process. Ron Hayes, however, was his primary target.

O'Hara started carefully with Hayes by visiting the Alaska Rainbow Lodge and fishing with him on several occasions. Over the next two years, O'Hara continued to befriend Hayes and over time managed to become one of his closest confidantes. By the third year, Hayes was ready to let O'Hara in on his clandestine hunting operation.

In the fall of 1987, Ron Hayes flew for five days over the Katmai National Park on the Alaska Peninsula searching out the largest brown bear he could find for his good friend Adam O'Hara. Several times he'd land and glass a bear and say to Adam, "I don't like the hair on that one, let's keep looking. I want you to have the best bear out here."

Finally, he found a monster bear, dropped O'Hara off, and proceeded to drive the bear right to Adam for an easy and sure shot. Adam later told me, "I couldn't believe it. He drove that bear right down my throat."

The bear measured nine feet and was the hammer that cracked Hayes's operation wide open to federal law enforcement. In early 1988, Hayes was arrested, and the U.S. Fish and Wildlife Service thoroughly searched the records of the Alaska Rainbow Lodge. Their search resulted in the seizure of illegal animals from dozens of hunters who thought their illegal kills were strictly confidential.

Pilot Michael Tessier, who turned federal witness, died from falling off a cliff before the investigation was completed. The pressure of the investigation drove the wife of one of Hayes's guides to kill herself. As for Hayes, he lost more planes: two Cessna 206s, two Piper Super Cubs, and a Cessna 185. He served a year in jail and paid a one-hundred-thousand-dollar fine. Finally, Ron Hayes got the message that wildlife crime was serious.

I began to consider that Bob Bowman was a Ron Hayes wannabe. Perhaps he wanted to be King of the Hunting Hill where the richest clients came for their treasured trophies along with a guarantee of remaining untouchable. His guides and pilots probably worked for the cheap thrill of seeing animals slaughtered and for the lure of easy money. I knew that the mixture of big money clients and abundant wildlife meant that there was a good chance that animals were being killed illegally.

Even so, the case still bothered me. I wasn't Joe and I wasn't Adam. I wasn't sure if I could live in camp with armed bad guys, while maintaining a cover that was linked to a loose cannon like my informant, Roy. Besides, I wasn't very confident about flying around in small planes that were flown by hot-dog bush pilots. Add that to the uncompromising Alaskan wilderness and the fickle weather and you had conditions that could have serious or even fatal consequences. There would be no contact with the outside world. No backup. No fall-back position. No nothing. I knew that if my cover was blown, I could be left for bear bait. This was a case looking for a thousand ways to go bad and I'd be crazy to take the assignment. As I thought of how to break it to Eicher, all I could hear was tobacco being spit into a cup.

"I'll think about it," I said, my voice cracking.

"Look," said Eicher. "If Bowman's not stopped he'll keep killing animals until the last one is gone. His killing could set wildlife wherever he hunts back for decades. Wildlife can only tolerate so much exploitation before it starts to decline. I'm telling you, Bowman is pushing the envelope."

"Tim," I said, "I'd really like to help you, but I've got to spend my time establishing myself in Wisconsin. You know, with the state officers, and the U.S. Attorney's Office. I've got to get busy here."

"That's bullshit. You've got cold feet. You're the only woman in this out-fit who can make this case. You've got the experience and the guts. You made great cases in the past and you can do it again. Forget about what Moore tried to do to you. Yeah, I've heard all the crap. It's over. Larry Hood is not going to stop you. This is your case, girl. Go for it."

As far as I knew, I was the only female agent with hunting-camp experi-ence, and Eicher was in a bind to find a way to catch Bowman. He didn't have years to work an agent in with Bowman, he needed to move now. But I was still hesitant. I started to tell Eicher that I prefer working cases where there was better evidence and an informant who wasn't such a loser, when he cut me off.

"Look, here's something that's not in the report. In 1986, one of Bowman's own hunters called the Alaska Fish and Wildlife Department and reported violations he'd witnessed. He was with a party of nine hunters from Texas and West Germany, and said they over-bagged bear, caribou, and sheep, and wasted wildlife. He claimed if the critter wasn't big enough, they'd leave it, fly around, find something bigger, and blast it. Bowman got away with everything because the hunter refused to cooperate in an investigation. He wouldn't even provide his own name. But it shows that there's some evil shit goin' on inside that camp."

This new information cut through me like a hot knife. If half of it was true, I wanted to choke Bowman with my own hands. A visual image seared my conscience of wildlife being slaughtered on the tundra as an airplane buzzed overhead, while Bowman radioed to the ground ordering the hunters to leave it because it wasn't worth taking home. I could see him chasing a grizzly until it was too tired to run any farther while a nearby hunter emerged from the brush and shot the exhausted bear. I imagined the wild animals within Bowman's reach being knocked off one by one. Eicher was right: Bowman had to be stopped. If he was sniffing out undercover agents, he'd probably be looking for an agent setup that had been used in the past. A woman hunter had never been used and was definitely a good angle. I was clearly the only option.

Finally I said, "This will be hard on my family, but I can't stand to see this kind of wildlife slaughter continue. I'm in."

"Good," said Eicher releasing a breath of air. "Grab up Roy and get back up to The Bear's Den. Get to know Moose a little better and book hunts for both of you. I can justify asking for the money after your contact the other night. The key is to get inside that camp."

"Moose insists that I hunt a sheep. He even said he'd find me an easy one."

"No way. A sheep hunt is too expensive. I want someone on a bear hunt, and that alone will be seven thousand with the license. Tell Moose you want to hunt caribou for thirty-two hundred. My budget is ten thousand dollars, but going over a little won't hurt. I'll get the money for a down payment in a day or so."

"Speaking of hunting bear, Roy is fully convinced he's the man. He told Moose he and I were going together. Roy did a great job with the intro, but he's not an agent and I think he drinks too much. We need to come up with a replacement pretty soon."

"Okay. Go ahead and book him in with Moose for now. We'll switch him out later. You're not going to Alaska with that guy. I'll find you a good agent.

But I gotta tell you, if you're successful, this could be hard-ass work that will literally chew up a year of your life."

"Now you're trying to talk me out of it," I spewed.

"Naw, you can do it. There are others around here who don't think so, but I do."

As I hung up the phone I thought about how life could change in a heartbeat, sometimes without your consent. I felt good about my decision though, even somewhat energized. Trying to stop Bowman was the right thing to do. Now all I had to do was tell Lonnie.

CHAPTER 4

Dead Animal House

"WHY YOU?" asked Lonnie when I told him about the Alaska assignment.

"Because no one will suspect a woman hunter is really an undercover agent. Besides, Moose James and Bob Bowman are serious wildlife violators, and I want to stop both of them."

"How long will you be gone?" asked Lonnie.

"About a week, I think."

"You know, I've flown a lot in small planes on duck-population surveys in Canada, and it's no cakewalk. I came close to crashing and burning myself, and I was flying with highly trained government pilots. You won't be. And then there are the bad guys you'll be with."

"I know there are risks. But taking risks is the only way these poachers are going to be stopped. I have a good feeling about this, and I think I can pull it off, but only if I'm sure that you're okay with it."

Lonnie looked pensive. "You know I've never held you back and I'm proud of you for taking on this assignment. I'll take real good care of our little girl, you just be damn careful."

I gave him a hug and thanked him, as I'd done so many times, for his loving support. In a lot of ways Lonnie and I were like a military family who took our respective assignments in stride and considered them as an important part of the cause we had committed our working lives to. We never complained about our traveling. I covered for him when he was gone and he did the same for me. We were a team and we trusted one another to maintain a healthy balance between work and family. But on this assignment, more than ever, I was going to have to make sure I didn't leave him without a wife or leave Megan motherless. The stakes in this case were higher than any I had ever worked before.

The next morning I went into my office and called Roy and told him to meet me at a wild rice store thirty miles south of The Bear's Den the following Friday around one o'clock. We were going to book two hunts with Moose. Roy was ecstatic—he saw this as his first step to getting to Alaska.

After hanging up the phone I began thinking about who would be a good replacement for Roy. I considered agent Ron Boyars. No, he looked too much like a cop. Acted like one, too. What about Jay Wilson from Michigan? No, he was too young—we wouldn't make a believable couple. Eric Shoemaker was about my age, but he didn't hunt.

I quickly realized I couldn't think of anyone to replace Roy. With an agent force of approximately two hundred, and nearly a quarter of it supervisors who didn't do investigative work, it was difficult to come up with an agent who was about my age, could hunt big game, *and* work undercover. The U.S. Fish and Wildlife Service wasn't like the FBI with more than ten thousand agents of almost any description and attribute. We were extremely limited. I decided to talk to Eicher about it later with hopes that he had a better idea.

I set up the VCR and watched the tape Moose had given me. It was a slightly edited promotional video Bowman shot for his hunting operation. The first scene showed Louis from Houston, Texas, with a dead ram that had thirty-nine-inch horns. Then there was Fred and his wife with two sets of sheep-horn trophies with forty-one- and forty-two-inch curls. The tape went on to Lloyd with a forty-two-inch ram, to which Bowman shouted, "Holy Smokes, there ain't too many of them left around here." I counted thirty-five dead sheep on the tape. Each reduced to its own short story of inches.

Sandwiched between the sheep hunts were a dozen moose hunts. One in particular showed a hunter straddling the neck of a dead moose on a rocky, river bed. "Ride 'em cowboy!" he shouted as he bounced up and down on the carcass. "Sixty-four inches, can't beat that!" shouted back Bowman from behind the camera. In another moose hunt, there was the sound of a rifle shot and then Bowman's voice from behind the camera. "Hit him again! Get closer!"

A hunter holding a pistol straight out in front of him entered the frame. Slowly he approached the downed moose. Suddenly the massive animal bounded straight up over the willows like a raging bull.

"Shoot him," shouted Bowman.

A shot sounded and the wounded moose fell back into the willows. The hunter hollered, "What do you want me to do now?"

"Don't ask questions, just do," hollered Bowman. "Watch him. Get ready to shoot. He's still alive."

The moose lurched out of the willows again, but there was still no shot.

"Get up there and finish the damn thing off," yelled Bowman, his voice strained with frustration.

Apparently, the hunter's gun had malfunctioned. At that instant the moose jumped up and charged the hunter. The camera fell to the ground and the film only showed the legs of Bowman and his client as they ran for their lives. Finally, a shot sounded.

"Shit," said Bowman gasping, "he almost got both of us."

"Now there lays dead a two-thousand-pound monster," said the hunter as if he had just single-handedly slain Godzilla. Bowman picked up the camera and it shook as he laughed along with the hunter.

I noticed in particular that there were only two bear hunts on the tape consisting of brief footage of hunters crouched next to their dead bear. Bowman guided a lot of bear hunters and it was odd that he didn't have more of them featured. I made note of the wing of a Super Cub that appeared with the bear hunt footage.

Finally, two full minutes were devoted to Moose James. He was lying in the snow wearing several layers of shirts and chest waders. Next to him was the pure white carcass of a Dall sheep. The perfectly symmetrical curl of his horns crowned his head royally.

"Yeah, I'm happy," said Moose. "But damn tired. Could have shot a bigger one, but I passed it up and had to take this one. He's not bad. He'll make a great full-body mount. Here's to you son of a bitches back at The Bear's Den drinking light ones."

The tape contained more carnage than a war movie, but it lacked the basic details of when, where, and how the animals were killed. Nothing on the tape proved definitively that Bowman was a wildlife criminal. The tape proved, however, that I needed to get to Alaska and see for myself what was really going on.

* * *

The following Friday, Roy and I walked into The Bear's Den. I looked at my watch and noted the exact time—5:11 P.M. The faint but reassuring vibration of the recorder against my chest told me that the tape was rolling. The bar buzzed with voices and cigarette smoke swirled around the grizzly on display. Most of the faces in the bar belonged to rowdy, summer migrants vacationing in the North Woods, along with a few of the full-time residents I thought I recognized from our last contact.

Moose glanced in my direction and swung his arm toward the back door. "Come on up to the house. We can't talk in here. What a madhouse!"

Getting into Moose's house was exactly what I wanted to do and I readily accepted the invitation. Roy and I followed Moose up the hill behind The Bear's Den to a modest-sized two-story wood-frame home. Two snowmobiles and a duck boat were parked on trailers alongside the house. The open door of a detached garage revealed the back of a black, four-wheel drive Dodge pickup truck with a heavy-duty hitch. He had all the toys for an outdoor boy. Just behind the house I could see a twelve-foot wooden gambrel, an apparatus built like a swing set used to hang big game for gutting, skinning, and butchering. I cringed at the thought of the illegal animals that had undoubtedly hung there.

"I'm going back up to Alaska to guide for Bowman in about a month. I can't wait," Moose remarked as we approached the house.

"How long will you be up there?"

"Two weeks. Not long enough I tell you. Come on in. I'll show you trophies that will knock your eyes out."

Moose opened the unlocked front door and we walked inside. Out of sheer habit my eyes locked onto the wildlife trophies that crowded the living room leaving little space for anything else. A moose head with what appeared to be a seventy-inch rack took up an entire wall, and a seven-foot grizzly hide took up another wall. A fully mounted mountain goat and a mountain lion sat on either end of a worn couch. There were no conversation chairs, end tables, a coffee table, or even a dining room table. Every inch was occupied by mounted animals.

Roy was truly impressed. "What a great place. Look at all this."

Moose took in a deep breath, full of pride. "I just ain't happy unless I'm huntin'. I love overpowering these beasts who have all the instincts to outsmart me, but I still get 'em. It's the best damn feeling on earth."

I handed Moose the Bowman videotape he had given me. "Thanks for the tape," I said. "It really got us pumped up."

"Yeah," said Roy. "The huntin' looks absolutely fantastic."

Moose folded his arms. "So, what's it gonna be? Two sheep and two grizzlies?"

"Not so fast." I said trying to come off as a real client. "I've got a few questions. If we sign up, will you guide us?"

"Absolutely. All the guides are good, but I guess I'm considered the best. I've been there the longest and know the country. I can get you the biggest critters in Alaska. No sweat."

"That sounds great," piped in Roy.

"Moose," I said. "The brochure claims that a moose hunt takes several days. I don't want to spend that kind of time on one animal. I want something big, and I want it quick."

"That ain't a problem. I promise you'll get a moose the same day the season opens. They're real easy to shoot. Just like shooting at that wall," he said pointing to his living room wall.

"I've got to have a big moose," I said folding my arms. "What happens if I can't find one that suits me?"

"Lady, you'll have a hundred to pick from, and the biggest one is yours. Guaranteed. But you really should shoot a sheep, too. If you don't shoot a sheep on this trip, you'll be begging me to go back up just to get one. I know you will."

"I want a trophy that takes up a living room wall. A sheep just isn't that big."

"Sheep are huge. A full mount is bigger than a couch. What about you Roy? You want to shoot a sheep?"

"Naw, I'm a bear hunter. I want a monster bear."

I knew Roy meant exactly what he said.

"How long will it take Roy to get a bear?" I asked.

"Bear are tougher. It's usually a four- or five-day hunt. But everyone gets one. Guaranteed. You guys should think about a caribou, too. They're all over the place, and they're easier to shoot than a moose." Moose raised his arms as if he was shooting a rifle. "Bam! Got one."

I broke in changing the subject. "I'd like to know a little more about the camp."

"Sure. The camp's got plenty of food and all the essentials. Bob's wife, Marianne, is one of the cooks, and she's the best. Sometimes we even have lobster. There ain't no roads to the camp so everything has to be flown in. Sometimes the planes are in the air ten hours a day with hunters and supplies. It's expensive to run a camp like Bob's, so when you think about it, the cost of the hunt isn't that bad."

"What about the accommodations?"

"First class all the way. Bob's got a couple of Quonset huts set up with bunk beds, and a separate cabin with beds. Everything's got heat. The guides and pilots stay together. Bob and Marianne stay in the main cabin where the kitchen and radiophone are."

"Boy, this sounds really exciting," I said exaggerating my enthusiasm. I slid my hand inside my purse and pulled out a certified check for sixty-five hundred dollars made out to Bob Bowman, and handed it to Moose. "Here's our down payment, made out the way you said."

"Great," said Moose scribbling on a yellow pad. "Okay, I'll put Roy down for a grizzly bear and you Jayne for a moose."

"And you'll guide us. Right?" I asked.

"You bet. It'll be fun."

"Uh . . . I'd like a receipt. Just for my records."

"Sure." Moose tore a page out of his yellow pad and quickly wrote a receipt. Silently, I groaned. The government bean counters wouldn't like this one bit—an unsigned receipt on notebook paper. They never understood what it was like dealing with the bad guys.

I continued to take a mental inventory of the menagerie: white-tailed deer, mule deer, antelope, caribou, a timber wolf, and at least six bighorn sheep shoulder mounts.

Moose gave Roy and me highlights of each conquest. "Yeah, I got this muley in Colorado three years ago. It's probably a Safari Club International record; I just never got it officially measured."

Of course not. What poacher would risk taking an illegal deer into the game and fish department to get it measured?

On top of the television set, I noticed a photograph of two teenaged boys with dead deer. "These your sons?" I asked.

"Yep. Duke and John. They both hunt their asses off. Great shots, both of them."

Just then I felt the click of the tape recorder. I had to change tapes. "Can I use your restroom?" I asked.

Moose pointed the way, and when I came back out he and Roy were in a deep conversation about the points on an elk rack. Roy seemed like he was truly envious of Moose. I went into the kitchen to look around and I noticed a baby bottle lying in the sink—definitely a misplaced item. Then I jumped back at the sight of a live fawn standing trembling under the kitchen table, the only shelter it could find. His eyes were motionless, but his ears twitched slightly, tracking sound, and I could see his chest thumping wildly from the stress of being in this horribly alien environment. I felt incensed that Moose had taken this innocent, young of the year animal and condemned it to a world of Formica and linoleum.

"Roy," I called out. "Come look at this."

Roy walked in the kitchen. "Holy Moses!"

Moose was right behind Roy. "When he gets bigger I'm gonna release him so my sons can hunt him."

"That's really great," I said.

I wanted Moose to think that I approved of exploiting wildlife. Even though the possession of a live fawn is against state law, turning Moose in for the live deer would jeopardize the rest of the case. Just then, I heard the front door open and close quietly. A woman shuffled into the kitchen, totally indifferent to the guests in her home.

"Hey guys," said Moose, "this is my wife, Peg."

Roy and I said hello. She nodded in our direction but said nothing. I gave her my full attention. She was Moose's age, but her forty years had been harder than his, as revealed by a sad face that had long lost its bloom. The top half of her hair was a mousy brown, while the rest was a frizzled, platinum blond. Her short torso strained against size-fourteen pants while her shoulders were locked in a permanent slump. Hands that had swollen veins that popped out like earthworms through hard and cracked skin told the story of woman who spent hours washing bar glasses in steaming hot water. A woman with no inspiration left in her life.

Peg went to the refrigerator and took out a baby bottle filled with milk. Still, without a word, she sat down at the Formica topped table and offered the bottle to the yearling who took it eagerly. I got the picture. Whatever Moose dragged home, dead or alive, she took care of it. She had probably eviscerated a thousand ducks, butchered tons of game meat, cleaned a hundred guns, and fed a whole legion of Moose's hunting buddies. The house she lived in was nothing more than a mausoleum for Moose's dead animals, and it seemed that a good portion of the family's income must have gone into mounting them.

My heart went out to this woman. She spent her life serving, cooking, cleaning, and sending Moose off on hundreds of hunting trips. I wondered what kind of family life could possibly exist here. And there was no light ahead. Her sons were growing up to be just like their dad.

"You have a nice house," I said to Peg.

"This isn't a house," she said sarcastically.

To break the tension, I turned to Roy. "We'd better get going."

When we got outside I felt a sense of relief. I had seen enough dead animals for one day.

"Thanks a million for showing us your trophies, Moose. It was super," I said.

"Just looking at your stuff makes me bloodthirsty as hell," added Roy.

Moose grinned, enjoying the accolades. Then his expression changed. "You know, Jayne, it ain't even natural for you to go all the way to Alaska and not shoot a sheep. I don't understand it, and I'm going to talk you into it no matter what it takes."

Moose's intensifying pressure to hunt a sheep was becoming a problem. Moose was right of course. No serious hunter would go to Alaska and not want to hunt a Dall sheep, especially if she had the hunting skills I claimed to have. In order to make things look right, I needed to book a sheep hunt. But Eicher had specifically told me not to.

"I don't know. A sheep hunt is kinda out of my budget."

I immediately regretted my words. Moose thought I had plenty of money to hunt. Meanwhile Roy was silent, letting me sink or swim on my own.

Struggling for damage control, I said, "You're right, Moose. But let me think about it. I'll call you next week and let you know."

Roy and I crawled back into the Corvette. I waited until we were a half-mile away before retrieving the tape recorder from under my shirt.

"Did you get everything?" asked Roy.

"Yeah. He's being very careful not to talk about anything illegal, which is the only reason he's not in jail right now. But he's agreed to be our guide and I bet Moose goes all out for his good buddies Roy and Jayne."

"I hope so. You gonna hunt a sheep?"

"It really bothered him that I didn't jump on it. I'm going to ask Eicher for more money for a sheep hunt. I can just hear the bean counters screaming already."

_____

CHAPTER 5

Undercover Tap Dancing

"COME ON EICHER," I said from my office phone. "You can't expect Moose to buy our story if I refuse to hunt sheep."

"Do the best you can. We only have enough money for two hunts. Turn on your best charm until Moose sees things your way."

I raised my voice. "You're no help! I tried to tell him that a sheep trophy wasn't big enough for me, and that Roy only has his sights set on a huge bear. Moose won't accept the fact that we only want two animals. If we don't look and act like the hunters we claim to be it'll hurt our cover. Help me out here."

"You gave him the six grand, right?"

"Right."

"And he's happy, right?"

"No. He's not happy. He can't understand why I don't want to hunt sheep. To him, it makes no sense. I've still got a whole year to string this bastard along and if Roy and I don't buy into his game plan, we're going to start looking damn suspicious."

"All right, I trust your instincts. If you think you need to hunt a sheep to maintain your credibility, that's enough for me. I'll call Porter today and see what he says."

Porter, who was the SAC for Alaska, had little field experience and no undercover experience, and he always had his eye on his budget. I didn't think there was much chance that he'd understand my dilemma.

As I hung up the phone I could feel the tense muscles in my neck. I hated fighting management. To me, cases were about catching poachers. That was what fish and wildlife agents were supposed to do. I didn't care how much money was spent on a case, but I knew Eicher was in for a fight. Squeezing money out of management was like trying to suck beef stew through a straw.

A week later, Eicher called back. "I talked to Porter and he's not crazy about authorizing more funds. But, he said he'd think about it for a couple of more weeks."

My voice turned dead serious. "Tim, this can't wait. I don't want to raise one suspicious hair on Moose's bald head so when the time comes, he'll think nothing of breaking the law when he's with us in Alaska. It's incredibly important that we maintain a sterling relationship with this guy."

"Calm down girl," said Eicher. "I'm not giving up yet."

"What about the State of Alaska? Can they float us some bucks?"

"I asked, but they can't, for reasons I can't go into now."

"What do you mean by that?" I shot back.

"They've got something going that doesn't involve you. It's a big secret."

"Okay," I said sourly. Eicher was withholding information from me and it stunk.

"Are you mad?"

"I'll get over it."

"Good. I'll talk to you later, take care."

Hanging up the phone, I felt I was being invaded from all fronts—Moose, Porter, and now Eicher.

By the first week in September I still hadn't heard from Eicher. It had been nearly six weeks since I'd last talked with Moose. I couldn't wait another day and decided to make a move on my own.

I pulled a small tape recorder out of my desk drawer, put in a new tape, and hooked it to up the telephone handset with a suction-cup device that picked up telephone conversations. It was the cheapest equipment money could buy, but it worked most of the time. I wrote out a short script on a piece of paper, and on the top I wrote "JAYNE" in big letters—so I wouldn't slip up and use my own name. Then I called The Bear's Den.

"Hiya Jayne! What's up?" said Moose.

"How did it go up in Alaska?"

"Great. There was a 100-percent take on bear, the biggest one measured seven feet, but there's still a lot of big bear left."

"What about the sheep hunts?"

"Fantastic! Seventeen sheep hunters got sixteen sheep for the season. Two of them were forty plus inch rams."

"Wow! Well, you talked me into shooting a sheep. I want to do it."

"Hey, that's great. I already told Bob you guys were gonna hunt sheep and caribou, but Bob wants you to shoot the caribou and Roy the sheep."

"You mean we're already booked?" I said, trying to hold back my surprise.

"Oh yeah. I wasn't gonna let you guys get away without shooting at least four animals. It ain't even worth the trip if you don't."

"Thanks Moose. Thanks a lot. I really mean it. But you know my heart was set on a sheep. How come Bob wants me to shoot a caribou instead?"

"Don't know for sure. That's what Bob wants, and he's the boss."

This unexplained change was unsettling because it wasn't something normally done with paying clients, but I went along with it. "Whatever works," I said.

"How come one hunter didn't get his sheep?"

"Oh, that was Joanna Hightower."

"A she? Couldn't she shoot?"

"Not on this hunt. She's a sportswriter and a big-shot hunter from West Virginia. Her picture is in all the hunting magazines 'cause she holds a couple of Boone and Crockett records. Anyway, Bob put her on three good sheep and she missed all of them. On top of that, she was a pain in the butt. I guess Bob ain't taking any more chances on women sheep hunters."

I then understood why Bowman didn't want me on a sheep hunt. Darn her anyway.

"I promise I won't be a pain," I said forcing a laugh. "Roy and I will be up to see you soon. We want to hear more about the hunts in Alaska."

"Sure, come on up. Maybe we can do some duck huntin'. My sons just built a new duck blind on my lake. There's about two thousand ducks sitting on it all the time."

"That would be great," I said remembering that Moose hunted ducks over bait. "We'd *really* like that."

"Yeah, I'm leaving tonight to hunt bighorn sheep in Montana, and then I'm headed to Arizona for a desert bighorn. I'll be huntin' right on the edge of the Grand Canyon."

"Be sure and tell us all about it."

"You bet."

I hung up the phone and stopped the tape recorder. *Amazing*, I thought. Moose had used his casual, but ubiquitous charm to maneuver Roy and me into more hunts. This of course made him look better to his boss who wanted all the paying hunters he could get, especially ones who were considered safe bets.

Now I had another problem. If Porter didn't approve the additional funding and we had to back out of the extra two hunts, Bowman would be furious, which would jeopardize our relationship with him. Worse yet, when Porter found out what happened he might even shut down the entire operation. I went to bed that night wondering if I'd ever get to Alaska.

———

CHAPTER 6

Inside The Bear's Den

IT WAS FRIDAY, OCTOBER 18, 1991, and cold fronts had dominated the weather for several days. With the waterfowl and big-game seasons in full swing, I was working seven days a week. On the day before, another agent and I served a search warrant on the house of a hunter who had shot a caribou illegally in Canada. Along with the mounted head of a caribou and two dozen pictures of that hunt, we seized evidence of other illegal hunts.

I was in my office filling out paperwork when Roy called. "You're not going to believe this shit."

"What?"

"I called Moose to ask him if he'd take us out duck huntin', and he's out duck huntin' right now."

"So what?"

"He's with Bob Bowman."

"You're kidding?"

"No. I just talked to Peg; she told me. Bob bought a new diesel truck in Minneapolis and is driving it to Arizona for the winter. He stopped up at The Bear's Den to hunt with Moose."

My mind raced. "How long is he going to be there? Did she tell you?"

"Two more days. Then he's headed south."

"We have to get up there. Tomorrow."

"To hunt ducks?"

"No, to meet Bowman. This is an opportunity to see who we're dealing with."

"Shit, I don't know if I'm ready to meet the big guy yet."

"Well, get ready," I said. "It's important that we look him in the eye. Wait until this afternoon and call Moose back. Make up a reason for us to be in the area, and tell him we'll drop by."

"Okay. What time?"

"Say four o'clock. I'm supposed to do an interview in Rice Lake at noon. Can you meet me at the Holiday Inn at three?"

"Sure. I'll tell Moose that we're on our way to a wedding in Minneapolis. I'll call you back if Moose says he won't meet us. Otherwise it'll be a go."

"Good job, Roy. Thanks."

My day was already crammed tight. I had to get out an overtime report, a travel voucher, and pack up four dead eagles to send to the wildlife forensics lab for necropsies. This would give me about two hours to buy dry ice, drive out to the airport, ship the birds, and exchange the government Explorer for my personal car, and pick up Megan from her after-school childcare program before it closed.

When I got home with Megan, I returned three phone calls that had piled up on my answering machine and cooked a chicken dinner. At the dinner table I broke the news to Lonnie that I wouldn't be home the next day for his birthday.

Once again the bad guys were calling the shots in my life. On my anniversary in November I was usually in the field somewhere trying to catch a wildlife violator. I worked most Thanksgivings and now I was taking off on Lonnie's birthday. I felt like a total heel and vowed that I'd try to make it up to him. But I couldn't control what the bad guys did or when they did it, which made balancing work and home life even more difficult, and there was no end in sight.

On Saturday, October 19, I pulled into the Holiday Inn parking lot at Rice Lake at twenty minutes before three. I had just finished a tough interview with a man suspected of using the insecticide Furadan to poison eagles. I laid the front seat flat and stretched out. Closing my eyes, I let the accumulated stress of work, home, and road time ease out of my body. As waves of drowsiness swept over me, three high-pitched beeps of a car horn snapped me awake.

Reluctantly, I sat up and gave a slight wave to Roy who had pulled up so close to the Explorer I couldn't open the door. *What a funny guy*. He backed up, and I got out and climbed into the Corvette.

"You look like hell," he said.

"Thanks."

"You shouldn't kill yourself. It ain't worth it."

"Come on, let's get this thing over with."

We pulled up to The Bear's Den at 4:00 P.M. sharp. Judging by the jammed parking lot there had to be a Packers game on TV. Right from the start I was preoccupied with what time I'd get home. I figured we'd leave the bar no later than five o'clock. That would give us an hour with Bowman and I'd be home by ten at the latest. I had put the tape recorder in place and stuck my finger on it to make sure it was running by its vibration. Roy and I got out of the Corvette and I prayed that we'd both be good liars today.

Walking inside I was reminded that Moose never missed anyone who crossed his threshold. His voice boomed across the room before the door closed behind us.

"Hey, you guys, over here!"

We shouldered our way around the pool table where a crowd had gathered over the hotly contested football game. Roy and I quickly claimed the only two empty seats that were across the bar from each other. From the happy howling that emanated from the back of the room, I knew the Packers were winning. Moose shoved a Korbel and Coke in front of Roy and a draft beer in front of me. He put his right foot up on a beer cooler and leaned on his knee.

"You should see the sheep I got on my last trip. Big bastard, I tell you."

"He ain't lying one bit," said a stubble-faced man sitting next to me who wore a Carson Construction cap and a shirt that read, "Eat, Sleep, and Fish." "I seen the pictures."

"You got 'em here?" I asked, doing some fishing myself.

"Naw. They're up at the house. I'll show 'em to you."

"Where's Mr. Bob?" asked Roy.

"He's gone, but he'll be back."

"Tell us more about your sheep hunts," Roy said between sips.

"Oh shit. The second one was one hell of a hunt. Up and down, down and up, all over the place. That damn sheep didn't want to get shot. But I got him.

That's what I like about sheep huntin'—it's real mental. Mental and physical. I lost at least twenty pounds right here." Moose patted his expansive belly.

Roy slid off his stool and walked over to me. Leaning toward my ear, he whispered, "Ever hear so much bullshit?"

Meanwhile, I scratched for details that would verify anything about his hunt. I'd already done a records check and knew he didn't have sheep permits to hunt in Montana or Arizona. "Say, how much do Arizona and Montana sheep permits cost these days?"

"A damn bundle," was all he'd say.

There was something wrong with Moose's sheep hunts, if he even went on them. He could have hunted on Indian land, which wouldn't have come up in my search. But still, his claims seemed dubious.

The stubble-faced man sitting next to me dragged lazily on a cigarette. The smoke spiraled up in the air and eventually made its way into my nostrils. A pyramid of cigarette butts piled up in an ashtray, a growing monument to the amount of time he'd spent in The Bear's Den. I looked at my watch. It was after five o'clock and still no Bowman.

Roy was sitting with his elbows resting on the bar, a drink in hand, looking content since he was being paid to drink. His eyes drifted in no particular direction, and the same small smile hadn't left his face for at least thirty minutes. I sipped my warming beer as stubble-face elbowed me. In a thick-tongued voice, his curiosity about the woman next to him came out.

"Where 'bouts you two headed?"

"Uh, Minneapolis, we're supposed to go to a wedding."

"Man, I don't go to that place unless it's absolutely a life or death matter."

"I don't blame you. It's pretty crowded."

"Ugh. People run around there like a bunch of crazy ants. I don't want no part of it."

"Yeah, but it's a wedding, so I guess that's important enough."

"Shit, I'd tell whoever was gittin' married to send me a video."

I laughed and again looked anxiously at my watch. Was Moose, the master manipulator, leaving us in a quandary for the purposes of his own entertainment because he knew our true identities? I wondered if Roy was feeling the same trepidation.

Finally, a man with white hair, thick as an Indian blanket, walked through the back door. He hesitated, as if he didn't want to be there and his eyes darted in several directions as if he was checking for danger. I knew Bowman had white hair, but this couldn't be him. According to his driver's license he was five feet, ten inches. This guy was shorter. Moose settled the issue.

"Hey, Bob. There's some folks waitin' for ya."

Finally, this is the man I want to take down.

"Things took me a little longer than I thought," he said.

Roy and I swung off our bar stools at practically the same moment. As I looked to Moose to take the lead, he left his station behind the bar and joined Roy and me. Moose's introductions were quick and direct. As I shook Bowman's hand, I looked straight into his clear, hazel eyes watching for a shrinking of the pupils that can signify mistrust. Although I didn't pick up anything, his handshake was weak and noncommittal, his smile seemed forced, and his speech was uneven, not at all like the firm, compelling voice I had heard on the videotape. *What on earth was wrong with him?*

I forced an upbeat voice, "It's great to meet you."

"You a good shot?" he asked, his eyes piercing mine like a laser.

"You bet she is," interjected Roy.

"Can't she talk?" sniped Bowman.

I answered quickly. "I sure am. I've been hunting for years."

"Good. I don't need no crappy shots. I just had a lady hunter in my camp who missed some good sheep. You can't get good animals if you can't shoot 'em."

Bowman asked a few more careful questions about our backgrounds. Sometimes asking them twice as if to check for discrepancies. Roy explained our van leasing business. As cautious as Bowman was, he seemed at ease with our story. Then he switched the subject to the equipment we would need.

"You're only allowed forty-seven pounds worth of gear, and that includes your gun. No more. Less if you want. Here's a list of what I'd recommend. If it's not on the list, leave it. That includes booze. I don't want it around the pilots."

He gave each of us a sheet that reminded me of a packing list for a scouts' camping trip. Moose went back to his business at the bar leaving Bob, Roy, and me standing in a little huddle.

"Sure, Bob, thanks," I said.

"No problem," added Roy.

Bowman glanced at Roy. "What kind of gun you got?"

"Uh, I got a .300 Mag. It shoots real straight."

"Good. What about you Jayne?"

"A Browning .270."

"Good."

I tried to assess Bowman's reaction to us. He was guarded, circumspect, and cagey as a coyote. He'd be hard to catch.

Bowman hadn't moved far from his spot by the door. It was clear that he wasn't going to sit down, have a drink, and chat things over. His mind was on business, his body stiff as a pool cue and his shoulders thrown back like they had been fused into place. As I felt his scrutiny bearing down on us, I tried to lighten things up a little.

"Moose has sure told us a lot about the great food and accommodations at your camp."

"Yeah," said Roy. "He's been trying to talk us into an Alaska hunt for years."

"Oh yeah. How long have you known Moose anyway?"

"Going on seven years."

With Roy's comment I felt my breath cut short. This was an outright lie and I glanced to see if Moose was within earshot. Roy had known Moose for two years at best. This inconsistency could kill what little credibility we seemed to have. Bowman took a handkerchief out of his pocket and wiped it across his lips.

"Yeah? Well that's good. Listen, just as soon as you get home, I want you guys to call Scott Olsen. He's my ticket broker in Seattle. He'll make all your plane reservations and send you your tickets. They might not be in your real names. All you have to say is that the tickets were donated . . . uh . . . just do what he tells you."

I couldn't believe it. Roy's seven-year comment seemed to have turned things around. Bowman was now pulling us in on what sounded like an illegal travel scam. Although he still seemed to twitch at odd moments, he was opening up.

"When you get to Prudhoe Bay I'll have you booked with Duane at Deadhorse Charters. He and I got an agreement. I give him all the charter business to my camp and he don't drop off other hunters in my hunt areas. He takes care of me and I take care of him."

"Great!" I said. "Do you hunt with your clients?"

"No, I'm usually too busy spotting animals and placing hunters. I fly a Super Cub at low altitude so I don't miss nothing. Hunters though, they can't fly and shoot the same day. That's the law in Alaska. They have to wait. So I get everything spotted for them. I've got great guides who really deliver. That's why my business is so good. I advertise complete satisfaction and I deliver. Most outfitters don't. They just bullshit about everything."

"We heard you were good," said Roy.

"Okay, I gotta go, but I'll tell you what, I'll give you guys a four-species rate since you're a couple. That way your caribou hunt will be free. Roy, I want you to shoot a bear the first day in camp; in case there are problems, we'll still have time to recoup. You'll have plenty of time to get a sheep."

"Sounds good."

"Jayne, you'll shoot your caribou around the twenty-eighth of August, and then when the moose season opens on September first, we'll put you on a good moose."

"I can't wait," I said, grinning widely.

"Nice meeting you, folks. Glad you booked when you did 'cause I'm almost booked for the '92 season already."

"Wow!" I said extending my hand to Bowman's, which felt colder and clammier than before—a sure sign of nervousness. I struggled to make sense of this.

Bowman pivoted on one foot and marched out the same door he came in. I watched through the window until I saw him climb into a two-tone Dodge diesel pickup truck that threw gravel as he wheeled it out of the parking lot.

Roy shuffled up to me and squeezed my shoulders. "Man and wife team? How do you like that?"

I turned my head and muttered, "It stinks."

"What a hoot. Let me finish my drink, then we'll go."

I glanced nervously at my watch. It was almost eight; if we left now I would probably be home by 1:00 A.M. I went back to the bar where Moose was shuffling glasses.

"Can we take a look at your sheep hunt pictures before we go?"

"Love to, but I can't leave this place right now to go get them. Next time, okay?"

"Sure."

"So, what'd you think of Bob? Nice guy, huh?" asked Moose.

"He's really nice, Moose. But he seemed a little uptight. Is he always like that?"

"Naw, he don't like bars. He's in recovery, if you know what I mean."

Now everything fell into place. I've heard of ex-alcoholics getting pretty uptight in bars. Every minute he spent with us must have been pure torture. Finally, I saw Roy gulping down the last remnant of his drink.

"Gotta go, buddy. Thanks a lot. I'll be in touch."

"You be good. See ya. Have a good time in Minneapolis."

"Minneapolis! I almost forgot!" I grabbed onto Roy's arm and pretended like I was using all my strength to drag him out of the bar. This gained a roar of laughter from Moose and the boys, which I thought was a good way to end our "official" visit.

Roy's spirits were high as he started driving toward the Holiday Inn in Rice Lake. "We're doin' great, don't you think?"

"It looks like we're good to go on the hunts. But Moose wouldn't talk much about his sheep hunts."

"Yeah, he never showed us his sheep pictures."

"He was just too busy to go get them."

"He's sure a secretive little bastard," muttered Roy.

"That's why this Alaska trip is just as important for nailing Moose as it is for getting Bowman."

"You know though, there's something I don't get. Those two don't seem anything alike. It's hard to imagine they're such hot friends," said Roy.

"They're not friends; they're crooks. Bob trusts Moose to keep his sure-fire hunting methods secret. Think about it: as much as Moose talks about hunting, he doesn't say a damn thing about violating. Even though he has to be."

"So what did you make of Bowman?"

"He's not in love with us—we've got more schmoozing to do."

"That's *your* department."

The truth was I wasn't sure how to gain Bowman's confidence. He was a hunter, adept at patiently stalking his prey, learning its every inclination so that when the time came he would be a step ahead. Bowman didn't blindly accept everyone who crossed his path. He was wary of anything that could cause trouble and, like a fox inspecting a trap, he would only take a step when his instincts told him everything was okay. Bowman isn't going to think we're legitimate just because we said we were. We were going to have to show him.

Roy rolled down the window and let loose a spitball. "Listen, I got a buddy I'm going to stay with tonight. Why don't you get a room at the Holiday Inn in Rice Lake. It's too late to drive all the way back to Madison."

I looked at my watch, "I know, it's a five-hour drive and it's almost nine now."

The Holiday Inn was booked but the clerk gave me numbers for several other area hotels. They were all booked as well.

Frustrated, I hung up the phone. "Why can't I find a room?"

"It's the FIPs," replied Roy.

"Who?"

"The Fucking Illinois People. They're all up here looking at the leaves or some bullshit like that."

Even though I was wrung out from the day I decided to drive home anyway. I cranked up the engine and turned up the radio as loud as I could stand it. After about a hundred miles, however, my eyes felt heavy. Finally, I pulled into a rest stop—without any argument from my ego. I scanned the parking lot for a spot where I wouldn't be bothered and parked. Locking the doors, I crawled into the backseat, pulled a coat over me, and collapsed with every intention of staying there for no more than an hour.

The next thing I knew a sharp light pried through my closed eyelids. I slowly raised my head and peered out the windshield. It was full daylight and people were walking around. Glancing into the rear-view mirror, I winced at the crease lines running down my puffy face. *Better crank it up and get home.* Maybe I'd get there before Lonnie woke up.

Nearly three hours later, I walked into my kitchen, running my hands over my crumpled shirt to straighten it. Lonnie was fixing waffles for Megan, who was in her pajamas glued to the cartoons on the family room TV. His face was etched with worry. He glanced at me sternly as I walked in.

"I've been worried sick about you."

"I'm so sorry. I tried to get home last night. I just couldn't. I was too beat to drive any farther."

"So where did you stay?"

"At a rest area. I slept in my truck."

"Nice."

"I didn't have any choice. All the motels were full."

"Do you realize how worried I've been? I had no idea where you were, and no one to even call. I can't believe it. You act like these jerks you're trying to nail are more important than us. Hell, your mother called this morning. What was I supposed to tell her? That you were working on a case at some bar? Keep me posted when you're going to be out like that."

"Lonnie, I was working. And you're right, I should have called."

"I'm going out to walk the dog."

As Lonnie went out the garage door with Trapper, I went into the family room and sat on the floor next to Megan and kissed her cheek.

"Hi, sweetie."

She hugged my neck. "Mommy! I'm glad you're home."

"Me, too. Can I watch TV with you for a while?"

"Oh, yes!"

We sat together, holding hands. While Bugs Bunny danced circles around hunter Elmer Fudd, I thought about Bowman. He was bright on my radar screen and I was determined to find out just how legitimate his so-called "guaranteed" hunts were.

_____

CHAPTER 7

The Banana Club Lesson

"I DID IT." Eicher's voice over the phone was upbeat. "I got the money."

It was already December and after two months of agonizing silence, Porter finally approved enough money to cover a combination bear/sheep hunt for Roy and a combination caribou/moose hunt for me. Eicher had convinced Porter that Bowman had offered a deal we couldn't refuse. Still, the total bill for the investigation would be around twenty thousand dollars.

"Great! Roy and I will finally be Alaskan big-game hunters. Thanks, Tim."

"I did it just for you."

"Yeah, yeah," I laughed.

"Have you found an agent to replace Roy yet? I'm still concerned about his drinking."

"You said you were going to find a replacement."

"I can't think of anyone. Besides, you should pick someone you're comfortable with."

"I seriously can't think of anyone who would be good on this assignment. Moose and Bowman have accepted Roy and me as a twosome. If we substitute another agent, it might upset the integrity of our cover, which at the moment is the strongest thing we have going. As nervous as it makes me, I think it's important to maintain the cover as it is."

"But what about Roy's drinking?" asked Eicher.

"Bowman instructed both of us not to bring any booze into the camp. So, if Roy doesn't drink at the camp, theoretically we should be all right."

"Funny Bowman won't allow booze in the camp. Drinking is usually the main entertainment after a long of day of flying and shooting."

"He said he doesn't want alcohol around the pilots. But I learned that he's a recovering alcoholic."

"That's interesting. Okay, we'll keep Roy in, but tell him if he screws up this investigation I'll personally kick his ass into his next life."

"I'll be right behind you. As for now, I'll do my best to control him."

"Okay, stay in touch."

Later that day I called Roy and gave him an update on the Alaska case. He was thrilled over the developments and then surprised me by asking me to help him with a case that the state had contracted him to work on.

"What kind of case is it?" I asked.

"I've been trying to get this dirt-ball fishing guide to take me on an illegal fishing trip. He's over-limiting on walleye like crazy and I think he's selling, too."

This was strictly a state law case that I wouldn't normally get involved in, but I felt the more time I spent with Roy, the better off we'd be when we got to Alaska.

"Okay, I'll help you. What do you want me to do?"

"Go with me to the Banana Club. My target's gonna be there next week and I wanna buddy up to him. It'd sure look better if I was with a woman."

"All men look better with a woman," I laughed.

"Great, Jaynie. Next Friday at nine-thirty?"

"Sure."

After the phone call I smiled to myself. Roy was calling me by my undercover name all the time now to make it a habit. I had to give him credit for that.

When I arrived at the Banana Club in a small town outside of Madison, I realized that Roy had failed to mention what a dump it was. I parked the Explorer under a railroad trestle and hoped to hell that it wouldn't get stolen. All I could see was a dark joint about the size of two double-wide trailers with several small windows. As I slipped out of the Explorer I sensed this place wasn't comfortable with strangers.

My chest tightened with apprehension as I walked up to the door and went inside. The overwhelming stink of marijuana and cigarette smoke, the dank smell of beer, and the cacophony of high-voltage hard rock music assaulted my senses from every direction. Looking around, I noted that my red plaid shirt, blue jeans, and Timberland leather shoes contrasted sharply against the spaghetti straps, three-inch heels, and tighter-than-skin skirts that were the primary female attire. A couple of motorcycle gang members looked at me as if they wanted to take me on for violating the dress code.

As I made my way toward the bar I smiled weakly, hoping like crazy that Roy was there. Then I saw him, looking as if he'd been there forever.

"Hey! Have a seat. What do you want?"

The hell out of here.

"A beer I guess."

A buxom barmaid appeared. "Draft or bottle, honey?"

"Uh, draft. Anything will do."

As usual Roy was perched over a Korbel and Coke. I shoved my stool as close as I could to his—sending what I hoped was a message to potential suitors that I was taken. It was the first time Roy looked even remotely appealing to me.

"So, is your guy here?"

"Yeah. He sittin' over there." Roy nodded his head so slightly that I had no idea who he was referring to.

"You gonna talk to him?"

"Yeah, soon. So how have you been?"

"Fine. Couldn't you have found a nicer sewer to meet this guy in?"

"It's not that bad. I think it's kinda homey."

"Yeah, for prostitutes and drug dealers. If you ask me, this place is begging for a drug bust—just what I need right now."

"You worry too much. Relax."

Roy ordered another drink and I swiveled on my stool to catch the entertainment behind me. About ten people packed together, and in various states of sobriety, cavorted and howled in a high frenzy to the music. I turned back to Roy. "Where's your guy again? I can't stay very long."

"He's over there, talking to the big blond."

"Get him over here. Let's get this over with."

"I will in a few minutes. I need more time."

After ten more minutes I got up. "This is ridiculous. I'll be right back."

I went to the restroom, washed my hands, and splashed cold water on my face. A hooker wearing an eighteen-inch skirt pushed me out of her way to spray her hair and redo her mascara. I went back out into the bar only to find that the frenzy had grown to almost delirious proportions. *What was going on?* The answer was a red tube-dress that landed on the floor right next to me. Just then I saw the tassels on a woman's breasts twirling, while men stuck money in her g-string. I quickly went back to the bar and grabbed Roy's arm firmly, getting his immediate attention.

"Listen you big son of a bitch, how *dare* you bring me to a dump like this."

His jaw dropped. "Hey, man, what's the matter with you?"

The tube-dress woman, who had by now found her dress, shoved her way to the bar. "'Scuse me, I need another drink."

"I can't believe you brought me in here. I'm leaving." I marched toward the door, too furious to notice that Roy was following me out to the parking lot.

"Jayne, come back."

My face was hot with rage and my whole body trembled.

"You didn't bring me out here to help you with your contact. You did it for some kind of a cheap thrill. Well you can shove this whole thing up your butt. I've never been so mad in my life."

"Jeez, I didn't know . . ."

"You didn't know what? That I've got standards of common decency and don't enjoy being in places that maggots would find disgusting? You and *your* contact, what a bunch of crap."

"I really am working on a fish case."

"Do you *have* to work your fish case in this dump? You could have met this guy somewhere else. But you picked this place so you could come down here and entertain yourself. And then you dragged me into it. What crap! And another thing, if you screw up my case I'll kick your head in, so you won't be able to spell Alaska, much less go there. Do you understand?"

He reached out to touch me. "Come on, calm down."

"Keep your hands off me!"

I turned and stormed off to the Explorer. Roy called after me, but I ignored him. My emotions were in overdrive and I was afraid of what else I might say. I started up the Explorer and with my hands shaking on the steering wheel I pulled out onto the street. I felt degraded and had no one to blame but myself. I should have never trusted Roy. I already knew he liked these crappy joints and this incident had just reinforced that knowledge.

After a few minutes I was on the main highway and headed home. Entering my house through the garage door, I eased off my clothes, leaving them in a pile on the cement floor where they wouldn't stink up my home with their bar stench. It was about eleven o'clock when I took a shower, slipped on a clean nightgown, and slid into bed next to Lonnie. I put my arm around him and thanked God that I had someone so good in my life.

As the hours ticked by, I still couldn't sleep. I was stuck with an informant with a careless attitude who I didn't trust. Sure, he could get me into the Alaska camp, but he could also easily get me killed.

CHAPTER 8

Ambushed

"READY ON THE RIGHT. READY ON THE LEFT. Ready on the firing line. FIRE!" Upon the command of the range master more than a hundred 148-grain hollow-point bullets pierced human-silhouette paper targets.

It was June 1992, and one-half of the U.S. Fish and Wildlife special agent force had been summoned to the desert outback of Mirana, Arizona, for its annual in-service training. The facility was at the Evergreen Air Station, once an active military airfield, since converted to an overflow training facility for federal law enforcement officers. It was a Thursday morning just before lunch and the temperature had already reached 101 degrees. I was on the range with my colleagues requalifying with our duty weapons.

The first time I held a gun was in April 1975, during Criminal Investigator School. In those days it was held on L Street in Washington, D.C. The ten male U.S. Fish and Wildlife agents I trained with in D.C. were raised hunting small game and deer, and were already proficient with firearms. While they breezed through the preliminaries, I had to be taught everything. I took my training very seriously though, because I knew that if I was going to be accepted among the ranks, good marksmanship was extremely important.

Most of my new colleagues thought that the firearms program would wash me out, but with the days and weeks of practice, I improved my score from a basic marksman to Sharpshooter, and finally I was awarded the much-coveted Expert Certificate. Everyone was surprised. One night I called my mother in Florida and told her that I had finally shot an "Expert." There was a long silence before she laughingly replied, "Did you kill him?"

When the thirty-six-round qualification course was over, the range master gave the command for us to unload and holster an empty weapon. At another command, we marched in unison to the front of the range to score our targets. Mine scored out with 296 out of 300 points, which meant my reputation as a deadeye would stand for another six months.

"Not bad, Annie," said a voice from behind my left shoulder.

I turned around and saw Tim Eicher. I almost didn't recognize him without his Stetson cowboy hat and western-style plaid shirt. He was wearing a T-shirt and a ball cap to protect his decidedly bald head. I would never tell him that his aviator sunglasses and abundant mustache lent him a captivating look.

"Thanks, I can kill 'em when I want to."

"No kidding. Say, you got a minute?"

"Sure. How did you do?" I asked scanning the row of targets for his.

"Don't ask."

We walked over to the firearms shed where I emptied the few live rounds I still had in my pocket into a box, and then walked around to the back of the shed where we captured the only shade at the range. Just then Ken McCloud, a herpetologist-turned-agent, walked by.

"Hey, you guys going looking for lizards tonight?" asked McCloud.

"Naw, I got better things to do than to turn over rocks in the dark for creepy crawlies," drawled Tim.

"I'd go," I said, "but I went last night."

"I must have missed you," laughed Ken. "We're going for gila monsters, could be a hot night."

"Next time, buddy," chuckled Tim.

Ken shot his right arm up in a wave and kept walking.

Eicher and I had been talking all week about our strategy for the Bowman case and I assumed he wanted to talk some more. He leaned one shoulder against the wooden slats of the shed, with his thumbs hooked in the pockets of his jeans. His head hung lower than usual and I sensed something was wrong.

"Uh, there have been some new developments in the Bowman case."

"Shoot. Pun intended."

"I got a call this morning. The State of Alaska sent an undercover into Bowman's camp this spring for a wolf hunt. He did pretty well, so Porter doesn't think we need to continue the investigation."

I was stunned, like someone close to me had died. Beads of sweat ran down my back as I tried to remain calm until I heard the rest of Tim's story. I couldn't believe it. Had the untouchable Bowman really been caught? Had it been that easy? I took a deep breath and froze the expression on my face to conceal my feelings of having the rug pulled out from under me.

"Tell me about it," I said evenly.

"There's a state warden from back east who had always wanted to hunt in Alaska. He's buddies with the Alaskan Fish and Wildlife chief and he worked out a deal for him to hunt with Bowman this spring."

"How did this warden manage to get into Bowman's camp? I thought you had to have a reference from the Queen of England to hunt with Bowman."

"The chief sent the guy to a sport hunting show in Las Vegas last summer. He met Bowman there. I guess they hit it off and Bowman took him in. Bowman checked out the warden's story and he passed muster. It was a good piece of work."

"I see." I nodded, hoping that Eicher wouldn't notice my twitching lip. "So what happened?"

"Basically, Danny Bridges, one of Bowman's guides, took him and a pharmacist on a wolf hunt. Bowman put up his Super Cub, spotted a black wolf, and wagged the wings of the plane to mark its location. Danny and this pharmacist were on a snowmobile and Ted, the undercover warden, was on another machine by himself. Danny dropped the pharmacist off and herded the wolf right to him. The pharmacist shot the wolf, but didn't kill it. The wolf was still going so Danny picked up the pharmacist and they chased it down and killed it. Danny may have shot it again, I don't remember. Then Ted shot a wolf that Bowman spotted for him as well."

"Nice."

"Yeah. Well, they're both Alaskan Airborne Hunting Act cases. Bowman used the plane to spot wolves and aided in killing them. Porter doesn't think we should invest more time and money into our case. He wants you to try and get refunds for your hunts. After all, Alaska Fish and Wildlife has their man."

I wasn't giving up yet. "Has Bowman been arrested?" I asked.

"No. He hasn't received a citation yet, so he doesn't even know he's been caught."

"Will this case shut his hunting operation down?"

"No. It's not enough. But it's enough to fine him, which is better than nothing."

I felt jilted. This case had become part of my life and now it was over? What about all the work I had put into gaining Moose and Bowman's confidence? The bullets I'd sweat keeping Roy's and my cover tight? Now, finally, the hunts were booked, the fees paid, the airline reservations made. Everything was set to go in less than six weeks. This case was very important, and I damn well wanted to pursue what was left of it.

I took a worn Kleenex from my front pocket and blotted it around my face. "Are you actually satisfied with a case on a guy who wagged his wings over a wolf?" I asked sarcastically.

"The case is not that bad. Neither of these guys could have killed their wolves if Bowman hadn't found them from the air and signaled to the ground where they were."

"What if Bowman says he wasn't signaling and that his plane had a bad case of the hiccups? What if Danny-the-guide says he knew where the wolves had been hanging out and took the hunters right to them?"

"It didn't happen that way. Bowman kept the wolves out in the open so Danny could get at them. Bowman's been suspected of doing this from the air for his hunters for a long time. Now the State can prove it."

I stretched the sleeve of my T-shirt and wiped where the Kleenex had missed. The smell of gun powder was still on my hands and shirt and I figured I was probably smearing lead residue all over my face.

"What you've got is a traffic ticket for a guy who uses a plane to spot hundreds of animals in the wilderness and serve them up on a platter to his hunters. A ticket is not going to stop Bowman. He'll laugh it off like a bad joke. Just like Hayes didn't stop the first time he was caught, Bowman won't stop. Besides, what about Moose James and the other violating guides and pilots inside Bowman's camp? This case will never touch them."

"Maybe not, but Porter's looking at saving money. I can't argue that, especially when neither you nor I can guarantee that we can top what the state warden did."

"Top a wing-wagging case? Spare me."

"I don't blame you for being pissed. Look, it's just a case."

"No, it's not *just* a case. Bowman is killing every animal within Super Cub flying range of his camp and I know I can stop him."

"How come you're so damn sure all of a sudden?"

"Because I can feel Bowman's gluttony grinding in my gut and the only way I'm going to get rid of it is to put him and his trigger-happy friends out of business. I know I can get the job done. Tell Porter that all the money he saves by not continuing the investigation is going to cost Alaska a lot of wildlife. I think an administrator could live with that, but I'd be surprised if you could."

I'd hit a nerve. Unable to look me in the eye, Eicher turned away and stared across the desert, strewn with prickly pear and ocotillo with lingering red blossoms. In the distance huge cargo planes, retired from numerous military missions, sat dormant on a cracked and weedy airfield.

Tim turned back to me. "If you do go and it doesn't work out, and all of Porter's money goes down the rat hole for nothing, I'll be getting my paycheck in Chicago."

"Hey, at least the weather will be better."

Eicher slammed a clenched hand against the shed, "Shit! Can't you see I'm stuck?"

"Tim, listen to me. You've got a chance to do the right thing here. Don't let Porter and his cheap-ass attitude about his budget stop us from putting Bowman and that two-bit Moose in jail. There's nothing wrong with the wolf case. But it's not enough. You said you really wanted to stop the killing. Let's do it."

"Have you always been such a pain in the ass, or is this a more recent development?"

"You'll talk to Porter?"

"I'd rather have three root canals."

I put my hand on Eicher's shoulder. "Tim, remember when you called me and talked me into this case. You said the fate of wildlife in the Brooks Range hinged on shutting Bowman down. Remember that. If we let Bowman get by with this wolf case we condemn more animals to die under Bowman's wing and the guns of his clients. C'mon, do the right thing here."

Eicher's peeled off his sunglasses. His eyes met mine and I could almost see right through them. "Okay. I'll talk to Porter. I gotta pick the right time though. He told me to shut this case down so he's not gonna be happy."

"Good. I'm going to get cleaned up before lunch. Let me know how it goes."

"Sure. See you later."

I had put Eicher in a hell of a spot and although he'd pulled out of many tough spots before, there was no guarantee he could save this case.

At home in Madison, Wisconsin, Megan threw a rubber dog bone while Trapper slid across the kitchen to retrieve it. I tossed utensils on the kitchen table while water boiled in a pot for spaghetti. The evening news blared from the TV set in the adjacent family room. As I grabbed a gallon of milk out of the refrigerator, the phone rang. I slammed the door shut with my foot, slid the milk onto the table, turned down the stove, and picked up the phone.

"Hello."

It was Eicher. "Hey, girl, I got news."

"They're moving you to Chicago?" I said as I stirred a pot of spaghetti sauce that spattered red on my white shirt.

"Real funny. I've been working on Porter for a week and I talked him into continuing the investigation."

I put the spoon aside. "I haven't heard from you in three weeks. I thought for sure the investigation was off."

"Naw. Just 'cause I'm in Alaska doesn't mean my cowboy charm doesn't work. Porter's all for it, so you need to get packing."

"Confess Eicher. How did you do it?"

Eicher hedged. "I went out on the limb a little, but it's not a big deal."

"Tell me."

"I promised Porter that you'd deliver several felonies for him."

"You did what?"

"I told him that it was a sure thing that you'd come up with several felonies. You gotta realize that Porter has a huge ego. He wants to look good, and a big case with felony violations would do the trick."

I pushed Trapper away from my feet and paced the floor. "You know that's impossible."

"Yeah, I do. But Porter doesn't. Besides what's he going to do to you? Fire you? You don't even work for him."

"No, but this puts pressure on me that I don't need. In fact, I'm feeling it already."

"Calm down. The goal is to get you to Alaska. I just did what was necessary. Don't worry, Bowman and Moose are first-rate crooks, they'll screw up."

I did worry. My neck was on the line to make this case. If a twenty-thousand-dollar investigation went down with few or no prosecutions, Porter would blame me. The reality was that if Bowman and Moose had any suspicions about Roy or me, they'd make sure everything we did or saw was completely legal. But there was no backing out now, and even with trepidation surging in my heart, I had to go to Alaska and give it my best.

BOOK II

CHAPTER 9

King Informant

AUGUST 27, 1992, MADISON, WISCONSIN. I had just turned forty years old the week before when the day finally arrived to fly to Alaska. It was a Saturday, so Megan and Lonnie were home. Roy was due any time to meet me and to drive to the airport in Chicago.

I rolled up USGS topographical maps of Alaska I'd been studying and put them in a closet. I had used them to memorize the names and locations of rivers like Lupine, Ribdon, Toolik, and Kavik, so I'd know them when the bad guys mentioned them.

As I checked my duffel bag one last time I noticed something was missing. "Where are my boots?" I asked anxiously.

"Haven't seen them," said Lonnie.

Racing though the house I searched the bedrooms until I found Megan in the office planted in my boots, peering out the window with my binoculars. She had done this since she was two years old. Unpacked my bag as I packed it. It was her way of saying that she didn't want me to go.

Gently, I convinced her to relinquish my gear. I held her in my arms and said, "I'm going to be home real soon and then I want to hear all about what you've been doing in school."

"Promise."

"I promise." I kissed her on the cheek. "Let's go find daddy."

Lonnie was in the living room checking my gear making sure my real name wasn't on any of it.

"Jayne Dyer" appeared boldly on a duffel bag, and on a tag that was on my gun case. My only other gear was a small backpack. All together my gear weighed exactly forty-seven pounds.

"Have you double-checked your ID cards?" asked Lonnie.

"Yep. Triple-checked."

"Your airline tickets?"

"Jayne Dyer on all of them."

I stopped. Lonnie's questioning was a sign that he was worried. Even though I had gone on undercover hunts before, he knew this was different. This one would be longer, the country more unforgiving, and the situation in the camp completely unpredictable.

I sat down next to him on the couch and put my hand on his knee. "I want you to know that I'm going to be very careful up there. Nothing means more to me than you and Megan, so I'm not going to do anything reckless. Remember, I'm a professional."

"I know you are, but you can't blame me for being a little worried," he said.

I stood up and looked out the window. "You just take care of yourself and Megan. I'll be fine. Hey, here comes Roy."

When Roy came to the door Lonnie shook his hand and gave him a courteous smile. Lonnie wasn't concerned with my traveling with him since I'd traveled with male agents my entire career. Lonnie helped us load our gear into my Explorer, gave me a big hug, and went back into the house to be with Megan. As Roy and I pulled out of the driveway, Lonnie stood in the doorway with Megan in his arms while she waved good-bye. She was so beautiful and happy, and I was starting to miss her already. My throat tightened as I fought to keep my emotions from showing.

En route to Chicago, Roy and I encountered some unexpected traffic that made us late getting to the airport.

"Drop me off at the American Airlines door and I'll stand in line with the gear. Park the Explorer and meet me inside," I said.

"Sounds good. I don't want to keep them bears in Alaska waitin' for me."

Inside the terminal I dragged his gear to the American Airlines counter. *This stuff weighs a lot more than forty-seven pounds.* Roy showed up a few minutes later.

"Gee, that was fast. You must have found a close spot."

"I parked in short-term."

"Short-term! We're going to be gone more than a week."

"I know. But I didn't want to risk missing the plane."

"You had plenty of time to park in long-term parking. This is going to cost a fortune. Especially in Chicago."

"You feds have plenty of money."

"Darn it anyway, Roy, I've spent my entire career conserving the government's money, and you act like it's yours to just blow as you please."

"We're goin' to Alaska. That's all that matters right now."

A pounding headache started to build as I thought about Roy's bullheaded attitude. Roy thought he was "king informant," and he could do what he wanted. And it wasn't over. At the airline counter Roy's gear weighed in at 137 pounds. American Airlines wanted money for excess baggage.

"You're going to have to leave something here," I said.

"No way. I need everything I packed."

"Do you have any booze packed?"

"No, I promise."

I looked back at the line of people waiting anxiously for Roy and me to hurry.

"Okay, I'll pay the fee, but you weren't supposed to bring this much."

"I just packed what I needed."

I slapped down the eighty-five-dollar fee in cash. Roy and I grabbed our boarding passes and headed for the gate. Even though I wanted to ream Roy out for his attitude, my number-one rule was not to fight with my partner before an undercover contact. The resulting tension would bleed over into the contact and could have a negative impact on the case. We were supposed to be boyfriend and girlfriend on a once-in-a-lifetime Alaskan hunt. We were supposed to be happy. I swallowed my ire and remained congenial. But as we settled into our seats, every time I looked at Roy I had this irresistible urge to choke him.

Midnight. *Tap-tap.* Slowly the door to room 203 at the Anchor Inn in Anchorage, Alaska, drew open. Roy and I walked into a room feebly illuminated by two lamps with crooked lampshades. The smell of stale air overpowered with room deodorant swept into my lungs. As a frequent traveler, I'd smelled the stuff many times.

I nodded first to Tim Eicher who stood with one of his roping boots perched on the heater box next to the window, which was draped shut with a heavy plastic curtain. The dark shadows in the room made me feel like I was about to meet the legendary Deep Throat, a feeling intensified by the dim figure of a man seated in the corner.

"This is Ralph Collins, Chief of Law Enforcement for the Alaska Fish and Wildlife Department," said Tim.

As my eyes adjusted to the dark, I could see Collins, a balding man in his mid-fifties, heavy set, with the pasty-white skin characteristic of people in northern climates. He barely rose from the chair as he reached across the table to shake my hand.

"Nice to meet you," he said. He nodded to Roy. "You, too." Collins wasted little energy in making Roy and I feel welcome in his home state.

"My pleasure, Ralph," I said, forcing a smile.

"So," Collins said sitting back down. "Are you two up for this assignment?"

"As ready as we'll ever be," said Roy shrugging his shoulders.

Collins studied me carefully. His left eye squinting critically as if he expected me to somehow prove to him right then and there that I was capable of penetrating Bowman's ironclad camp. I ignored his unspoken demands.

Eicher broke the silence. "Hey, guys, it's late. Let's get this over with. You need to show the Chief your creds."

I pulled the leather wallet out of my jacket pocket and laid it open on the table revealing a large gold badge and accompanying credentials with my photograph. Collins raised his eyebrows slightly.

"Okay, raise your right hand."

Collins pulled a small piece of paper out of his front pocket and read an oath citing various Alaska laws and judicial codes. Finally he read the last line.

"Do you promise to faithfully execute your duties to the best of your abilities, to protect the natural resources of the State of Alaska, to protect your fellow officers and citizens of this state from bodily harm, and to tell the truth at all times?"

"I do."

"Does this mean we're married?" joked Roy.

"Don't wish that on yourself," chuckled Eicher. "It means that for the purposes of this investigation she's a commissioned Alaska State Trooper. She now has the authority to investigate state law violations. Hopefully there will be a bundle." Tim picked up my badge and put it in his briefcase.

"I don't know about this," said Collins as he slowly folded the sacred oath. He looked at me. "I'm warning you that this could be an extremely dangerous assignment, and I don't have the manpower to bail you out if something goes wrong."

I met his eyes. "We know that. We're going in anyway. Tim, you gonna take us to the airport tomorrow?"

"Yeah. I'll pick you up at your hotel at 5:00 A.M. Roy's gonna bunk with me."

I walked toward the door. "Good. See you tomorrow. Nice meeting you, Chief."

Eicher touched my shoulder. His voice a little softer. "I need one more thing."

"What's that?" I asked, turning around.

"Your gun. Do you have it?"

"Of course I have it. Right here." I patted the fannypack around my waist.

"How'd you get it on the plane?"

"I left it in my checked bag."

"Well, give it to me. You can't take it with you."

"I know, I forgot." I took the Sig Sauer 9mm pistol out of the fannypack and gave it to him.

"Better give me the fannypack, too."

Quickly, I unhooked the strap and handed it over. "There. No gun, no credentials."

As I walked out into the dark Alaskan night to go to my hotel with no badge and no gun, I felt like a warrior going into battle without a sword or shield. On this assignment, my wits would be my only weapon and protection, and they'd have to be very sharp.

A few minutes later I arrived at the Regal Alaskan Hotel where Bowman had reserved a room for Roy and me. In my suite, I pulled back the baroque bedspread and slid between the luxury sheets. The bedside digital clock blinked 1:16 A.M., reminding me that I had less than four hours of this unprecedented luxury. But sleep always eluded me when it was mandatory. Breathing deeply, I tried to relax.

During the night, a vision of the Waubay marshes in South Dakota crept into my brain. I was slogging through the marsh easily as I had done many times sneaking up on illegal duck hunters. As the muck slid up on my chest waders and my legs churned the mire, the pungent smell of the marsh entered my nose and inched its way down into my lungs. Although it stunk, it was a smell that grew on you over time.

After a while, the muck became thicker, sucking at my thighs, pulling me deeper into the sludge. Sweat beaded on my face, my chest heaved, and my heart pounded from the effort. A voice told me to quit. *But I can't, I have a job to do. I have to get there.*

With every fiber of my body I fought the sludge, but I could barely keep from being sucked into the marsh. The voice said to give it up. It insisted that I wasn't going to make it. *No. I have to keep trying. I'll get there.* The mud closed around my chest, pressing against my lungs, making it harder to breathe. *Keep going.* Then mud seeped over the edge of my chest waders and began filling them. I sank even deeper. *Don't die!* As the mud crept up higher, the alarm rang. I awoke exhausted. *That was one hell of a dream.*

I rolled out of bed and made some coffee in the pot that was on a service table. Then I took a quick shower. Afterwards I stood in front of the mirror, combing my hair, and stared at two bloated cheeks holding up the bags under my eyes. *What a wreck.* I poured some coffee in the plastic cup, grimaced at the first bitter sip and dumped it down the sink. After running the hotel's blow-dryer through my hair a few times, I took a black passport holder that held a small notebook and a stubby pencil and clipped it around my waist. That would be my concealed recorder for this assignment.

I pulled on the same tan field pants I had worn the day before and checked in the mirror to see if the passport holder was visible under my pants. *No.* Then I put on a dark purple long sleeved turtleneck with a fuchsia flannel shirt over it. *Color. I want these guys to know I'm a woman.*

Ten minutes later, I was standing outside the hotel when Eicher pulled up with Roy in an unmarked Dodge pickup truck. Eicher hopped out, said hello, and flung my gear into the back of the truck while I slid in the front seat next to Roy. It was a tight squeeze but bearable. At the airport Eicher dropped us off in front of the main terminal with our gear at our feet.

"Good luck guys," he said. He then gave us our "short instructions." "Call me the minute you're out of the camp. If you're not out by September sixth, me and six other agents are going to check on that camp and see what's up. If there's any sign of trouble we'll haul you and Roy outta there."

Inside the terminal, Roy and I stood in line to check our bags. I leaned over and spoke in a low voice. "We're in role now. From now on, we're who they think we are. Roy and Jayne, big-game hunters. Got it?"

"Right, boss."

"Don't call me boss."

Two hours later I pressed my nose against the Plexiglass window of the jet and tried to take in as much of Prudhoe Bay from the air as I could. It was smaller than I had thought, but there was no mistake from the cluster of smoke stacks and pipelines that the town existed for one reason: oil. The runway caught us from out of seemingly nowhere, and before I knew it we were out on the tarmac, surrounded by a dull, gray industrial metropolis of grimy metal. Even the air smelled ugly.

We collected our gear inside, at the only baggage carousel in the modest-sized terminal. Lined up at the ticket counter were two hunters with loads of gear and a cache of hunting trophies consisting of moose antlers intertwined with caribou antlers, taped together with what looked like miles of duct tape. A huge duffel bag that was probably stuffed with bear hides. Long gun cases that probably held twelve-hundred-dollar hunting rifles. I wondered if they had been at Bowman's camp. I wondered if they had hunted legally or had illegal kills.

Roy and I and trudged back outside with our gear where Roy voiced his first priority to a young oil worker standing nearby. "Is there a bar around here?

The man laughed. "There ain't no bars here. Prudhoe's dry."

"You got to be kidding."

"That's okay," I said. "Let's go find our ride."

"Who you lookin' for?" asked the worker.

"A charter service run by a guy named Duane."

"Yeah, I know him. He's just across the lot, where the trailers are. He's in the second one on the right."

"Thanks, buddy," said Roy. "I can tell you right now, I couldn't live in this place."

Roy and I found the nondescript trailer with a sign on the door that read: DEADHORSE CHARTER—COME IN.

Leaving our gear outside, we opened the creaky door and walked inside. A man in his late thirties sat hunched over a gray metal desk and held a phone to his ear. If he knew he had company, he didn't let on. While waiting for him to notice us, I took a moment to study him. I saw a skinny, shot-in-the-ass kind of guy with shoulder-length, oily-brown hair and a four-day stubble beard. He was wearing stained denim pants and a sooty thermal underwear shirt covered with a navy-blue down vest. His body odor was so thick I could almost see it.

Finally he got off the phone. "You guys the Dyers?"

"Uh, I'm Jayne Dyer. This is Roy. We've got reservations to get flown into Bowman's camp."

"Yeah, I know. I've been waitin' for you. I'm Duane."

As we shook hands, I caught a whiff that made me think that he probably had breakfast with Jack Daniels.

"We can leave just as soon as you pay me six hundred dollars," said Duane. "It's a forty-five-minute flight and I'm fueled up."

The three of us clamored down the metal steps of the trailer to where the gear lay. Duane picked up my duffel bag with one hand.

"How much does this weigh?"

"Forty-seven pounds, on the dot."

He picked up Roy's two bags, one at a time.

"Hey, man, you can't take all this shit."

"Hey, man, I need all that shit and I'm takin' it."

"Then I'm charging you an extra two hundred, so that's eight hundred dollars total."

"That's a rip-off," I protested.

"Lady, I'll be lucky to have enough gas to get back home. That shit is heavy."

"Roy, this really ticks me off. Leave some of that stuff here. You knew all along there was a weight restriction."

"I ain't leaving nothing. I need my gear. Pay the man so we can go."

"I got by with forty-seven pounds. How come you couldn't have?"

"Jayne, just pay the man."

"No. It's too much money. Leave some of your stuff here. We'll pick it up on our way out."

"I ain't doin' that. It might get stolen. Besides I need it. You got the money. Pay him."

Duane's cracked lips pursed together as if he was holding back. Then he said, "Lady, you got about three seconds to make up your mind. I got hunters waiting on the other end to be brought back."

I ripped seven one hundred dollar bills and two fifties out of my wallet and pushed them into Duane's open hand. He shoved the money in his pocket and said, "All right you lovebirds, follow me."

Duane's plane was a small Cessna with two seats up front and one in the back. I crawled into the back, sank into the seat, and appealed to my higher power. *Just get us there.*

As we pulled off the runway, the Alaskan tundra stretched beneath us into an expanse of rich, low-lying vegetation, and we soon spotted a large herd of feeding caribou. What I assumed would be a wild ride with Duane turned into a phenomenal nature tour. Duane tipped the wings of the aircraft to give Roy and me a better view of a grizzly bear loping across the tundra, and a few minutes later he took the plane slightly off course to check out a pair of moose with huge racks standing in some willows. A few minutes later we saw several hundred more caribou and two grizzly sows with young. Seeing the wildlife calmed my nerves and reminded me why I was even in Alaska. But it all ended much too soon.

As Duane circled the plane above a nest of white tents and Quonset huts he yelled above the engine noise, "That's Bowman's camp. The river below us is the Ivishak. You should go fishing while you're here."

Roy eagerly nodded his head. Duane bounced the Cessna on the gravel runway, which was part of the riverbed, and brought it to a stop. I spotted Bowman standing with two other hunters. Bear hides were taped in round bundles, with Dall sheep horns secured on top. Inside the Cessna, the three of us sat quietly for a couple of minutes waiting for the prop to stop spinning.

Meanwhile I eyed the two hunters. One of them looked vaguely familiar. He had a medium build, with a light-haired Nordic look common to people in the Dakotas where I'd been stationed for eight years. I strained to see through the window of the plane. Even his gestures seemed familiar. The way he threw back his head and laughed and the way he shuffled his feet. I felt my insides go cold. *I definitely knew this guy from somewhere.*

———

CHAPTER 10

A Bad Day to Die

WHAT WERE THE CHANCES OF SEEING SOMEONE I knew at this outpost in Alaska? Slim to none?

Once we unbuckled our seat harnesses Duane popped open the door and got out. Then Roy and I hopped out of the plane onto the river rocks.

Roy stretched his arms wide as if to take in the entire cosmos. "Damn," he said breathing in deeply. "This is where them big bears live to die."

"Remember, you're not on vacation," I said in a low, rigid voice.

"Quit being so damned uptight would you?"

Ignoring him, I walked away from the plane toward the river, pretending to look at it. I wanted to play it safe and avoid the familiar-looking hunter.

"You still pissed at me over the gear?"

"Leave me alone for a minute."

"Whatever."

Not daring to turn my back, I heard Duane greet Bowman, and introduce Roy to the two hunters. One of the men said he was from Alpine, Texas, and the other said he was Jerry Hoff from South Dakota. *Jerry Hoff*. This name was burned into my memory. I had written him a five-hundred-dollar citation for shooting an over-limit of geese along the Missouri River near Pierre. It had been a couple of years earlier, but I remembered the case because Hoff had threatened to call the governor and have my job. If Hoff got a good look at me, he'd remember me. After all, I was the only woman federal wildlife agent in South Dakota. In fact, most hunters I contacted in the field remembered me.

Here I was only minutes into the operation and my cover was on the verge of being blown. I strolled back and forth along the river bank wishing the hunters would get their gear loaded and get the hell out of there. Meanwhile my eyes pored over the landscape. Mountains cut across the sky like a jagged wood saw, forming a small part of the Brooks Range, which is the largest east-west mountain range in the Western Hemisphere. There were no crowns of lush trees or emerald forests, only a vision of grays and browns, with a sprinkling of snow that looked like powdered sugar. Stretching to the foot of the mountains was a carpet of low-lying lichens and mosses that had defied eons of paralyzing freezes and still managed to color the landscape with warm hues of chestnut, mustard, and olive. Even thought it was all beautiful, I was too tied up in knots to fully appreciate it.

Finally, I heard the Cessna's engine roar to life. From the corner of my eye I saw Bowman trot away from the plane. I didn't dare approach Bowman and Roy until the plane had turned around. The takeoff was sluggish and the plane seemed to grunt as it finally became airborne.

"Too close," grumbled Bowman. "He barely made it that time. Too much gear. Damn hunters never listen to me when I tell them not to bring every single thing they own."

I cut Roy a glaring look.

He turned his back to me and picked up his bags and gun case.

"C'mon," said Bowman, "I'll show you guys to your tent."

As we hiked briskly along, Roy, who was already panting, asked, "Is there anything left for us to kill? Or did Moose get it all."

"There's plenty left for you to kill, but Moose ain't comin'."

The news startled my already jittery nerves. "Why not? He promised to be our guide."

"He came up with a sheep permit in the Lower 48. We got plenty of good guides here. Don't worry; you'll get your animals."

But the fact that Moose had backed out did worry me. He had been adamant about being our guide. Was he on to us? Had he told Bowman? Or was I just overreacting because of my near-miss with Jerry Hoff? I didn't dare ask Bowman any more questions about Moose. That alone would appear suspicious. I'd find out about Moose from someone else.

As we walked, voices drifted from the first chalky-colored Quonset hut we approached. "Is that Spanish I hear?"

"Yep. I got three hunters here from Spain. They don't speak no English, and they're complaining their asses off, but I don't know what about," snarled Bowman.

I smiled. "I can help you. I speak Spanish."

Bowman looked at me, his mouth dropped open in disbelief. "Roy, wait here. Jayne, come with me."

I followed Bowman inside the two-room Quonset equipped with army beds, a heater, and little else. The Spaniards were in the back room with clothes, wine bottles, and boxes of imported chocolate strewn everywhere. The sight of a woman caught their immediate attention.

One of them looked at the other and said, *"Qué lindisima mujer!"* (What a pretty woman!)

Bowman looked at me, pointed at the men, and said, "Well, talk."

"Uh . . . sure. *Hola. El Señor Bowman me dijo que ustedes nescesitan una traductora."* (Hello. Mr. Bowman tells me you need a translator.)

Skipping introductions, the largest of the three men, with dark eyes and thick dark hair combed back from his forehead, pointed a finger at Bowman and exploded in a torrent of Spanish.

"Tell him that my back hurts and I can't hunt at the spike camps anymore. I can't sleep on the ground. I need a bed and I can't take all the hiking up and down mountains. My back is killing me. And the food is terrible. We want all our hunts done from the main camp. No more of the bullcrap spike camps."

The second man, in his late fifties with a mellow face and deep-brown eyes, took an unlit cigar out of his mouth. *"La comida en el campamento portal es fatal."* (The food in the spike camp is garbage.) "I won't eat any more of it. Tell Mr. Bob that when I came out here I expected to hunt with my son." He put his arm around a young man in his twenties with a soft, moon-shaped face. "My son gets left here while I'm out in the middle of nowhere. I came here to be with my son. The situation right now is very bad. Tell him that."

I turned to Bowman and translated a gentler version of the Spaniards' complaints.

Bowman's face turned a light crimson. "Tell 'em this ain't no Riviera resort and the only way they're going to kill critters is to get out there where the critters are. Tell 'em they're eatin' what everyone else is eatin' and I can't make no exceptions. As for the spike camps, they ain't supposed to be luxurious. What the hell? And as for that kid flying around in an airplane for a ride, forget it. I got too many hunters to put on animals and he's just dead weight. If he don't hunt, he don't fly."

"Gentlemen, Mr. Bowman says that nothing can be done about the food at the spike camp. It's difficult to prepare good meals in the wilderness. And he can't fly non-hunters in his plane, because there's not enough room."

"*Uufff,*" said the big man.

"*Es ridículco,*" said the older man.

The son, thin and pale, was dead quiet.

The big man spoke again. "Did you tell him that I hurt my back hunting a sheep? I can't hunt for several more days, at least."

When Bowman heard this translation he became even more infuriated. "And that's another damn thing. These guys can't shoot worth a shit." He pointed at the big man. "A guide put him within thirty-five yards of a good sheep and he wounded it. My guides spent fourteen hours tracking the damn thing and never found it. I can't put up with that shit. I want good, clean shots. I want both these guys to sight in their guns. They refused to do it when they got here."

I explained to the Spaniards about their guns and they grunted with indignation. They said there was nothing wrong with their guns, and besides they didn't know anything about sighting them in. I explained that I had to sight my rifle in and would sight in their guns at the same time. I had seen a makeshift range on the riverbed when we landed.

The big man and the older man looked at each other and seemed satisfied. "*Bueno,*" said the big man. "*Vamos por nuestras armas.*" (Good. Let's get our guns.)

Tempers cooled and finally Bowman made introductions. He nodded to the big man and said, "This is Pedro. He owns a fancy restaurant in Spain, and his partner here is Carlos. We call him 'El Doctor,' because he's a doctor. The kid, Carlos Jr., is his son. We just call him 'Junior.' "

I shook hands with the Spaniards as they issued thanks for my coming to their rescue. I told them to bring their guns down to the riverbed in a few minutes.

Outside, Bowman and I joined up with Roy and continued into the camp. Bowman stopped at a wall tent, made from white canvas in the shape of a one-room cabin. It had a wooden door with part of a caribou antler for a door handle.

"There's your tent. Drop your gear and then go sight in your guns."

The interior of the tent was clean with two single beds set on a wooden floor. A small sink was plumbed into one corner, and an oil burning heater sat in another.

"Boy-o-boy, this is great," grinned Roy.

"Not bad," I conceded. I especially liked the fact that we weren't housed with other hunters. This would give us the privacy we'd need to discuss the investigation.

Roy shut the door, "What was going on back at the Quonset hut?"

"Three of Bowman's hunters are from Spain. They don't speak English and have been bitching about the conditions around here for days. I think Bowman warmed up to me a bit. He needs me to translate for him."

"Oh man, this is getting good already," cooed Roy as he began laying his extensive hunting wardrobe out in piles on the floor.

I uncased my Browning .270, grabbed six shells, and headed out the door. "Come on down to the range when you're ready."

"Sure thing."

The Spaniards were already gathered on the riverbed at a wooden shooting bench. Quickly, I put in some earplugs and took each of their rifles, making a special note of the makes and model. Pedro had a .300 Winchester Magnum, El Doctor had a 7mm Mauser, and Junior was also shooting a 7mm Mauser. All the guns were equipped with good scopes. I fired rounds at a target set about one hundred yards away, each time adjusting the sights until the shots formed a tight ring. When I was done with the Spaniards' guns, I sighted in my own, and then told them that I was going to get my partner Roy to get his gun sighted in.

Halfway back to the tent I ran into Bowman. "Hey," he said, "I was just looking for you. Get your hunting gear and meet me at the plane in ten minutes."

"W . . . why?" I stammered.

"We're goin' sheep huntin' that's why."

Flustered, I continued on to the tent but stopped short and turned around. "I'm not even booked to hunt a sheep. I'm supposed to hunt caribou and moose."

"Well, that just changed. You're huntin' sheep. Now git."

My heartbeat kicked into high gear. What's wrong with him? He was fine a few minutes ago. Were these sudden changes a bad sign? When I got back to the tent, Roy was still organizing his gear—he had that much stuff. I explained to him what had just happened.

"What the hell? You just got here. Where's he taking you?"

"I don't know."

I grabbed a pair of hunting pants, boots, and some cold-weather hunting gear including a Gore-Tex camouflage jacket that I stuffed into a backpack. I was moving so fast my head felt like it was spinning. "Where's my camera?"

Roy handed it to me from the bed and I dropped it into my pocket. "When are you coming back?" he asked.

"In a few days, I guess." I put my hand on Roy's shoulder. "Just keep real close track of everything that goes on around here."

"I'll try."

"Do better than try. This is important."

I slung the backpack over my shoulder and let the cabin door bounce shut as I trotted down the embankment to meet Bowman at his red-and-white Piper Super Cub. His head was lost under the opened engine cowling. He was talking to the engine like it was an old mule that wouldn't budge. "C'mon you old son of a bitch."

Looking on was another man who I hadn't met yet, but I had seen his picture in Eicher's file, and one glance into his cold, dull eyes confirmed he was Billy Howe.

Howe was one of Bowman's pilots and a guide, and according to Eicher's information he'd killed more wildlife than a hundred hard winters. There was nothing special looking about him, but for an outdoorsman his body appeared spongy and soft. His roughened skin made him look like he was well past the fifty-yard line of life, although I knew he was only forty-eight. Eicher told me that he was what they called a "squaw man," which meant he had a common-law Inuit wife who cooked, cleaned, and provided for his every need. It was known that many squaw men humiliated, intimidated, and abused their wives.

"Hello," I said brightly. "I'm Jayne."

Howe's piercing eyes locked onto me like a pair of lasers.

I broke from his gaze. "Bob, where do you want me to put my stuff?"

"Try behind the backseat," muttered Howe. Already I could feel a quiet, cool hatred emanating from this man.

"Sure thing."

Bowman was still grumbling to himself under the cowling. I wondered if the plane was even airworthy. I assumed that the planes at the camp were maintained and often repaired by the pilots who were like backyard mechanics. Finally, Bowman slammed the cowling shut and walked around the plane inspecting it for gas or oil leaks. He then pulled on the elevator on the tail to make sure it moved freely.

I climbed into the backseat and buckled in. Just before shutting the door on my side, Howe gave me a profoundly suspicious look. I was gripped with the idea that Jerry Hoff had seen me and called back to tell Bowman that I was a federal agent. I was flying out of the main camp with Bowman and had no idea what to expect next.

Bowman cranked the engine and the prop came to life. Slowly the plane moved forward, the spongy tires rolling over the river rocks like a dune buggy. After about three hundred feet the plane had built up enough speed and we were airborne. I was used to flying with highly competent government pilots and so far I had no reason to feel confident about Bowman.

There were two pedals on the floor that he worked alternatively. These operated the rudder. A small wheel in the middle of the console was the trim that leveled the plane once we were airborne. He controlled the altitude with a floor mounted "stick."

I also noticed a Garmin GPS unit installed in the instrument panel that would provide longitudinal and latitudinal coordinates for locations Bowman wanted to mark. Eicher had told me that he suspected Bowman of spotting wildlife from the air, marking their location with a GPS, and then taking his hunters right back for an illegal kill.

Suddenly I felt the plane bank and lose altitude. "Look," shouted Bowman. I pressed my face against the plastic window and saw a grizzly bear on the ground. Bowman dropped the plane to about two hundred feet, and began pursuing the bear from behind. Sensing the danger, the bear broke into a run.

Harassing wildlife from the air is a violation of the federal Airborne Hunting Act but I could tell that Bowman was quite practiced at it. After a few minutes he gave up on the bear and the Alaska oil pipeline came into view. Bowman followed it until we came upon a graded gravel runway marked with an austere looking building. He landed the plane, pulled up to a gas pump, and shut down the engine.

Finally he said, "This is what we call 'Happy Valley.' It's an inspection station run by the Department of Transportation for the oil haulers. I need to get gas."

Bowman crawled out of the plane and inserted a gas hose into one of the plane's wings.

"How many gallons do the wings hold?"

"Sixteen gallons on each side."

"Is that enough to get you around this country?"

"Naw. I stash gas wherever I can. That's what I'm doing now. Picking up gas cans to stick out in my hidey holes."

Bowman headed for the DOT building and I followed. The building was reminiscent of the drab buildings on the military bases I had grown up on. A large room with tiled floors that smelled of Pine-Sol. The cinder-block walls were painted a light olive green, the metal desks were gray, and the chairs were covered with hard plastic, olive green, of course. It was Sunday so everyone was gone, but everything had been left wide open. Maybe locks weren't needed on the tundra.

Without explanation, Bowman disappeared into a back office. Nervously, I waited alone.

Ten minutes later he returned and asked, "Tell me more about this van business you and Roy have in Chicago."

My stomach churned. "We're not actually in Chicago, we're just north of there. Our business is called 'J and M Leasing.' Mainly we lease panel vans. Lots of businesses use them on maintenance jobs and to haul equipment. We rotate them out on a regular basis for repair and painting. That's about it."

"Why don't people just buy the damn things? Why rent?"

"Renting is usually a stronger option for small companies that don't want to get bogged down with maintaining a vehicle fleet. They don't want to hire a staff of mechanics."

Bowman's face didn't flinch. *Good. So far, he believed me.*

"How many of these vans do you lease?"

"We usually have thirty or forty out at a time."

"Where do you buy 'em?"

"At the Chicago car mart."

"What do they cost? On average."

Shit!

I hesitated, "Oh, the cost varies. Roy takes care of all that."

Not good. If Bowman asked Roy the same question, I didn't think Roy could pull off a credible answer. I may have saved my own butt for the moment, but I put Roy in a tough spot. I worried that Bowman had picked up on my hesitancy and I looked for a diversion.

"Hey, I'm itchin' to hunt. When are we going?"

"In a minute," Bowman growled.

I followed him outside to the plane and watched as he pumped gas into the wings. Then he trotted to a nearby shed and brought out three five-gallon gas cans and filled them up. He stashed the gas cans behind my gear. As I crawled into the backseat, I felt like I was flying in a Molotov cocktail. The fumes from the gas sickened me.

Bowman pulled himself into the pilot's seat and put on his headset. The prop churned and within about ninety seconds we were airborne again. This time we headed north, deep into mountain country. The magnificent scenery of peaks and valleys calmed me down a bit, but that all changed when Bowman landed the plane on the barren riverbed.

He leaned forward in his seat and popped open the door and shouted, "Okay, get out."

My mouth went completely dry and my throat tightened, nearly closing up completely. Reluctantly, I crawled out of the backseat of the plane with my rifle and hopped to the ground.

The engine was still running as I backed away from the plane to escape the blowing dirt and held a hand over my eyes. Bowman popped open his window and shouted, "I'll be back."

I was unconvinced. This would be an extremely easy way to get rid of me. Bowman could say I went out hunting and "got lost." This was exactly what Ron Hayes threatened to do to agent Joe Ramos. My brain was dulled by disbelief as I tried to keep thoughts of impending gloom from engulfing me.

The tail-dragger turned practically on a dime and took off in the same direction it had landed. As it sprung into the air, I took out the small camera from the pocket of my hunting jacket and snapped a picture. In case Bowman didn't come back for me, there would be some evidence of what had happened to me.

As Bowman's plane disappeared into the pale blue sky I couldn't shake the gnawing feeling that he thought that Roy and I were cops. I was alone in a wilderness the size of Texas with a rifle and two candy bars in my pocket. An hour passed. I sank down onto a rock as I mulled over the events of that morning. There was Jerry Hoff, the hunter I saw at the main camp. Then, without explanation, Bowman changed my hunt and pulled me out of the camp. And there was the way Howe looked at me—as if he knew what was up. On top of everything, I had completely blown one of the questions Bowman had asked me about the van business I supposedly ran. *Am I overreacting to these things?*

Two more hours. I walked in circles—too anxious to stay still. There was still no plane in sight.

I'd promised Lonnie I'd take care of myself, and already I was wondering if I was going to survive the next few days. Images of my daughter swam around me. I felt her little arms locked around my neck as I carried her around the house. She always knew she was safe with her mother. As her sweet child's voice echoed in my mind, the enormity of what I had gotten myself into dumped on me like a crushing avalanche. My mind went back to when a nurse first laid Megan into my arms. The years I'd struggled over my career melted into a stream of nothingness. From her first breath, her gentle spirit showed me what was important in life. Love and family. Now I was on the verge of blowing it all because I was so intent on being a hotshot agent. Why couldn't I be a normal mother?

Abandoned on the tundra, I felt the tension well up into my gut. I bowed my head against my rifle, and asked my higher power to give me strength and to help me out of this situation. I'd been in bad ones before, but I'd never felt the helplessness that I felt now. I wished from the bottom of my heart that I'd never taken this assignment.

CHAPTER 11

A Woman in Camp

I HEARD THE BUZZ OF A PLANE before I saw it. Suddenly, Bowman's red-and-while tail-dragger popped up over the horizon. Was he back to pick me up or back to put a bullet in me?

He landed the plane nearly on the exact spot where he'd taken off. As he rolled to a stop he popped open his window and shouted, "C'mon, I found you a forty-incher."

My heart banged in my chest as I ran to the plane and pulled myself into the backseat with my rifle clanging at the side.

"Don't dent up my plane."

"Sorry—where are we going?"

Bowman jerked his head toward the backseat, "To a spike camp down-river. I got two guides set up who can set you up on the ram in the morning."

A spike camp is a bare-bones camp that can be moved quickly to follow the best hunting. Apparently Bowman had guides stationed at spike camps waiting for hunters.

I noticed that the three five-gallon cans of gas that Bowman had loaded into the plane at the DOT station were now gone. He had undoubtedly stashed them somewhere for later use when he was spotting or chasing animals and didn't want to go back to the DOT station to refuel. To spot and chase animals, he had to stay in the air. It now occurred to me that the reason

Bowman dropped me off was to conserve gas. Extra weight in the plane burned more fuel. I wished he'd just said so.

A few minutes later, he began circling. I saw two tents set up along the river and two men with their faces turned toward the sky. Bowman lowered the plane and dropped it down on a rocky flat. The plane bumped along about half the length of a football field and then rolled to a stop about thirty yards from the tents. Bowman got out first, and then I grabbed my gun and my backpack and jumped out, too.

Together, we hiked briskly to the camp where Bowman made the introductions. "Jake, this is Jayne. Danny, this is Jayne."

Jake was a tall, ruggedly handsome man in his early twenties with dark stubble that shrouded his strong jaw and dimpled chin. He stretched out his hand and smiled, "I haven't seen a woman in a long time."

Danny, a small-boned man with dark hair and dark eyes, walked past me without a word. He stomped into a new camouflage dome tent and came back out a few seconds later with a goose-down sleeping bag. With the bag in his arms he walked over to a weathered orange tent, and threw it inside. Still ignoring my presence, he returned to the camouflage tent and came out with a backpack and a pair of boots with thick lug soles, which he also threw into the shabby tent. His movements were jerky and the expression on his face was icy and stern. I finally realized that Danny resented being evicted from his new tent by a woman.

"Listen to me, Jayne," said Bowman. "I flew Danny up and showed him two good sheep. He's gonna take you up in the morning on foot, and I want you to take the bigger sheep. Understand?"

"You bet," I said.

So, this was the way it was. Every animal Bowman spotted from his plane was living under a death sentence. The law stated it was illegal to fly and hunt the same day, so technically what Bowman was doing was legal. But still, I was struck by the blatant lack of fair chase. In most hunting operations, the hunter would be dropped off at the spike camp with a guide and they would go out on foot and hunt their quarry—with no aerial spotting. The sheep I was about to pursue was as good as dead.

"Danny, I want that sheep dead here tomorrow. I'll be back at noon to pick her up. Understand?"

"Sure, Bob. I'll take her up there. If she can shoot, we'll have it dead."

"She says she can shoot. Right?"

"If I can see it, I can shoot it."

Bowman turned to leave, but stopped short to have his last say. "If either one of you lay a hand on her, I'll slap your asses into next week."

"Don't worry about us," said Jake, cracking a grin.

"Okay, then. See you tomorrow." Bowman walked back to the plane. The three of us stood silent as we watched it take off and shrink into the sky.

Jake offered me some coffee, and Danny offered me some moose jerky. I declined both. Nerves had killed my appetite. Jake said he would start dinner after it got dark.

"I hope you like instant beef stroganoff," warned Danny.

"Shut up, Danny. It ain't that bad."

No wonder Pedro complained about the food.

The three of us sat perched on rocks and talked for a while. There was no campfire, which made the camp feel even more austere. Jake told me he was from Wisconsin and had been raised on a farm. While he was growing up he killed much of the food he and his family ate. Deer, rabbit, and waterfowl. He glanced around at the mountains appreciatively and said that guiding hunters in Alaska was the best job in the world. Except for the fact that he was away from his young wife, he was in heaven.

I said I was in Alaska to shoot a trophy sheep. I told them a little about my hunting past, and said I was divorced and was in camp with a business partner. Neither Danny nor Jake seemed more than casually interested in my story.

Then the conversation turned to hunting laws.

"We gotta wait to hunt in the morning 'cause it's illegal to fly and hunt on the same day," explained Jake.

I groaned inside. If they took me on a legal hunt I wouldn't be able to build a case against Bowman. But I reminded myself to be patient. Things could change.

"I've never guided a woman before," said Danny.

"I don't bite."

"I've been bit by lots of women, including my ex."

Danny went on to say that he was part Inuit Indian. The Inuit—long known as "Eskimos" by outsiders—are the aboriginal inhabitants of the North American Arctic, from the Bering Strait to East Greenland. Inuit men were considered master hunters and artists. I imagined that Danny had grown up hunting whale, seal, and big game, and was now being paid well for his traditional knowledge. When he wasn't guiding hunters, he roofed houses in Palmer, Alaska.

"Danny and me just spent four days with two of the worst hunters we've ever guided. They were from Spain. They didn't speak English and on top of that were really crappy shots."

"You must mean Pedro and El Doctor," I said. "I met them earlier today."

Jake and Danny looked at each other like they wished they had kept their mouths shut.

"They seemed arrogant as hell."

Relief spread over their faces.

"One of them missed two good sheep, then wounded a third one," added Danny. "I tracked that sucker for ten hours and never found him. I've never lost a sheep, but I sure lost that one. I still might find him someday though. I'll keep lookin'."

This made sense to me. I had read that the Inuits believed that the spirits of those who had died lived on in animals, objects, and in natural forces. For this reason, they believed in maintaining a harmonious relationship with nature. I surmised that out of respect for the animal, Danny wanted to find out whether the sheep Pedro had shot survived. Danny wasn't about to leave a dead animal in the field and allow its meat to rot.

I left my guides and took a short walk down to the Sagavanirktok River, which Danny called "the Sag." I stood on the edge contemplating the rocks in the riverbed, round and polished from several hundred years of continuous washing. The water, clear and cold, danced over them in the shallows, but in the middle it moved deeply and mysteriously. *Just like Bowman,* I thought.

The unmistakable sound of an airplane disrupted my thoughts. I looked up and saw it flying along the river toward the camp. I trotted back to the spike camp where Jake and Danny were speculating on who it might be.

"It's not Bob," said Jake, checking the plane through binoculars.

"I think it's Howe," said Danny.

"Yep, you're right," agreed Jake. "What's he doing here?"

I flinched. Billy Howe, the man who would probably jump for joy if I were eaten alive by bears. His sudden appearance couldn't be good. The plane circled the spike camp with no signs of landing.

"What the hell does he want?" Danny wondered aloud.

"Hey look," shouted Jake. "He just threw something out."

A white box that looked like a small Styrofoam cooler tumbled through the air and bounced twice on the ground.

"Ouch," said Danny. "I hope nothing broke."

Seconds later the plane veered back up the river into the deepening twilight.

Running, I reached the box first. I tried to rip the tape off so I would be the first to see what was in it. Just in case there was a note about me. But Jake and Danny were right behind me with hunting knives out and ready. After they cut the box open, we were speechless for a few seconds. Inside were steaming slices of hot turkey, a huge mound of mashed potatoes smothered with gravy, buttery rolls, and globs of peach cobbler. The aroma made me instantly ravenous.

"Yahoo!" hollered Danny. "This has to be from Marianne and Rhoda. They must have made Billy bring it out to us."

Marianne was Bowman's wife and Rhoda was the cook at the main camp. If this was their doing, I was eternally grateful. The three of us sat on the ground and huddled around the box, grabbing the plastic forks that lay on top of the food. Digging in, Danny said it was the first decent hot meal he'd eaten in more than a month.

"Jayne, you're probably the reason we're eatin' so good tonight," said Jake between gulps.

"Yeah," agreed Danny. "Maybe a woman in camp ain't so bad."

I welcomed the return of my appetite as the warm mashed potatoes and gravy slid down my throat. The food was delicious, but more important, I'd survived a bizarre and unpredictable day, and hadn't been left for dead by Bowman.

As I watched Jake and Danny laugh and gulp down platefuls of food, I had to admit I liked them. They didn't strike me as wildlife poachers, and I wondered if they were an unwitting part of Bowman's plan. Maybe he'd deliberately planted me with a couple of Boy Scouts to make sure I didn't see anything illegal.

———

CHAPTER 12

Across the Line

AT 9:00 P.M., I SLID INTO MY SLEEPING BAG inside Danny's new tent. The long day's strain on my nerves had drained my energy. In spite of how tired I was, I propped up a flashlight and wrote every detail of my harrowing day in the small notebook I carried.

An hour later, I hid my notebook in the passport holder that was still strapped to my body and rolled over, counting my blessings. For the moment I was okay. Grateful, I allowed myself to sink into a deep sleep.

In what seemed like only moments, I heard Jake's voice, "Jayne! You in there? It's time to get up." I slowly gathered my wits, "Yeah, I'm here." I shined a light on my watch, it was 3:30 A.M. "Are we going now?"

"You bet, in ten minutes."

These guys are nuts. Nevertheless, I peeled off my long johns and pulled on some field pants. They were ripped and patched from all the barbed wire fences I'd climbed over sneaking up on hunters. My waterproof leather hunting boots had covered some ground, too, stalking hunters in snow and ice, hiking countless miles on other hunts, and sneaking through the woods at night to get samples of corn from baited ponds. A green-and-tan plaid flannel shirt under a Gore-Tex camouflage jacket completed my "uniform" as I emerged from my tent to go to work.

Jake and Danny had boiled water for the instant coffee and instant cook-in-a-bag oatmeal. I went into the bear-proof food box, grabbed a couple of cereal bars, and stuck them in my pocket, just in case. I doubted that I'd need them because the plan was to be back by lunchtime with a dead sheep.

"Here's the deal," Jake explained. "Danny's gonna take you up the mountain where Bob spotted that big ram yesterday. He knows exactly where it's at. All you have to do is climb up on the backside of the mountain and you'll be right over him. You should have a close, easy shot."

"Great! I'm ready when you are."

"I ain't going," said Jake. "We don't need two guides to get a sheep that's as good as dead. I'm going to do some scoutin' south of here, 'cause when you get your sheep, there'll be a bunch more assholes out here wanting to get theirs."

This disappointed me some. I wanted Jake to go along, I felt more comfortable with him than with Danny. But finding more sheep up in those rocks was their job and with only me to guide, they had a little break. It only made sense for Jake and Danny to split up.

Jake picked up a spotting scope, stuck it in his pack, and trained his eyes on the vast land that lay ahead. As he trekked out of camp I wondered if he would encounter a grizzly bear, fall and break a leg, or tumble into a rushing river. These were standard hazards in the Alaskan bush, but hunting guides regarded them as minor inconveniences. I refused to consider that any of these perils applied to me.

Minutes after Jake left camp, Danny pointed the way to the three-thousand-foot mountain where we would pursue my Dall sheep. I was in good physical condition and felt up to the challenge.

Danny and I set out in thirty-five-degree temperature. The air was calm, so there wasn't a chill factor to worry about. In South Dakota, I'd worked in twenty-below-zero temperatures with a thirty-mile-an-hour wind. *This will be a cakewalk.*

For the first hour we hiked north along the rocky bed of the Sagavanirktok River. I struggled to keep my footing while Danny walked effortlessly, as if he was on carpet. He then cut northeast across the tundra where I met a new friend—frost boils or "pingos." These were spongy twelve-inch mounds of ground-hugging vegetation that grew closely together in hillocks. Walking on them was like walking on a spongy mattress where every step twisted in a different and painful direction. I quickly realized that my waterfowl boots didn't have enough ankle support for this type of terrain. In spite of the discomfort,

I was still going strong, staying directly behind Danny and flaunting my physical stamina.

Three miles later we reached a tributary of the Sagavanirktok that ran east. The water appeared to be waist deep and was running steadily. I scanned the river up and down looking for a shallower place to cross. Then, for the first time all morning, Danny spoke. "Hop on. I'll carry you over."

"You mean on your back?" I asked incredulously. Danny wasn't much bigger than me.

"Sure. I did it for the Spaniards—they were heavy bastards, too."

Danny hated the Spaniards; I had to do better than them. "I can get across myself. Isn't there a better place to cross?"

"Jayne," said Danny impatiently, "this is where we're at, and this is where we're crossin', so hop on."

"No, I'm crossing myself."

Danny splashed into the water as if he didn't care if I made it or not. I waded in cautiously as the water slid up to my waist. The bone numbing glacier water made me gasp. I gritted my teeth and dug my feet into the sandy river bottom to hold myself against the current, which was more than strong enough to sweep me downstream. Danny looked over his shoulder to check on me as I struggled across the last stretch. It took me ten minutes to cross. As I shuffled up onto the dry bank, Danny smirked. "Good thing you made it."

I wanted to rest, but Danny was ready to go. After another thirty minutes of hiking my guide stopped in his tracks and pointed to a dry creek bed. "This is where we killed a black wolf last spring."

I couldn't believe it. He was talking about the wolf Bowman had spotted from the plane so the pharmacist and his guide, who I now realized was the same Danny I was with, could kill it. While Danny trudged ahead, my thoughts traveled back to the previous spring. I had read about the hunt in a report and knew the details. In my mind I heard the buzz of Bowman's plane and saw the wag of its wings pinpoint the wolf running for its life. Then I heard the rifle shot. A rocky ledge and dry creek bed brought everything I already knew together in a short mental video. I could see the snow, the now crippled, bleeding wolf, and Danny and the pharmacist on a snowmobile as they ran down the wounded wolf to finish it off. In this case, an undercover agent happened to be a witness. But how many silent places were there like this where such illegal kills had been so savagely wrought, and no one ever knew?

As I watched Danny hiking in front of me, my emotions turned to anger. He was no Boy Scout, nor was he a harmonious Inuit hunter. He was a poacher who would kill for a dollar, and I was going to watch every move he made.

Danny and I hiked another four miles to the back side of the mountain where the sheep were supposed to be. Huge jagged rocks formed the base of the three-thousand-foot mountain. I could see that about halfway up the terrain changed to gravel and spotty vegetation.

Danny turned to me, "Can you climb?"

"Sure."

He started up and I followed. I felt strong, barely noticing my rifle bouncing against my back. Instinctively negotiating hundreds of footholds, I stayed with Danny for the nearly three hours it took us to get to a position just below the crest of the mountain.

Danny's mouth curled into a cunning smile. "We're real close to where me and Bob seen the big ram yesterday. He's around here real close, so we gotta move real slow and real quiet. When I tell you to get ready, get a shell in the chamber and get it pointed to where I tell you."

Even though I nodded confidently, apprehension was building inside, making my stomach churn. I knew I'd probably only have a few seconds to get the sheep in my scope and get off a good shot. Sheep were quick to take off. If I didn't make the shot, my credibility as a hunter would crumble.

Slowly, Danny crawled his way to the top, which was like a broad soccer field loaded with boulders and scrubby plants. My senses sharpened for anything that moved or made a sound. So far there was nothing. We made our way to the ridge where I looked down at the silvery tributary we had crossed. From this altitude I could see that it cut deep through the mountains and came out in a lush, grassy valley.

To my surprise, Danny broke the silence. "Want me to take your picture up here?"

"Sure, that would be great," I said, handing Danny my cheap point-and-shoot camera.

Standing against the backdrop of an impossibly blue sky and pristine wilderness, I smiled. The camera clicked, and as my eyes broke from the camera lens to beyond where Danny stood, I picked up the slow-motion image of horns rotating like radar. Then I picked out the white face and body of a Dall sheep, and a second one standing next to him. These were the first Dall I'd ever seen. Their gleaming coats and unbelievably majestic horns nearly took my breath away. These animals were truly monarchs of the mountains. Still as stones, their inquisitiveness about Danny and me seemed to outweigh their desire to flee. I was surprised that they stood as still for as long as they did.

"Danny," I said in loud whisper. "Don't move. The sheep are right behind you."

"Son of a bitch," he hissed, jerking his head.

Instantly, the sheep turned on a dime and charged east across the mountain. Within seconds they vanished completely from sight.

"This pisses me off," hollered Danny. "The bastards saw us long before we saw them. They was probably watchin' us take pictures."

A "real" client would have been furious with Danny. Stopping to take pictures in the middle of a stalk on a couple of trophy rams was unforgivable. But I decided to let Danny off the hook and said, "Well, at least we found them."

"Lot of damn good that's gonna do us now. They're gone. Shit, Bob's gonna kill me for this."

I pulled out my binoculars and looked in the direction where the sheep had fled. "So, what do we do now?"

"We gotta find the sons of bitches, that's what," Danny spat out, disgusted with himself.

Without a word, he marched off in front of me on a desperate mission to find the sheep, and not just any sheep. It had to be the big one, the one that had just outwitted him in the game between the hunter and the hunted.

I watched him as his eyes scanned the terrain, looking for any predictable path our prey may have taken. Every cell in his body seemed absorbed in what to do next. I sensed that man's earliest hunting instincts were deeply entrenched in Danny. And as impossible as it seemed, he'd eventually find the sheep.

After hours of hiking across the mountain, we split up. Danny headed for the bottom while I stayed above to look for the sheep. He walked the drainage and then changed direction, angling along the side of the mountain, staying well above the drainage. By now, Danny was a small figure, moving steadily over the rocks. He stopped and perched on an outcropping as I imagined him trying to out-think the sheep. *Them sheep were spooked bad . . . they might be hanging out under a cliff . . . it'll be hours before they move again. Got to fig-ure a way to intercept them bastards . . . they can't get away again.*

By now we'd been away from camp for more than eight hours. Bowman had probably stopped at the camp and left by now. His next trip back would likely be the next day. My still-wet feet throbbed from their relentless pound-ing on rocks.

I perched on a boulder and peeled off my boots and socks. My socks were still soaked so I wrung them out and stretched them on a rock to dry a little. Then I indulged in a cereal bar and let my bare feet bask in the sun. Lying across the rock, I closed my eyes and imagined myself at home, reading a book to Megan under her bedcovers, my feet warm as toast. We were laughing and giggling. Suddenly, Danny's voice snapped me out of my daydream.

"You see anything?" He had appeared out of seemingly nowhere.

"No. How about you?"

"I can't find them down below. Let's climb back up to the top, farther east."

That hit a nerve. "Climb back up. We climbed to the top once, then halfway back down and now you want to go back up again? What for?"

"I think they went over the top, but higher up."

"They might have gone anywhere. Do you have any idea how big this country is?" Of course he knew, much better than I did.

Danny ignored my bellyaching. "You can stay here if you want, I'll find the sheep, and then come get you."

Grumbling, I grabbed my socks and boots and put them back on. Danny could do something illegal and turn into a suspect at any minute—I had to stay with him. "No, I'm going with you."

I followed Danny on what I considered a futile exercise. Sure, we'd get back to the top and find out that the sheep weren't there, either. The top of the second summit was about three hundred feet higher than our first one. We were now walking in snowpack left over from the previous winter and maybe even the winter before. My little waterfowl boots felt as adequate as bedroom slippers. My sore feet were now beginning to blister.

Danny pointed as he spotted a group of sheep tracks. "Them sheep were here."

I felt a glimmer of hope. "That's great, how long ago?"

"Don't know. These prints could have been made yesterday."

My spirits slid back down. Danny went through the snow just like he did water, brush, and everything else—like it didn't exist. But I had to push and plow through it, using all my physical reserves to stay with him.

Soon we were in thigh-deep snow that was crusted on top. Just punching through it required at lot of strength, so I resorted to walking in the holes Danny had already made. Exhausted, I plunged one leg into a hole and felt my foot wedge between rocks buried several feet below. Teetering, I fell into the crusty snowpack and felt pain surging through my left shin.

Danny, stopped and turned. "You all right?"

"Yeah," I grumbled as I brushed off the wet snow.

"Just stay there, Jayne. I'm going to look around some more. I'll come back and get you."

"No, I'm coming, just give me a minute." I put some weight on my left leg, and although it was throbbing, I knew it wasn't broken. Pressing my fingers along my shin, I found tender flesh. "Ouch!"

"Jayne, you gotta be careful; 911 don't come this far. If you get hurt, I'll be hauling you out on my back."

He was right. An injury, even a minor one, could be disastrous. "Okay Danny, I'll wait here. Sure you can find me again?"

"I'll find you."

So, he left me. My leg was in pain and my gut was gnawing with hunger. All of this, and I wasn't even close to killing a sheep or making a case. Danny was gone for ninety minutes. When he came back I asked anxiously, "Did you find the sheep?"

"Naw, them sheep were spooked so bad, they ain't gonna show their faces until tomorrow. I still think they went over the top and are on the north side. We won't be able to get to 'em before dark. Let's head back down."

I felt relieved as we began to hike down the mountain. But as we started back I realized that going down the mountain was going to be hard on my injured leg.

Danny was about forty yards ahead of me when he motioned frantically for me to catch up with him. Maybe the sheep had made a miraculous reappearance. My body was in no mood to move quickly, so I half slid and half sidestepped down the rocky slope. When I reached Danny, he was crouched behind a huge boulder.

"Do you see the sheep?"

"Get close to me and stay real low."

Then I heard the *whir* of a small plane but didn't think much about it until I saw Danny peering at the sky from under his hunting cap. I followed his gaze and saw the plane. It was larger than the Super Cubs at Bowman's camp and was flying almost directly overhead.

"Don't look, and don't move," he whispered.

There was something about this plane that bothered Danny. When the wings of the plane banked slightly I caught a glimpse of the Canada goose and rainbow trout emblem of the U.S. Fish and Wildlife Service on the fuselage. My heart quickened. This was a wildlife refuge plane patrolling for poachers. This meant we were on the Arctic National Wildlife Refuge and that we'd been hunting illegally all day.

The plane passed, apparently without seeing us. Refuge personnel didn't know I was in the area working undercover, so there was no reason for them to be flying the refuge except as a routine matter.

After the plane was well out of sight, Danny stood up and continued down the mountain. He didn't say a word about the plane and neither did I. I didn't want him to know that I now realized we were hunting in an illegal area. Danny was now a suspect, and if we returned the following day and killed a sheep on the refuge, I'd have a case against both Danny and Bowman.

It was another three hours before we hobbled into camp. Jake was already there, boiling water for that evening's Mountain House instant dinner. Jake and Danny immediately fell into a conversation about their days. Jake said he covered a large area south of our camp and didn't see sheep. Not even tracks. Danny recounted our long day with a few added expletives about the elusive sheep.

After hearing the story, Jake did nothing to make Danny feel any better. "Jeez, Bob's gonna whip your ass when he finds out you spooked that big ram. That is if he don't kill you first."

"Shit," said Danny, "don't even tell 'im. Them sheep moved and that's all there was to it."

Jake looked at me. "Got that? The sheep moved."

"Of course they moved. I saw them do it."

Danny moaned.

"Don't worry," I said. "Your secret is safe with me. Say, don't you guys ever feed your guests?"

Spaghetti and meatballs was served up within minutes and the conversation turned to how lucky we were to be dining in the great outdoors.

After dinner, the sun was still high in the sky, but I was more than ready to turn in. I also got the feeling that Danny wanted to tell Jake about seeing the U.S. Fish and Wildlife Service plane.

I got up and limped to my tent when Danny said, "Look, I'm just about sure where them sheep went. We'll get 'em first thing in the morning."

"Thanks. Rattle my tent when you want me up."

On tender knees I crawled into my tent and dug out my notebook from its hidden pouch and began to write every detail of another perilous day. Even after what I'd been through, my spirits were high. I'd discovered that Bowman was sending hunters onto a wildlife refuge to poach animals, and in this case he had just sent a federal agent.

Special Agent Lucinda Schroeder, aka Jayne Dyer, hunting sheep on the Arctic National Wildlife Refuge.

United States Fish and Wildlife Service Special Agent badge number 203 carried by Agent Schroeder from 1974 to 2004.

Bob Bowman's hunting camp along the Ivishak River in the Brooks Range, Alaska.

"Jayne" in the kitchen at Bowman's camp, which also served as the camp's "command center."

The camp's meat shed used to store game meat from illegal kills.

Bowman in his Super Cub after he dropped "Jayne" at a remote location in Alaska's Brooks Range.

Guide Danny at a spike camp just off the Arctic National Wildlife Refuge.

Danny hunting for sheep illegally within the confines of the wildlife refuge.

The top of the second peak during the first day of sheep hunting.

"Jayne" with the Dall sheep she illegally killed in the wildlife refuge.

Informant Roy with an illegal grizzly that was herded to him from the air by Bowman.

The illegal caribou shot by Spanish hunter Junior.

"Jayne" with a moose she killed in the Brooks Range.

An illegally killed grizzly, once proudly displayed at The Bear's Den, was seized by U.S. Fish and Wildlife agents.

Special Agent Tim Eicher.

———

CHAPTER 13

To Kill for Conservation

THE CLANGING OF METAL PANS OUTSIDE MY TENT sent me shooting straight up in my sleeping bag. I groped the folds in the rip-stop nylon of my sleeping bag for a flashlight. *What the hell's going on?* I flipped the light on and I heard Jake's voice outside.

"Where's the damn coffeepot? Is she up yet? Go get her up."

"I ain't getting her up," grumbled Danny. "You do it."

"Jeeez, Danny, we ain't got all morning."

"Hey guys, I'm up . . . I'm up," I moaned. I pointed the light on my watch: it was 3:45 A.M.

"We gotta cut out in twenty minutes," barked Jake. "So hurry."

I had slept in my clothes so there wasn't much to do except slip out of my bag and pull on the miserable leather hunting boots that had turned on me yesterday. I pulled the laces loose and gritted my teeth as I crammed my swollen feet into them, still wet from the day before. My feet were painfully sore, so I tied the laces just tight enough to keep the boots from sliding off my feet. I had to go back out into the bush and kill a sheep.

Every muscle in my legs and back ached as I stood stooped over in the domed tent. I groped around the sleeping bag for my flannel shirt and put it on over my T-shirt. In the process, my spine banged against one of the supporting metal poles, sending a bolt of pain down my back.

"Ouch!" I screamed.

"You okay?" asked Jake.

"Yeah," I said with a jaw clenched tighter than vice grips.

"Sure?"

"I'm okay. I'll be out in a minute."

For seventeen hours the day before, I had carried my rifle across my back. The constant pounding of the rifle against it was yet another source of pain that would live with me for days. Digging into my backpack, I found some ibuprofen and swallowed three tablets dry. This was going to be a brutal day; I didn't want to feel more pain that I had to.

I eased on my camouflage Gore-Tex jacket. Next came my camouflage hunting hat. I shoved my hair tightly under it and dropped sunglasses in my pocket for later. They were my makeup.

When I crawled out of the tent into the late August morning there was little more than a hint of light in the sky, which provided an eerie silhouette to the nearby mountains. The temperature felt like it was in the mid-thirties. Jake and Danny were huddled over a pot of water boiling on a single-burner camp stove. Danny handed me an open foil bag of oatmeal, poured water into it, and offered me a cup of instant coffee. Breakfast was served.

Despite all my aches and pains, I tried to buck up. No legitimate hunter would be grumbling after one rough day in the field. I couldn't either. Besides, Danny and I had spent the whole day hunting on a national wildlife refuge. Since I didn't have a permit to hunt there, the hunt was completely illegal. If he ordered me to shoot a sheep on the refuge, not only would I have a case against him, I'd have one against Bowman, since he had located the sheep initially, and had given the instructions to kill it.

I thought back to the times I'd arrested poachers on other national wildlife refuges and was struck by the irony that today I might be "poaching" a sheep on one. Danny thought the sheep had moved over the top of the mountain we'd hunted the day before. He speculated that during the early morning hours the sheep would be in the drainage feeding on the grasses that grew along the tributary. He wanted me to shoot my sheep there so we wouldn't have to do more climbing. Danny warned me that they'd only feed for a couple of hours; we had to leave the camp as quickly as possible.

To my surprise, Jake announced that he was going to hunt with us that day. I had the impression that Jake avoided the illegal stuff, but he knew that we were going to be hunting on a refuge. Maybe I had given him too much credit.

I hurried back into my tent and double-checked to make sure that my notebook was secure in my passport holder. I worried constantly about losing my notes. If anyone read them, the whole operation would be blown. My mind shot back to the undercover state warden's hunt report that quoted Bowman's declaration that he'd kill a game warden if he found one in his camp. When I got back outside, Danny and Jake were standing next to a spotting scope set up on a tripod.

"I thought we were in a hurry," I said.

Danny peered through the scope, and then Jake stooped over to take a look. Scanning far into the distance I could barely discern a large, dark mass, moving ever so slowly across the tundra. It had to be a bear, but I played ignorant.

"What is it?"

"A grizzly," said Danny. "A big one."

"Yeah," agreed Jake, "it's got to be one of the biggest ones I've ever seen."

"Should we take him? He'd sure be a good one," Danny said, taking another look through the spotting scope. "He's one big son of a bitch."

Jake glanced over at me. "I don't know. Jayne doesn't have a bear tag and neither do we. We'd go to jail if we got caught poaching a grizzly."

"Naw," countered Danny, "we'd have it back to main camp by nightfall and give it to a hunter who has a tag. It'd be a cinch."

"Yeah," nodded Jake, squinting as he gazed out across the tundra.

Danny turned toward me. His expression asked the unspoken questions: Would I turn them in if they shot the grizzly? Could I keep the secret? The grizzly had presented itself at an opportune time. No doubt Bowman had hunters coming into the main camp who would relish having a huge bear trophy like this one. After all, Bowman guaranteed his hunters would have the biggest and the best animals for their trophy rooms, and taking a shortcut would probably suit them fine.

If Danny and Jake shot this bear, it would save them a lot of hard-ass hunting later on. They were caught in a vicious cycle of supply and demand, where the seemingly infinite demand for high-quality trophies far exceeded the supply. For them, this was a "bear in the bank."

To protect the integrity of the case, I couldn't influence them one way or the other. If they wanted to shoot the bear, I had to let them. But I couldn't encourage them either. In this situation, however, Jake and Danny would only kill the bear if I went along with the plan. The silence between the three of us hung heavy while I evaluated the options.

There was the possibility that if either of them shot the bear and took it back to camp, Bowman might insist on using Roy's tag, since he was my partner. In that case, I would be a witness to the killing, tagging, and transporting of an illegal bear. Pictures, statements, and the bear itself would be the evidence for an open-and-shut case. Jake and Danny would probably go to jail.

But this would leave Roy without a bear tag, and he was scheduled to hunt a grizzly later that week with Bowman. Without Roy on a hunt with Bowman we'd lose our chance to catch Bowman using his plane to hunt. Although this bear presented an opportunity to catch Danny and Jake violating the law, they weren't the main targets of this investigation, Bowman was.

Jake and Danny still had their eyes fixed on the potential trophy feeding on what were probably wild blueberries.

"He sure is a nice one," said Jake, smacking his lips.

"Shit yeah," said Danny.

As I watched the bear nosing through the vegetation, I played tug of war with myself.

Finally, I said, "Come on guys, I don't want to spend time chasing a bear. I'm here to hunt sheep."

Danny snapped up the spotting scope and slammed it in the food box in one angry motion.

Jake swung a daypack on his shoulder, shot a huge spit wad on the ground, and shrugged. "You heard the woman."

He stomped out of camp, and Danny and I fell in behind him. Strung out like dots, we started out across the endless tundra in total silence.

An hour later the Alaskan sun exploded over the horizon, highlighting splashes of brilliant mustard-yellow wildflowers clear to the horizon. The snowcapped mountains glimmered like jewels against the blue sky.

Our brisk pace warmed me up, but once again the mossy frost boils sucked at my boots as my ankles twisted. Because of my bruised back, I held my rifle in front of me, infantry style. The rifle felt like it had gained ten pounds overnight.

Once again, we approached the Sagavanirktok River at a place where we had to cross it. I waded into the bone-numbing water, knowing my cold and wet clothes would remain with me for hours. Three long hours after leaving camp, we passed the mountain where we had hunted sheep the day before. We trekked another mile and a half when, thankfully, the spongy frost boils turned into a more rocky terrain providing more secure footing.

Finally, we reached the mouth of the drainage where Danny thought the sheep would be feeding. From a map in my mind's eye, I was sure we were well within the Arctic National Wildlife Refuge. There were no signs of course—this was one of the most remote places in Alaska.

Looking into the distance, I focused on what looked like sheep feeding along the water's edge. I grabbed my binoculars to get a better look and quickly realized that the "sheep" were actually boulders. If the sheep weren't here there was no telling where they were, and I wasn't sure how much farther I could go on my now swollen and badly blistered feet.

Danny and Jake, who were about thirty yards ahead of me, stopped, dropped to their knees, and pointed up the drainage. Hoping that they had spotted the sheep, I pushed myself into a jog and caught up with them.

"Do you see 'em?" I asked, panting lightly.

"Shit no," said Danny. "They ain't here. We missed 'em."

"What a pain in the ass this is," grumbled Jake. "I hope they haven't gone far 'cause we're going to have to climb to find the sons of bitches."

We set out across the small valley, splashing our way through a silvery tributary that was only a few inches deep. When we got to the other side, we hiked to the foot of the mountain we had to climb. I looked up—definitely Mount Everest.

Danny started up first. Carefully navigating every step, he moved one foot in front of the other in a zigzag pattern. Moving up in one direction and then the other, always at an angle, like a mountain goat. Jake and I followed.

While Jake made easy work of the climbing, I concentrated on making every step solid. My knees throbbed and my feet burned, making me unsteady and vulnerable to injury. I continued to climb, hundreds of footholds in the rocks and dirt, twisting back and forth up the mountain, even though my guides still didn't know where the sheep were.

We climbed for an hour. Every time I looked up, the top of the mountain seemed to move farther away. Every few minutes, Jake and Danny stopped and whispered to one another as though they knew something. Then Danny rotated his head in all directions as though he were picking up scent.

Danny and Jake suddenly interrupted our endless plodding and dropped to the ground in prone positions. I did the same. On my stomach with my rifle flung over my bruised back, I inched my way in their direction. As I eased closer I followed their fixed gazes up the mountain, but all I could see was a solid sea of gray shale — sedimentary rock formed millions of years ago by the fusion of beds of clay and mud.

Suddenly, my eyes picked up something that didn't match its surroundings. It wasn't flat shale, and more important, it moved. Then the sun flashed off something white. I pulled out my binoculars and focused on the unmistakable shape of a pure white animal with massive, curled horns. It was a Dall.

My heartbeat raced as I anticipated what would happen next. We were still out of gun range and to get closer we had to be extremely cautious. After all, this critter was already edgy. As Jake and Danny huddled to plan their assault, I could almost feel their adrenaline surge. Danny's eyes were locked on the sheep.

Covering his mouth he murmured, "That's the big one, the one Bob wants dead. We gotta get closer."

"Shit, it's wide open out here. He'll see us," whispered Jake.

"Let's stay way back, go around the mountain, and come at him from the other side," murmured Danny.

Jake stared into the sun and grimaced. "Too risky, if he sees us when we come over the top, he'll bolt. That's what happened to you yesterday."

Danny's head dropped at the reminder of the fiasco the day before.

Jake had an idea. "Let's go lower and wait for him to come back down this evening when they feed again."

Danny's voice had an edge to it, "With the wind blowing like this? No sheep is so fucking stupid that he's going to walk right up to us. He'll catch our scent and it'll be all over."

Jake mulled over Danny's comment and must have agreed. "Shit!" The curse exploded from his mouth with a spray of saliva. "We find the bastard and now we can't even get to 'im."

I knew what Jake was talking about. "Getting to 'em," was the biggest challenge of sheep hunting. Finding them was much easier than getting within gun range. Dall sheep hang out high in the mountains, scanning miles of terrain for threats. If they sensed something they didn't like, they'd sprint out of gun range within seconds. Avid sheep hunters spend years fantasizing about that ever-so-brief moment when they would finally have a good shot at a ram, especially a big one like this.

Every ounce of Danny's being seemed focused on the ram as if he were trying to read the animal's mind. "So far he don't know we're here. . . . Let's crawl, real slow."

"It ain't gonna work," muttered Jake.

"We don't have a choice. He ain't bothered by us now and might not notice anything if we move real slow."

I thought Danny had a point and whispered, "Let's give it a try."

Inch by inch, we wormed over the greasy shale that felt as slick as ice. For every three feet I moved forward, I slid back one. Occasionally, I felt the raw edges of the flat shale jabbing into my skin. I didn't dare utter a sound.

Finally, Jake pointed to a low ridge of shale jutting out of the mountain. Its highest point was about two feet, and was just enough to give us limited cover. We slithered toward the ridge and stayed behind it as though we were dodging enemy gunfire. I rose up slightly, pulled up my binoculars, and glassed the slope again. The ram still had not moved, but now there was a smaller one with him.

Danny must have seen him, too. "Take the big one. You're gonna have to take your shot from here, Jayne. Can you do it?"

"How far is it?" I asked.

"It's 250 yards, at least. It's not an easy shot. That critter picked some shitty country to get found in."

Jake spoke next. "C'mon, Jayne, you can do it. This is your sheep. Take him."

Two hundred and fifty yards up the side of a mountain and I'd have to take an offhand shot—without support to steady my rifle. All I could see was shale and the barely visible blanched shapes of two sheep. Slowly, I pulled the Browning .270 bolt-action rifle to my shoulder, and cautiously rose up. This was a government gun seized from a night hunter and I had only fired it to sight it in. I prayed that my reputation for raw accuracy would pay off now. It had to.

Through a Leupold nine-power scope, the ram appeared no larger than a quarter. I tried my best to get enough of a "picture" in my crosshairs for a clean heart-lung shot. This had to be a very good shot; I might not get another one. I had to kill this ram to convince Bowman and his outlaw crew that I was the serious hunter I claimed to be.

The tension made me hyperventilate slightly, causing the gun barrel to sway. I quickly forced myself to breathe slowly, deeply, and deliberately. As the gun steadied, I pushed the rifle hard into my shoulder and leaned forward slightly to take the recoil.

I shut my mind down even further, focusing everything on the shot. The ram was now at an angle facing me. I put the crosshairs just beneath and to the right of his chin, estimating that at 250 yards the bullet would drop about four to six inches. This should put the bullet directly into the heart and lung area.

I talked to myself, *Squeeze the trigger—don't jerk the gun.* Jake and Danny were still whispering orders, but I blocked them out. Everything had to go into the shot.

Okay, I'm ready. I slowly released my breath as I squeezed the trigger. An instant later, the butt of the gun slammed against my shoulder as the report shattered the silence.

"She hit it!" screamed Danny. "Wow! She hit it!"

Looking through the spotting scope, I saw that the smaller ram had vanished. The bigger one had folded onto the ground, his head still up. I could see his body. He may have moved at the last instant because he wasn't dead. I had to shoot again.

Danny, who had been on his knees, collapsed to the ground in a prone position. "Use my back as a bench."

Jake plopped on the top of Danny crossways, to make the human bench higher. "Go ahead," he said.

"Thanks, I'm okay." I couldn't get an accurate shot from a bench that was breathing.

Jake got up and glassed the ram. "That sucker is wounded bad. He ain't goin' nowhere. Take another shot, Jayne. Take your time and kill him."

Another draw to the shoulder, another sight picture, another tight breath, and another squeeze of the trigger. As the rifle kicked, the sound of the shot slammed against my ears and echoed through the mountains. Lowering the rifle, I saw Jake and Danny leaping in the air.

"She killed it! The son of a bitch is dead! What a fucking shot!" yelled Danny.

"Damn, I can't believe it!" hollered Jake. "The best darn shot of the century!"

"Them sheep didn't expect such a good shot to be on them today. This is great!"

Although they congratulated me with bear hugs, I was too exhausted to feel anything. I followed them as they led the way toward the fallen ram. Crawling and scraping our way across the slippery shale, we made the ascent to where the ram lay stretched across huge chunks of shale. Once again, I was amazed at the immense size of his horns and his glistening white coat.

"How much do you think he weighs?" I asked Danny

"Three hundred, easy."

Moving closer to my trophy, I saw blood near the front of his left hindquarter, indicating where my first shot had gone. I hated to kill a magnificent ram like this one for a case, and I wondered for a moment if I was any better than the crooks who killed animals for their own selfish agendas.

Danny peered into the ram's mouth to check his molars and then announced that the ram was an "old bugger" and wouldn't have lasted another winter anyway. I doubted that.

"Jayne, sit behind him, and hold up his horns," ordered Danny, holding an Instamatic camera in front of me. "Bob wants lots of pictures."

Picture-taking is a required ritual of trophy hunting. Photos provide indisputable proof of the hunt and, in this case, they would be used as evidence.

I pulled my small camera out of my pack and handed it to Danny. "Here, take some for me."

Climbing over the still warm carcass, I crouched awkwardly behind the ram and fingered the gashed and battered ridges of the horns that told part of his story. This guy had been a fighter. The tips of his thirty-seven-inch horns had been broomed off at least three inches, and were so worn down from his frequent fighting that they were no longer pointed but blunt like the ends of broom handles. He'd undoubtedly been a worthy opponent who didn't back down easily.

The thirteen-inch-round base of his horns told me he had been in good health and had successfully walked the survival tightrope of this harsh alpine environment for many years.

"Grab them horns and pull 'em towards you," shouted Danny.

The head was heavy and bulky. I grunted as I heaved it toward my chest.

"Higher," barked Danny.

I pulled even harder.

Danny chided me. "You ain't smilin', Jayne—you're supposed to be happy. Smile!"

I needed to be more careful. Normally, a hunter would be elated after a successful kill.

On top of my exhaustion, anger boiled slowly under my skin. Bowman and his greed for money were the root of all this. Had he not been running an illegal hunting operation I wouldn't be sitting on a mountain inside a wildlife refuge with an illegal ram. But it was better that it was me because I would put a stop to it. This ram would not be forgotten on a bleak, glaciated slope north of the Arctic Circle. He would be remembered. I wanted the death of this magnificent ram to serve a greater purpose by bringing Bowman and his guides to justice. The ram was dead but the spirit is stronger than the body, and I would carry the spirit of this animal for as long as I lived.

As Danny pointed the camera toward me, I forced a tight-lipped grin across my face.

—————

CHAPTER 14

Instincts on Point

JAKE ALREADY HAD HIS SIX-INCH HUNTING KNIFE pulled from its case that was attached to his belt. He knelt next to the animal with the gleaming blade poised near the breastbone. No doubt this knife had sliced through hundreds of carcasses.

"You gonna do a full mount?"

"No, a head mount. Just take the cape and horns." I was lying of course. Little did Jake know he was preparing evidence that would never be mounted and that would later be used against him, Danny, and Bowman.

With the skill of a surgeon, Jake made a clean and straight cut from the crotch to the breastbone in one fast motion and then held the cavity open while the gut pile poured out intact. Steam rose up from it, filling the air with a gamey odor I was more than familiar with. I admired how accomplished Jake was. I had been with poachers and hunters who created revolting messes by dumping blood and guts everywhere in an attempt to field dress a wild animal.

Danny moved in with his skinning knife. Carefully positioning it, he sliced a "T" between the ears and straight down the neck. He made the next two cuts at the base of the neck and ran them behind each shoulder, stopping behind each of the front legs. Without hesitating, he cut a curve under the two front legs to connect with the breast incision. The hide was now ready to come off.

Jake and Danny grabbed hold of the hide and yanked on it as hard as they could, and pulled it inside out.

"Jayne," said Jake. "Take my knife and cut away anything sticking to the hide so we can get this thing off."

As they held the hide back, I cut the connecting tissue. They then pulled on the hide, ripping it from the meat, which made a sound like leather being torn apart. The hide was completely detached within ten minutes.

When I returned Jake's knife, he quickly cut through the muscle covering the large neck joint immediately behind the skull, exposing the first vertebrae. He spent the next few minutes cutting the tissue around the joint, then twisted the head, and finally snapped if off with a quick jerk.

Danny worked on skinning around the ears and at the base of the horns. Then he removed a field saw from his pack and cut the skull plate loose, leaving the horns intact.

Finally, Jake drove his knife into the sheep's back and cut out the loin meat. Then came the two hindquarters, with the aid of the saw.

Jake and Danny wrapped the meat in light plastic sheets covered with dried blood from other kills, and crammed it into their two backpacks. I took some of the meat and stowed it in my pack to share the load. Danny insisted on carrying the cape and horns, which he crammed into his pack with the horns perched on top like a crown.

"Wolves will get the rest of him," said Danny wiping his knife clean on his pants.

Just then there was a distant hum of an airplane. As if on cue, the three of us turned our heads toward the wide valley below as a Piper Super Cub came into view. Because we stood at one thousand feet above the plane, it looked like a vulture riding the air currents.

"That must be Bob to pick up Jayne," said Jake.

"Yeah," said Danny. "He's gonna be mad that we ain't back yet. He wanted this sheep dead yesterday."

Jake picked up a rock and threw is as far as he could. "Dammit anyway. He can't expect miracles. Sometimes things happen. He better not give us any shit, this is damn hard work."

"I'll tell him about the trouble we had," I said.

"Bob's an asshole—nothing you say's gonna help," Jake sputtered.

Danny glassed the valley. "He's landed. Guess he's gonna wait awhile."

"Great," said Jake. "It's gonna take us another five hours to get back. He'll be really pissed by then."

Jake was right. Bowman was going to be furious. He had his guides on an assembly-line schedule. Downtime cost him money. He wanted hunters to get their trophies as quickly as possible to make room for the string of hunters waiting at the main camp for their turns in what he had turned into killing fields.

As my guides started down, I told them to go ahead and I'd follow. I wanted to be alone.

Carefully, I footed the shale on the downside of the mountain. As expected, my knees took a beating from every angle. As I negotiated my way, I sometimes resorted to sliding down the shale—although hardly graceful, it seemed a bit easier.

During my hours alone, I thought back to the life I had outside of this Alaskan drama. I thought about Wisconsin and Megan and how she was doing at school. She was learning to play the flute and her first concert would be in a couple of months. I couldn't wait. I also looked forward to getting home to Lonnie, going out to dinners and movies. Even walking Trapper was a simple joy I longed for. Even though my good life in Wisconsin seemed like a dream, I tried to remind myself that this life of blood, guts, and crooks was not real, and it would soon be over.

Two hours later, I saw Bowman's plane buzz up into the sky and break off into the distance. Apparently unwilling to wait any longer, he headed back to the main camp. More than likely he wouldn't be back until the next day, which meant I'd have another instant dinner and a night sleeping on the ground.

When I arrived at the camp three and a half hours later, the scene was like happy hour without the margaritas. Jake and Danny were in high spirits, laughing and telling jokes. Chunks of sheep meat were already sizzling in a frying pan. I walked straight to my tent muttering a few words of acknowledgment as I passed them. Inside, I collapsed on top of my sleeping bag. My body throbbed against the ground as I wondered if I'd ever get up again.

After several minutes I rolled over and realized that because so much had happened that day, I had to make notes. I removed the passport holder from under my clothes, found my notebook, and then reeled my memory back to what seemed like days earlier. I began writing:

On duty, 3:45 a.m. Met with Danny and Jake; they spotted a grizzly and wanted to shoot it. They talked about using someone else's tag to cover it . . .

"Hey, you want some?" yelled Jake from the cooking stove.

My heartbeat jumped. "Uh, no thanks, I'm really not that hungry."

I saw the zipper of the tent door slide and quickly shoved the notebook under my shirt. Jake's hand appeared through the opening holding a plate of sheep meat.

"Here, you earned it."

I took the paper plate. "Okay, thanks." As the aroma of the meat filled the tent, ravenous hunger took over. Using my fingers, I shoved the chunks of meat into my mouth as the grease ran off my chin. For the first time in my life, I felt a primal craving for warm meat, stirred by the inextricable connection between survival and the hunt. I now had a better understanding of the ancient hunt. It was life itself and the means by which humans managed to perpetuate themselves on earth for hundreds of thousands of years.

When the meat was gone, I had to admit that no meal had ever satisfied me more. Setting the plate aside, I picked up my pencil and notebook again.

We went to the 3rd drainage west of camp and on the north side of the Sag. Danny and Jake instructed me to shoot a Dall about 1/2 mile into the drainage. I fired twice …

"Hey Jayne," yelled Jake, "I think Bob's coming."

I crammed my notebook back into the passport holder, scrambled out of the tent, and immediately heard an airplane overhead.

Danny cranked his head upward. "Yep, that's Bob. Hope he's not too upset."

"To hell with him," said Jake in a voice tinged with genuine concern.

Standing outside the tent, I watched as Bowman flew by the camp low, then circled and went over the same spot again. The third time around, he dropped lower and came in for a landing on a stretch of rocky tundra. To me, every landing seemed like a miracle.

Bowman opened the pilot's side door, hopped to the ground, and started walking toward the camp. He was shouting, "Did you get him? Did you get the sheep?"

I limped quickly toward him, waving my arms and screaming, "Yes! I did it! I did it!"

Jake and Danny were right behind me yelling, "She got 'im. He's huge!"

When Bowman and I were finally within a few feet of each other he bellowed, "Damn, that's fantastic." He flung both his arms wide open and took me in like a big Russian. "Did you get pictures?"

"Sure did," I said.

Bowman squeezed me again and lifted me off the ground. "Did you get lots of pictures?"

I resisted the urge to fight him off. "Yes. Lots of pictures."

Then he turned to the two guides. "Where in the hell were you this morning? I waited for five hours."

What a lie, I thought.

"Them sheep weren't where they were supposed to be," said Danny.

"What the hell, I pointed them right out to you."

Danny stared at the ground. "They . . . they moved on us. They weren't anywhere near where you and me had seen 'em."

"I waited here for over five hours; I couldn't figure out what happened. So where the hell were they?" Bowman asked, his irritation escalating.

Danny and Jake jabbered nearly simultaneously as they explained where they had found the sheep compared to where Bowman had initially spotted them. I sensed that Bowman was confused, but he finally accepted their explanation. Then he turned to me with some urgency, and said, "Get your gear, we gotta go before it gets dark."

I hobbled quickly back to my tent and stuffed my gear into my pack and in less than five minutes was back outside heading toward the plane. Danny had already thrown the hindquarters of the sheep into the back. I threw my gear on top of the meat and squeezed into the backseat.

Jake handed me the horns. "Be sure and show these to those lazy, good-for-nothing Spaniards."

Grinning, I promised I would.

Bowman crawled in and cranked up the engine.

"Lean over my shoulder and grab those metal braces by the windshield with both hands."

"Why?"

"I got too much weight in the back and don't think I can get off the ground."

Great. Most pilots would take weight off the plane, but not Bowman. He was just going to shift the weight around enough to get the tail off the ground. I hoped he knew what he was doing; I didn't want to die in this eggbeater.

I followed his instructions and held my breath as the plane bounced along and struggled into the air. When we were finally airborne, I breathed a sigh of relief and was greeted with a glorious setting sun. Gliding along, I saw moose feeding on willows and caribou coming together in the last light of the day. A distant light at a pipeline station house flickered. I let my body sink into the seat and leaned my forehead against the window. For a moment, I forgot about the case, the bad guys, everything. Nothing existed but me.

My tranquillity was shattered when Bowman jerked his head toward the back and shouted above the engine, "You sure you got plenty of good pictures?"

"Yeah," I yelled back. But then it hit me. *Why does he keep asking about pictures? What is he going to do with them?*

After a few minutes, the plane broke out of the light clouds that were causing some chop and I saw the faint lights of the main camp. The area around it was pitch-black but in the flickering moonlight, the rocks in the riverbed shone a silvery gray. Bowman swung the plane around and put it down in a spot on the riverbed that was deep in his memory, a spot where the tail-dragger wouldn't hit any large rocks and flip over.

As the plane came to a rolling stop, I could see a light near the kitchen door, and the shadowy figures of a petite woman, Roy, and Billy Howe filing out. Roy made it to the plane first, just as I was prying my aching body out of the backseat.

"You okay?" he asked in a low, worried voice.

"I'm okay. Everything went fine."

Bowman walked around the front of the plane carrying my sheep horns. "Come look at these great horns Jayne got."

The woman introduced herself as Marianne, Bob's wife, and gave me a congratulatory hug while Roy and Bowman gloated over my trophy. Howe stood by silently as if he was waiting to be convinced that the horns were even real. His steel-gray eyes continued to show nothing but contempt for me. I had hoped that my sheep kill would convince the man that I was the hunter I claimed to be.

As I turned to walk toward the tents, Howe pulled me aside. "Nice sheep," he muttered, his eyes still crackling with suspicion.

I brushed him aside. "Gotta get these wet boots off."

Roy and I went inside the canvas wall tent in which I had yet to spend a night. I pushed the wooden door shut and closed the latch, which was the extent of our security measures. I sat on the floor while Roy went to his duffel bag and pulled out a flask.

"I told you not to bring any of that stuff."

"I just brought a little. It's almost gone. You want some?"

"Naw, I'm okay."

Roy joined me on the floor and spoke in a loud whisper. "Jeez. They wouldn't tell me where you were, who you were with, when you were coming back . . . nothing. I didn't know what the hell was going on. It scared the hell out of me."

"There was no way I could get word to you; all the phones were busy," I said sarcastically.

"Bowman could have told me *something.* That bastard just left me hanging. Marianne said you'd be back last night, and when you didn't show I asked Bowman about it. He blew me off and said he didn't know when you'd be back."

"Bowman flew into the spike camp this morning. Didn't he tell you?"

"Hell no. I saw him leave but I didn't know where he was going."

"Don't worry about it. Everything turned out fine. Look, my guides took me into the wildlife refuge. That's where I shot the sheep."

"Hot damn, I can't believe it. They took a federal agent on an illegal hunt on a national wildlife refuge. Wait till they find out."

"Shut up," I hissed. "It's the kiss of death if anyone hears you."

"Jeez. Don't be so paranoid."

"Be careful of what you say. You have no idea who could be outside listening. Sorry, I'm just exhausted. What did you do?"

"I went out with one of the guides on an all-terrain vehicle and shot the caribou you were originally booked for. It was a cinch. I wonder why Bowman put you on the sheep I was booked for?"

"Hell if I know." I didn't want to tell Roy, but I thought Bowman had done this because I was in much better shape. Looking back, Roy couldn't have hunted that sheep. I barely made it myself.

I went over to an army-style bed and threw my sleeping bag over it for extra warmth. At least tonight I'd be off the ground and would have a pillow. Roy was already rolled up in blankets in his bed.

Then I heard him mutter, "I've never slept in the same room with a girl without sleeping with her."

"Get used to it," I said.

As I tried to lie still, my mind was still jumpy, so I got up and walked over to the duffel bag I had left in the tent while I was on my sheep hunt. I unzipped it and went through the contents. Two flannel shirts, a pair of pants, plane tickets, socks, underwear, and a paperback book. The socks were near the top and I was sure I had packed them on the bottom. My pants weren't folded as neatly as I'd left them. I picked up the paperback and thumbed through the pages. My hands broke into a clammy sweat. The bookmark had been pulled out.

I cocked my head toward Roy. "Have you been in my duffel?"

"Hell no. Haven't touched it."

"Someone's been in this bag. I just know it."

"I hope they were looking for a badge, 'cause there ain't one in it."

I glared at him. "What about your bag? Has anybody been through it?"

"I don't know, and I don't care. I got nothing to hide."

"Don't you get it? The fact that someone likely searched our bags isn't good."

"Not to me. They didn't find anything, so they should be happy."

Maybe I was overreacting, but someone had their suspicions of us. If Roy and I were headed for trouble I wanted to know about it. Still on the floor, I sunk my head between my hands. Who would rifle my bag? The first person I thought of was Billy Howe.

CHAPTER 15

Todo Es un Secreto

THE NEXT MORNING WAS AUGUST 31, 1992. I woke up still worried that someone had snooped though my bag. Roy was still sleeping so I rolled out of my bed as quietly as possible, but when my swollen and bruised feet hit the floor, I couldn't help but groan. I checked my duffel again and there was absolutely nothing in it that would give me away. I was okay. But still, Billy Howe and his constant suspicions troubled me deeply.

Outside, it was a clear, crisp day, like late fall in Wisconsin. I looked up the thirty-yard hill to the outhouse. The red flag was raised, meaning that it was occupied, so I sat on a rock and waited impatiently. Nearly twenty minutes went by and the red flag was still flapping in the wind. Who in the world was in there? Slowly, I took painful baby steps up the hill and listened for any sounds emanating from the outhouse. All was quiet, except for the flapping of the flag. When I reached the outhouse I peeked through a crack to see if there was any movement inside. None. I tapped on the door. No response. I tapped again. Still nothing. Slowly I cracked the door open, and peered inside. From the bottom of the hill, a barrage of laughter erupted.

"Oye mujer! Que haces alli?" howled Pedro from down below. (Hey, woman! What are you doing up there?)

"Necesitas ayuda?" hollered Junior. (Do you need help?)

Very funny. The Spaniards knew the outhouse was empty. They had set me up. Entertainment north of the Arctic Circle was obviously lacking.

Muttering to myself, I entered the outhouse and slammed the door, the sound of the Spaniards' laughter following me until their voices faded into their Quonset hut.

I may have been the only woman hunter in camp, but I was also the only one with an impressive trophy sheep. Minutes later, I limped down the slope from the outhouse and went directly to the skinning shed. Inside, I found the horns from the ram I'd shot lined up with several other smaller sets. One of the sets had a tag with Pedro's name on it. Apparently he'd been on another sheep hunt while I was gone and was finally successful.

I hauled the horns from my sheep up to the kitchen and used a chair to prop open the outside door. I set the horns on the chair and then tore out a sheet of notebook paper. I scrawled "JAYNE" across it and stuck it onto the chair. Then I went inside.

The kitchen was warm with the aroma of frying eggs and bacon. Another woman stood over the stove while Marianne set the table.

"Good morning, Jayne," said Marianne. She nodded toward the woman by the stove. "This is Rhoda, my kitchen help."

Rhoda raised her spatula in acknowledgment. "Nice to meet you, Jayne. Heard you shot a nice sheep."

"Yeah. In fact I put it outside for everyone to see."

"Rubbing it in are you?"

"Yeah."

"Good for you—these men gotta know they aren't the only big shots around here."

Marianne moved about the kitchen quickly like a perky little bird. She was slender and very petite but augmented her height by piling her richly colored red hair on top of her head with a rubber band and a dozen bobby pins. She wore carefully applied false eyelashes along with heavy makeup that was unquestionably overdone for the circumstances. Nevertheless, although she was in her forties she was holding her own, and seemed genuinely kind.

Rhoda on the other hand was decidedly bland. Her drawn face was dominated by dark circles under her eyes and her teeth didn't gleam like Marianne's. Dull brown hair hung flat to her head and over her shoulders. Her bony figure was barely discernible through a well-worn T-shirt and faded Levi's that were held up with a man's leather belt. Her simple silver wedding band was scratched and dented. I later learned that she was married to a backwoodsman who insisted that she haul her own water. Although she was much younger than Marianne, her years had been harder.

One by one, guides and hunters filed into the kitchen. The first was Lenny, only about five feet, five inches tall, who wore a watch cap and had such a full beard that all I could see were his dark, beady eyes. He was the camp skinner responsible for fleshing hides and preparing trophies for shipment to clients' homes.

He extended his hand to me. "So, you're the lady who shot that big Dall. Congratulations, ma'am."

"Thanks. I'm really happy with it."

Bowman came out of a room adjacent to the kitchen and began issuing instructions to Lenny. The room was their bedroom, Marianne explained, which also had a private bathroom with a shower. She invited me to use it, but only because I was a woman. It was off-limits to the other hunters.

Next in the door was a sixty-five-year-old German hunter with thinning white hair and a stout build. He introduced himself as Wilhelm.

His English was limited but he smiled and held his hands about four feet apart. "You sheep?"

"Yes, my sheep," I said.

"Goot, verry goot," he said, patting me on my shoulder before taking a seat at the table. As he placed his hands in front of him, his Rolex watch glimmered in the morning light.

I could hear Pedro, El Doctor, and Junior chattering in Spanish outside. Looking out a window I saw them gathered around my trophy, nodding and pointing. As they filed inside the kitchen each one smiled at me saying, *"Vaya trofeo!"* (Great trophy.) I hoped that they were green with envy.

I fell into action by placing plates of scrambled eggs and biscuits on the table. Piles of bacon came next. Working in the kitchen was part of my strategy to become friendly with the women.

"You don't have to help us," protested Marianne. "You're a client. Please, sit down."

"I don't mind," I answered. "Besides, it makes me feel more like I'm at home."

"Don't turn any help down, Marianne," laughed Rhoda, "We'll give her extra food."

"She gets what everyone else gets," joked Bowman.

The light mood was broken when a Grizzly Adams look-alike stomped into the kitchen, the floor shaking from the force of his steps.

He plopped down in a chair at the table and scowled. "Rhoda! Coffee!"

Rhoda hurried over and slid a cup in front of him.

He took a sip and grimaced. "How old is this shit?"

"I made it this morning. It should be okay."

He shoved the cup across the table. "Well, it ain't."

Rhoda backed off and folded her arms across her stomach, her pale face unable to hide the pain she felt from the insult. So this was Gordon, her husband, who was also Bowman's head guide.

At that moment, Roy sauntered in with two other hunters, Larry and Ted from California. Larry and Ted claimed to be friends who were on sheep "hunts of a lifetime." Something about them struck me as odd, but I couldn't put my finger on what. Ted said he had been a deer hunter since he was a kid and had always wanted to hunt sheep. A Dall hunt in Alaska was a dream come true. Larry claimed to be a long-distance marksman who practiced five-hundred-yard shots on a regular basis. But I knew from some very recent experience that hunting sheep requires tremendous stamina—and Larry was an overweight chain-smoker.

The lively conversation at breakfast was mostly about my sheep hunt. Again, I became an instant translator between the Spaniards and the rest of the group. Bowman seemed impressed with my language skills and I sensed that he was realizing I could be critical to his ability to communicate with the Spaniards. I wanted to capitalize on this because I wanted Bowman to *need* me.

Meanwhile, Pedro asked how long I had to endure the spike camp. El Doctor said he had never met a woman who hunted like me. Larry wanted to know how long my shot was. Through all their questions, Bowman sat at the head of the table smiling benevolently like a proud papa. My sheep kill was another conquest that fed *his* ego. He reminded everyone that he'd found the sheep and that he was the real reason I had such a magnificent trophy.

After breakfast Roy announced that he didn't feel well and went back to the tent. I lingered in the kitchen because it was already apparent to me that it was the camp's "information center," with Marianne in charge. The fact that I was a woman made hanging out in the kitchen appear natural.

There was a radiophone on top of the refrigerator and a wall-sized topographical map of the hunting areas. Several spike camps were prominently marked with flagged pins. I walked over to the map and found Jake and

Danny's camp and retraced my hunt. The Spaniards were standing right behind me examining the map.

"Uh-oh," I said.

"Hay problema?" asked Pedro. (Is there a problem?)

"Ven esta área?" I said, pointing out an area of the map. "See this area? It's a wildlife refuge . . . that's where I killed my sheep."

"That explains why you were able to get such a big one," whispered El Doctor.

"That's where the best animals are for sure. It's the same way in Europe," said Pedro.

I faced them with a contrived, worried look. "Please don't tell anyone that my sheep is illegal. Keep it a secret, okay?"

My strategy was to cut them in on my little secret so they'd be more likely to confide in me.

"Of course," said Pedro. "Don't worry, no one will ever know. Around here, *todo es un secreto*. Everything is a secret."

Pedro's statement caught my interest. He'd just alluded to more "secrets," which in my mind meant illegal activity. Naturally, I wanted to know more. The Spaniards and I fell into an easy conversation like we'd been friends for years. Pedro explained that his back was better and he was eager for Bowman to take him on a bear hunt. El Doctor said he wanted to hunt a bear and a moose. Junior wasn't a hunter. His father, El Doctor, had brought him to Alaska because in Spain Junior lived with his mother and rarely saw him. Junior kept his hands stuffed in his pockets and rarely said anything. Overall, he seemed like an emotionally vacant young man who didn't know what to do with all the "quality" time he now had with his father.

As we talked, I noticed that El Doctor was wearing a brand new four-piece coordinated olive-green woolen outfit from Orvis and asked him where he bought it.

"In Seattle," he said. "The airline lost my luggage so I bought a thousand dollars worth of new clothes."

He shrugged his shoulders and drew a breath through a Cuban cigar. "I bought a case of wine, too, and had to pay the bush pilot to bring it in on a special trip. I have to have wine, even if Mr. Bob doesn't allow it."

Switching my attention to Pedro I asked, "Are you married?"

As an answer he slid an imaginary ring off his finger, threw it on the ground, and spat. "Spew . . . that's what I think of marriage."

"I'm the same way. No more marriages for me." I wanted Pedro to think we had something in common.

"So," asked El Doctor curiously. "You like to travel around and hunt? Unusual for a woman. No?"

"American women are independent."

"Must be expensive," said Pedro.

"I have money. Well, my ex-husband has money and he has to give half of it to me."

"What does he do?" asked Pedro.

"Uh, he's an investor in Chicago. What do you do?"

"I own a restaurant."

"Five restaurants," chimed in Junior for the first time.

"No wonder you complain about the food here," I said with a laugh.

"The food around here stinks like crap."

"It's not *that* bad. But I do have one question. Why did you say that here *todo es un secreto*?"

Junior covered his eyes and turned away while his father smirked and took another puff of his cigar.

Pedro leaned forward close to my ear. "Because no one will say how they got their animals—it's all a secret. You'll see."

I shook my head as if I understood. Even though I felt an urge to dig for more, I didn't want to appear overly anxious. I said that Roy wasn't feeling well and that I needed to check on him. I promised to visit with them later.

At the tent, I found Roy lying flat on his back on his bed reading a paperback. "You okay?" I asked.

"Yeah, just feeling some jet lag I think. Anything going on?"

"I had a talk with the Spaniards. They've got plenty of money and don't seem too concerned about wildlife laws. We should keep a close eye on them."

Roy rolled over. "That's your job, I can't speak Spanglish and don't have time to learn."

I took a deep breath and hoped that Roy's downtime was temporary. I needed another set of eyes and ears to monitor what was going on in the camp. I also needed him as a witness to any illegal activity. But for now I could see that he was completely worthless.

"I'm going to take my horns back down to the skinning tent. See you later."

As I approached the kitchen shack, I noticed Larry and Ted, the two California hunters, standing outside talking. Larry was smoking a cigarette.

I nodded at Larry and said hi to Ted. Although I was within clear earshot, he acted like he didn't hear me.

"Hi, Ted," I repeated.

Larry took the cigarette out of this mouth and muttered, "Jerry, she's saying hi to you."

"Ted" looked up. "Yeah, hi. Jayne right?"

"Right."

I kept walking to process what I had just heard. Two guys hunting together and one under a false name. *What the hell was going on with that?* My first suspicion was that they were an undercover team sent in by the State of Alaska. After all, the State had put their guy on Bowman that spring. But surely they would have informed Eicher if they were going to do that again. I didn't know what to think. For now, my whole world was this hunting camp and the people in it, and I had to consider every possibility.

When I arrived at the skinning shed, Lenny, the skinner, was there with Wilhelm, the German hunter. Lenny was wearing his usual stocking cap and a flannel shirt with the sleeves rolled up revealing long-sleeved underwear. He also wore blue jeans and a blood-smeared plastic bib apron. He would have easily fit in on a commercial fishing boat. Wilhelm on the other hand looked like he was dressed for a leisurely afternoon at a fancy fly-fishing resort with his lambs-wool jacket and new leather boots.

"Would you guard these for me?" I said to Lenny as I set the sheep horns inside the tent.

"You bet. I won't let anybody take those."

"Goot, verrry goot," said Wilhelm, pointing at the horns.

"Thanks. I heard you got a nice sheep yourself."

"*Ja.*"

"Where is it?"

Lenny turned around, reached down to the ground, and grabbed a set of horns with a three-quarter-curl and definite points that were from a young sheep.

"These are his," he said. "Fine set of horns. I think."

"Yeah, they are," I said, smiling at Wilhelm. "Good, very good."

"*Ja,*" Wilhelm beamed.

"Where did you shoot it?"

He shrugged his shoulders.

I didn't know if Wilhelm didn't understand my question or didn't know where he had hunted the sheep. I made a mental note to ask him again later when we were alone. Then I looked at my watch. "Gosh, it's almost lunchtime; I'm going to the kitchen."

"I go, too," said Wilhelm.

As Lenny went back to fleshing the sheep hide, Wilhelm and I walked the seventy-five yards across the camp to the kitchen cabin. The day had warmed up nicely and by the time we arrived at the kitchen I noticed that Wilhelm was panting. How could this man hunt a sheep if he couldn't walk up a small hill? Somehow I had to find out exactly what had happened on Wilhelm's sheep hunt.

In the kitchen, Rhoda and Marianne were busy setting up the table for lunch, which consisted of sliced ham sandwiches with the works, a pasta salad, and a relish tray. Right away I made myself useful by helping them.

Pedro, El Doctor, and Junior were already seated. Roy came in a few minutes later with the California hunters. Bowman was at the head of table but didn't speak to anyone. He seemed more preoccupied than usual.

During lunch Wilhelm and I chatted in halting English phrases supplemented with short pantomimes. He explained that he owned a "washing business" that did the laundry for all the hospitals in the city where he lived. He pointed to his Rolex watch and told me it cost fifteen thousand dollars and then worked in the fact that he owned five Rolls Royces. I pictured Wilhelm living in a renovated seventeenth-century castle with an army of servants. Another reason I couldn't picture him on a death-defying sheep hunt.

Suddenly Bowman stood up and motioned to the Spaniards to follow him. He pointed to me and said, "Jayne, come here, I need you to talk to these boys."

"Sure." I stood up and joined Bowman and the Spaniards in the little huddle they had formed by the big wall map.

Even though Bowman spoke in a low tone, his voice had a sharp instructional edge to it. "Tell Pedro and the Doc I want 'em by the planes at two o'clock with just their gear and the clothes they're wearing. I'm taking them out for bear. Tell 'em I'm going to have to use the planes to help the hunts along or we'll be gone for a damn month. They gotta keep the part about the planes quiet. I mean strictly to themselves. And that means you, too. Understand?"

"Sure, Bob, I know nothing."

This was the moment I'd been waiting for. Bowman was now using me as a translator to communicate his unlawful hunting scheme to the Spaniards. I wasn't convinced that he completely trusted me, but he needed me, which forced him into cutting me in on his "camp secrets."

The Spaniards crowded closer to me as I translated Bowman's instructions. Pedro's strong cologne hung in the air while Junior's shoulder hugged mine. Bowman was being deliberately vague about "using the planes to help the hunts along," and I wondered if this was for my benefit. Maybe he hoped that I didn't know what this meant. But I knew exactly what he meant, and I translated his instructions directly.

"Mr. Bob says he's going to find your bear from the air, then herd them to you so you don't have to hunt for weeks."

Pedro and El Doctor nodded and smiled at each other with complete approval.

"The problem is that hunting bear from an airplane is illegal; you could find your butts in jail if you get caught. So you've got to keep this very quiet. Not a word to anyone—except to me of course," I added.

"We understand completely," said Pedro, laughing. "See, I told you, *todo es un secreto.*"

"Yes, I know. Be down by the planes at two o'clock, *punto.* Don't pack any clothes; just wear what you have on. Okay—you'd better get going."

Just then Bowman pulled me aside for additional low-voiced instructions. "Would ya tell Pedro not to wear that stinking cologne on the hunt? It scares off the animals. He's been wearing it ever since you showed up."

"You've got to be kidding."

"No, I'm not. Tell him to wash that crap off," said Bowman impatiently.

"Sure, Bob, I'll tell him now."

Just as the Spaniards had made it out the kitchen door I caught up with them and relayed Bowman's message to Pedro as tactfully as I could.

"*No hay problema,*" shrugged Pedro.

Junior, who was standing behind Pedro, shot a quick wink at me.

I went back into the kitchen to help Marianne and Rhoda clean up, hoping to generate some conversation that might glean additional information about Wilhelm and maybe the California hunters.

While I was drying and stacking dishes I told the story about "Ted" not knowing his own name.

"That's easy," she said. "His real name is Jerry Warner. He was substituted at the last minute for another hunter who couldn't make it."

"Isn't hunting on someone else's license illegal?"

"Technically yes, but it's such a shame to let a sheep tag go to waste. Sheep permits are hard to get you know."

Maybe Marianne accepted the substituted-hunter story, but I didn't. I knew from the intelligence information that I received prior to coming to the camp that Bowman checked out his hunters. Bowman probably accepted the original "Ted" and then Jerry Warner was switched in at the last minute as an undercover operative leaving no time to check him out. This "bait and switch" tactic was commonly used in undercover operations. I'd thought of doing it myself by switching another federal agent in for Roy.

"So what should I call him? Jerry or Ted?"

"Call him 'hey you'," chimed in Rhoda.

I shook my head. "I don't know how you two keep all this straight."

"Don't worry about those guys," said Marianne. "They've already gone out on their sheep hunts and will be gone for days."

They still worried me. I considered that Larry might be a cooperator. Most game wardens didn't have time to perfect the long-distance shooting skills Larry claimed that he had, and most wardens didn't smoke. "Ted" however was a problem. I didn't like the fact that he had slid in at the last minute. I decided to stay clear of Larry and "Ted" and have Roy talk to them when they got back. As it was, I was talking to too many people.

I changed the subject. "Wilhelm sure got a nice sheep for an old man."

"No kidding," said Rhoda. "Gordon had to shoot it for him. That old fart can't walk three feet without gasping for air, and he can't shoot worth a shit either."

Rhoda's words were music to my ears. In two seconds she confirmed my suspicions.

"I think that's true of most Europeans," I said without any basis.

"Why's that?" asked Rhoda.

"Ah . . . they don't have the space to shoot long distances. All their shooting is done at short distances. It's a whole different story over here."

Rhoda believed me. I probably wouldn't have gotten away with such an absurd explanation if I'd been talking to one of the guides. Even though Rhoda had given me the basic information I needed to make a case against the German, later I'd need confessions from Gordon and Wilhelm to make the case stick. These would come much later, after the undercover portion of the case was over.

Then I changed the subject to a more personal one. "Rhoda, I noticed that Gordon pushes you around. Why do you let him do that?"

Rhoda began nervously wiping her hands on her apron even though they were already dry. "He doesn't treat me bad. He just gets upset when the hunting doesn't go right. It don't usually last long."

"You're a great lady and I think if you put your foot down, he'd stop. You deserve better."

"Jayne's got a point," said Marianne. "I've never said anything, but Gordon treats you like dirt sometimes."

Rhoda plopped down at the table and looked at Marianne and me. "How do I get him to stop?"

"Tell him that you're sick of it and you'll leave him in the dust if he doesn't stop. Tell him that the clients are even noticing and you're not putting up with another minute of it," I said.

Rhoda's face looked pained. "I can't leave him."

"Just *tell* him that," suggested Marianne. "That's the only way he's going to take you seriously. I know Gordon. His head is harder than permafrost, but he *needs* you and will do anything to keep you. Jayne's right, you've got to put a stop to this crap."

Rhoda's eyes welled up. "I really do hate it when he yells at me."

"Then make him stop," I said. "Marianne and I will back you up." I sat next to Rhoda and handed her some Kleenex. "Look at me: I'm as good of a shot as Gordon is and he knows it. Tell him that if he doesn't start treating you better, I'm coming after him."

This made Rhoda laugh. "Okay, I'll talk to him before he leaves with Bob and the Spaniards."

"Good. Then he can think about what you've said while he's sleeping on the ground in the bush."

Rhoda looked at me. "I've never had anyone stick up for me like this before. Why are you doing it?"

"Because you're one gutsy woman who I happen to admire. Living off the land in Canada is tough and you deserve to be happy doing it. If Gordon isn't making you happy, then kick his butt until he does."

By now Rhoda was laughing again and seemed to have built up enough resolve to deal with her husband. Both Marianne and I gave her hugs for good luck before she went back to her Quonset to confront Gordon.

I went back to my tent to find Roy once again lying on the bed, finishing up a book he'd been reading for days.

"Anything going on?" he asked.

"No, except Pedro and El Doctor are going out west this afternoon to hunt bear. Bowman's going to hunt from the air, Wilhelm's sheep is illegal, and I think 'Ted' might be a warden."

Roy sat up on the bed and looked at me. "Not bad. You know I'm gettin' sick of waitin' around here for Bowman to take me out. I should be out there right now tracking down the big one."

"The rich boys get taken out first."

"Yeah. Ain't that the way things are."

"You know, Roy, while you're waiting around here doing nothing, you could be helping me out. If fact, the California hunters just left on their sheep hunts. I want you to talk to them when they get back and find out about their hunts."

"Hopefully, I'll be out huntin' myself."

"What's the matter with you anyway? You've hardly been out of this tent since we got here."

"I dunno. I'm sweaty and a little shaky. I just don't feel like talkin' to nobody, and besides, you're doing just fine."

"I'm feeling a lot of pressure out there alone. Get it together, would you? You're supposed to be my partner."

"Okay, I'll do better. I'm going up the hill for a while." He heaved himself up out of his bed and headed out the tent toward the outhouse.

I couldn't believe that on top of the pressures of operating covertly inside the camp I had to deal with Roy. I couldn't figure out exactly what was wrong with him. Was he genuinely sick? Was all he really wanted out of this to hunt a grizzly and the rest of it didn't matter to him? Or was he just plain scared? But whatever was going on with him, I couldn't let him get to me. I had to keep focused on the case.

From the window I could see Pedro and El Doctor by the riverbed with their gear, apparently in high spirits. Maybe they had been drinking some of their wine. I ran a brush though my hair and then ambled down by the planes where Bowman and Howe were doing their preflight checks. Gordon was busy loading gear behind the backseats. I noticed a plastic bin stocked with freeze-dried entrees and wondered how long Pedro the restaurateur would put up with this fine cuisine.

Pedro took the backseat of Bowman's plane while El Doctor and Gordon both stuffed themselves into the backseat of Howe's. Two pilots, two hunters, and one guide. This was going to be a hunt where the "f" was going to be omitted from "fair chase." An air chase was illegal of course, but it produced easy trophies when you needed them in a hurry. I would have given anything to be there, but could only watch as the two Super Cubs lifted into the sky until they were no more than floating specks on the horizon.

Junior followed me back to the kitchen like a puppy who expected to be played with. What was I going to do with this kid? I reached for the Scrabble game and told him I'd teach him how to play. Since the Spanish language uses more vowels than English, we quickly ran short of them. But eventually we finished a game and as I reviewed Junior's words I noticed that he'd spelled out, *vida, sin, amor*. Life without love.

After Junior left the kitchen, I popped open a can of Pepsi and sat at the table to visit with Marianne and Rhoda. I noticed that Rhoda's mood seemed lighter.

"How did it go with Gordon?" I asked.

"When I told him I didn't like him yelling at me, we got into a fight. But when I told him that you were noticing what an asshole he was to me, that seemed to make a big difference."

"Good. Did he agree to knock it off?"

"He said he didn't want to lose me and admitted that maybe he took bad hunting days out on me too much."

"What a pathetic excuse," I muttered.

"I think the timing was perfect," said Marianne. "He's gone and Rhoda didn't have to kick him out."

We all laughed and I was especially glad that Rhoda was feeling good about having stood up to Gordon for one of the first times in her marriage.

"Say, I heard you're gonna be famous," said Rhoda winking at me.

"Like how?"

"Didn't Bob tell you?" said Marianne. "He's gonna put your picture with your sheep on next year's brochure. This is quite an honor you know."

The Pepsi stopped in my throat. *So that's why he wanted so many pictures.* With my picture on Bowman's brochure, there was the potential for every outlaw hunter, guide, or outfitter in the country to know who I was. The problem was Danny still had the camera with the film in it, and I didn't know when or if I'd ever see him. Somehow I had to get a hold of that camera, even if I had to steal it.

CHAPTER 16

La Amiga

THE NEXT MORNING THE WOODEN DOOR TO THE TENT creaked as I pushed it open and stepped outside to a sky the color of a robin's egg. The chilly nip in the air was a precursor to the much colder weather that was soon to come. By mid-September, my tent and the Quonset huts would likely be buried in snow.

On my way to the kitchen, my attention snapped skywards to the unmistakable pumping wing beat of a peregrine falcon. I caught a glimpse of the pronounced black cheek patch identifying it as a Peale's peregrine, an endangered species. With sheer joy and wonderment in my heart, I watched the bird soar across the sky. This was the first Peale's peregrine I'd ever seen in the wild.

In 1981, I arrested several falconers in Utah who had taken peregrine falcon chicks from eyries in Alaska. These nest robbers risked their lives to get these birds, rappelling hundreds of feet down rocky cliffs to eyries secluded in small caves. They typically wore hard hats to protect themselves from the female peregrine that would strike the heads of the intruders when they got close to the nest.

Peregrines are known for their incredible ability to dive-bomb prey and pluck it out of the sky at speeds up to two hundred miles per hour. Some North American peregrines have ended up in the hands of Middle Eastern sheiks willing to pay more than one hundred thousand dollars per bird, which secured a fat profit for nest robbers.

My spirits rose at the sight of this wild falcon. Just as my arrests had helped to stop the falcon robbers, I hoped that by stopping Bowman and his guides, the big-game animals in the Brooks Range would be free from poachers.

The delicious smell of hot food welcomed me into the kitchen. Corned beef hash, bacon, biscuits, and copious amounts of juice and coffee were already on the table. Marianne believed that good meals mitigated any shortfalls in the hunting. Given the vulnerability of most hunters to food, I figured she was probably right.

Roy was already at the table with Wilhelm. Both were digging into the food like it might be their last meal. Next to them was Wild Bill, a caribou hunting guide. Wild Bill was a twenty-eight-year-old Texan with a redneck drawl and an attitude that critters existed so he could "make death." A photograph of Wild Bill holding the heart of a caribou near his mouth with blood dripping off his chin was taped to the wall. On it was written, "Oh, my achey, breaky, heart!"

Marianne insisted that Wild Bill take his cowboy hat off while he was at the table. Matted hair formed a greasy band around his head like a toilet ring and his knotted beard looked like an inviting habitat for burrowing insects. I caught a whiff of his boots, which smelled like they had been dragged through piles of blood and guts.

No wonder he was at this outpost. Civilization wouldn't have him.

While I smeared homemade jam on biscuits, Junior sauntered into the kitchen and sat down next to me. He shoveled heaping forkfuls of corned beef hash into his mouth and complained about how he couldn't wait to get back to Barcelona so that he could go to discotheques and movies with his girlfriend. I figured that to Junior, the wilderness felt like a prison.

Roy scraped up the last bit of food off his plate, pushed his chair back from the table, and announced, "I'm going back to the tent for a while."

His words irritated me. It was obvious that he intended to spend another day in the tent loafing and napping. It didn't bother him one iota that he was leaving me out on a limb to make this case alone. If something went wrong, I could count on Roy being in the tent, counting sheep. Yet, he never missed a meal.

Seething, I kept quiet and cleared dishes from the table, but felt my face turn hot as Roy ambled out the door, letting it slam behind him. Meanwhile, Junior complained that he was so bored he planned to get drunk again that day. Lenny told me that while I was on my sheep hunt he'd caught Junior stumbling drunk, singing something that sounded like, "Johnny Walker is my best friend."

I asked Marianne if there was anything around the camp for Junior to do. She suggested that he go out on a caribou hunt with Wild Bill. When I translated this to Junior, he reacted enthusiastically. *"Si, si, si!"*

I looked at him with surprise. "Wait a minute. I thought you didn't hunt."

He held an imaginary gun up to his shoulder. "I want to blast something and show my old man that I can do it. *Zas-Zas-Zas!"*

Of course, hunting for love, I thought.

Wild Bill leaned over, picked up his hat, and slapped it on his head. "Yahoo! C'mon boy, let's go kill something."

Like a child eager for adventure, Junior followed Wild Bill out the door, chattering in Spanish about how excited he was.

Wilhelm stood up, bowed politely to Marianne as if to thank her for the breakfast, and went outside. I dumped breakfast scraps into a bucket and carried the dishes to Rhoda to wash.

After everything was cleaned up the three of us began making filled pastries and apple tarts. Soon the counter and table were covered with flour, brown sugar, spices, eggs, fruit juices, and apples.

"This will go so much faster with you helping," commented Rhoda.

"Don't count on it, I nearly flunked home economics."

"Still, you'll make it more fun," laughed Marianne.

Marianne and Rhoda knew exactly how to produce delectable treats from this wilderness kitchen, but I stuck to beating eggs and sifting flour. Even though our conversation was trivial it was also warm and caring. My bond with the women was growing stronger, yet little did they know of my true motivation.

Aside from being a cooking and eating place, the kitchen was like "command central" in a military operation. It was the camp's nerve center and the best place to keep track of what was going on. Marianne kept the whereabouts of the hunters, pilots, and guides posted on the wall map in the kitchen. Potentially important bits of information came in through calls on the radiophone.

When Bowman was in the field, Marianne was in charge, and she made all the decisions. I wanted to be in the kitchen as much as possible, and helping there was the perfect cover for gathering information.

Studying the wall map, I spotted where Bowman and the Spaniards were set up in a spike camp. The location was the Colville River. I committed this to memory.

"Does Bob hunt this area much?" I asked Marianne.

"Yeah, lots of times, but he's not actually allowed to use it. Another outfitter drew it this year and Bob drew another area much farther west. He doesn't have time to scout out a new area and fly his hunters back and forth all the time. The gas and time would eat up his business."

I knew that the Alaska wildlife department divided the state into hunting units and distributed them among the registered outfitters through a lottery. This helped to keep the wildlife populations stable and prevented the same outfitter from getting the same hunting area every year. Bowman was encroaching on another outfitter's area because it was closer to his camp and he knew the area better. I smiled to myself. Marianne was beginning to talk to me like one of her girlfriends. Perfect.

Suddenly Marianne screamed and ran to the window. "Would you look at this."

I darted to another window and caught the last flash of a pasty-white derriere as it plunged into the frigid waters of the Ivishak River. The backside belonged to none other than Wilhelm. Marianne and I stood laughing as we heard him bellowing a German song while rubbing a bar of soap all around his chest, face, and hair. Standing in waist-deep water, he jumped up and down, spun in circles, and waved his arms wildly as if he had gone totally mad.

"He's going to have a heart attack. He's too old for that cold water," I said.

"Don't say that. I don't need a dead body on my hands."

No more than a minute later, Wilhelm splashed through the water to shore. He trotted out of the river and like an old horse hobbled naked past the windows. I didn't know whether to laugh or be embarrassed for the old guy. Marianne, however, was indignant.

"How dare he run around here like that. I'm going to have a word with him. This isn't a nudist colony."

Later, I walked outside and found Wilhelm, fully dressed, taking in the expansive views of the Brooks Range.

"Nice day," I said.

"Ja," he agreed, smiling.

I noticed a small German/English dictionary in his hand and motioned to him to give it to me. I thumbed through it. Although communicating with Wilhelm was like pushing mud I was determined to get something out of him about his sheep hunt. Quickly, I assembled what I wanted to ask with a few German words. After a few minutes using my newly acquired handful of German words and his limited English, Wilhelm managed to tell me that he didn't eat or sleep at the spike camp.

If this was the case, Gordon had to have shot Wilhelm's sheep the same day he had flown, which was a violation of airborne hunting laws. I suspected that Bowman spotted the sheep from the plane and then landed close by for Gordon to shoot it.

I lifted an imaginary rifle in my arms and said, "Gordon shoot sheep?"

"Ja," said Wilhelm nonchalantly.

That was it. Bowman did the flying, Gordon did the shooting, and Wilhelm did the bragging. Some hunt. Any respect I had for the German gentleman evaporated into the pristine Arctic air. His only ammunition was his checkbook.

Overall, I was happy to have Wilhelm's confession of sorts. Later, we'd arrest Gordon and get him to admit that he shot Wilhelm's sheep illegally. I wasn't sure how Eicher would reach Wilhelm for a statement after he was back in Germany, but that was for another day.

Leaving Wilhelm, I went back to the tent to find Roy sprawled on his bed reading the same paperback he had already finished.

"I thought you were done with that book."

"I'm reading it again," he mumbled.

Even though the temperature in the tent was cool, sweat beaded on Roy's forehead. The paperback shook in his left hand, and his right hand quivered as it lay at his side. He'd been in this tent, on his bed, for days.

"Aren't you feeling any better yet?"

"Nope, I still got a cold."

"I just found out that Gordon shot Wilhelm's sheep for him. Wilhelm didn't even pretend to hunt it. I could have used you as a witness to this conversation."

Roy didn't take his eyes off his book. He turned, shifted his weight to one side, and muttered, "You can handle 'em."

I felt like I had been dealt a left hook out of nowhere. I was trying to keep track of people and their stories that swarmed around me like flies, and Roy wasn't a smidgen of help. Although I was on the verge of ripping into him, I realized that it would distract me from my real mission. More than ever, I had to stay focused. *Forget Roy.* He could lie there and rot—I had a job to do.

Pulling my notebook out of my hidden passport holder, I sat on the floor and jotted down notes about my conversation with Wilhelm. These notes would be the backbone of my case.

A few minutes later I got up. "I'm going back down to the kitchen."

"Have fun," Roy replied indifferently.

As I walked outside I wondered if I should be worried about him. Was he really sick? I figured as long as he was breathing and eating I wouldn't worry about him. I had enough on my mind as it was.

In the kitchen, Marianne was on the radiophone. "Hold on, Luís. Jayne just came in. Here she is."

I took the mike. "Who's Luís?"

"He's a hunting booking agent from Madrid. He booked the Spaniards here. Say something to him in Spanish."

"Hola! Soy la intreprete personal de Pedro y el me tiene pendiente de todo." I told Luís I was Pedro's personal interpreter and that he was keeping me at his beck and call.

Luis responded in English. "You sound like you have fun—I wish I could be there. Are you as beautiful as you sound?"

"Oh, yes. More beautiful than you can imagine."

"I'm on my way."

I gave Luís a girlish laugh and handed the mike back to Marianne, who told him that the guys were out with Bob hunting bear and they should be back that night.

"Very good," said Luís. "I'm very excited to hear how they do."

Funny, I was, too.

The late afternoon light slanted through the kitchen windows as I sat at the table with Marianne and Rhoda. We turned over rocks one by one, looking for impressions left millions of years ago by invertebrate marine animals. We had just returned from three hours of scouring the ancient Ivishak riverbed looking for a rare brachiopod fossil that might make us famous. Although each rock promised a startling discovery, nothing remarkable turned up. Rhoda knew a bit about fossils from a book she had read. She said that some of the impressions in the rocks were actually fossil traces of the burrows and tracks of certain organisms. I was fascinated with our scant fossil collection and tried to imagine what this part of the world was like some 3.5 billion years ago when it was a huge sea and later when it was home to prehistoric mammoths, whose ivory still lay buried beneath the very land we walked upon.

Our fossil party was interrupted abruptly when Wild Bill burst into the kitchen, his feet stomping and his voice roaring. "Stupid kid!"

Startled, Marianne sat straight up, her eyes wide. "What on earth is the matter?"

Wild Bill dumped himself into a kitchen chair and leaned over with his elbows on his knees. He wiped the sweat and dirt from his forehead with one hand. "The Spanish kid shot two caribou." Then he stood up, turned his back to Marianne, and erupted, "This pisses me off!"

Rhoda's mouth dropped open, but she quickly covered it. Her eyes shot back and forth between Marianne and Wild Bill as she watched the drama unfold.

Marianne's face turned crimson as she screeched, "Why did you let him do that? The limit is one. Bob could lose his outfitter's license for this."

"I know, I know," moaned Wild Bill.

"Tell me exactly what happened."

Wild Bill went on to explain. "There were about three hundred caribou in a bunch. I picked one out for him and told him to shoot it. He shoots it. It wasn't dead so I told him to shoot again. He fires the gun again and hits the one right next to it. If I'd-a known the kid was gonna do that, I'd-a clobbered him."

Marianne grabbed her hair with both hands. "Oh my God! Bob will kill me when he finds out."

Rhoda quietly collected the fossils on the table and stowed them inside a shoe box. Science class was clearly over. She walked over to the sink, took a handful of potatoes from an open sack, and busied herself scrubbing them.

The door swung open and Junior walked in. He timidly looked around the room, his face blanched as if Wild Bill's ranting had blown all the color out of it. I got up and put my arm around his shoulders and gently guided him to a chair.

"Que pasó?" I asked softly.

In a fearful, small voice Junior explained that Wild Bill told him to shoot two "cows," so he did.

I turned to Wild Bill. "He says you told him to shoot two animals."

Wild Bill's eyes blazed with rage. "I told that stupid little shit to shoot the first caribou twice. It wasn't dead yet. Then he hauled off and shot another one. There was nothing I could do to stop it."

Marianne's voice had a panicky edge to it. "I've got to get rid of the second caribou."

She looked at Wild Bill and me for concurrence. By law, the mishap was supposed to be reported to the Alaskan wildlife authorities. It was clearly a mistake, and Marianne would be better off reporting it than hiding it.

"Why don't you just report it as an accident," I suggested. "This sort of thing must happen all the time."

"No way!" shrieked Marianne. "I don't want any game wardens crawling around here. I've got to get rid of it. Now."

Marianne acted as if this was a murder scene that needed to be covered up. She saw the accidental caribou kill as a direct threat to her husband's hunting enterprise, which she was determined to protect at all costs.

Meanwhile, Junior tugged at my shirt. "What's going on Jayne? *No comprendo.*" (I don't understand.)

I decided to play with Junior's mind a little. "Marianne thinks you should be arrested, but I've convinced her not to call the authorities," I told him. "You'll be okay."

Junior let out a stream of air between his lips. "I didn't know this could be so serious. What would I do without you?"

"No hay problema," I said with a smile.

Marianne ordered Wild Bill to hide the caribou meat under a tarp behind the kitchen. The Alaska game wardens flew patrols and if they spotted an abandoned carcass they'd zero in on the camp and start asking questions.

She also devised a solution for the extra set of caribou antlers. "I'll make up a tag with El Doctor's name on it and put it on the antlers, so if we get checked, we'll be covered."

Marianne picked up the radiophone. Junior looked at me with fear in his eyes. *"A quien esta llamando?"* (Who's she calling?)

"No te preocupes," I reassured him. "Don't worry. It's not about you."

The call was about the caribou meat. Marianne contacted a friend of hers at the Department of Transportation pump line station and asked if he was interested in some caribou meat. I could tell that free game meat was always welcome and questions were never asked.

Marianne told Wild Bill she wanted the meat flown to the DOT station as soon as possible and added, "I don't want any talk about this, to anyone. Understand?"

Wild Bill pointed to Junior. "Tell that to *him*."

I translated to Junior that the caribou incident had to be kept secret, or else he would be arrested. Junior eagerly nodded his head in agreement and muttered the camp motto, *"Todo es un secreto."*

Unexpectedly, Billy Howe flew back into camp and said that Pedro was now being flown by Jack Watson, Bowman's third pilot. Watson, originally from Idaho, had finished up with the California hunters and had headed back out to help Bowman. Howe packed up the illegal caribou meat and transported it to the DOT station. This was a charge for the transportation of illegal game meat that I'd record in my notes.

Meanwhile, Marianne sat down at the kitchen table with a pile of Alaska Department of Fish and Wildlife hunt reports in front of her. The information in these reports would be used by wildlife managers to help maintain stable wildlife populations throughout the state. Bowman was required to file the reports indicating each hunter's kill and where it took place. I positioned myself at the same table, thumbing through a hunting magazine.

Also on the table was a letter from Caza Todo, the Madrid booking agency that had booked the Spaniards into the camp. It was dated August 12, 1992, and I could easily read it from where I was sitting. The beginning of the letter was about the fees paid by the Spanish hunters. From what I could figure Pedro and El Doctor each paid around thirty thousand dollars for their Alaskan adventure. Junior had paid an observer fee, but the cost wasn't mentioned. The last paragraph of the letter was of the greatest interest to me and when Marianne left the room momentarily I quickly scribbled it down, errors and all, and shoved it into my pocket.

> *I understand what you allways say about guaranties on your hunts and I totally agree with you, but let me also agree with you on your success*

ratio!! I do wish you all the necessary luck to be able one more time, to
keep your record at the same level as always, specially after all what we
had to suffer with these clients.

Looking fowardt to another group of satisfied Alaskan huntres,
Yours very truly, Luís Arroz

Luís's letter confirmed that Bowman was guaranteeing his hunts—in reality, an impossible thing to do—and that he was building a clientele that expected nothing less. This kind of "hunting" was devastating to wildlife.

Fifteen minutes later, Howe came in and ignored me, which suited me fine. He picked up the stack of papers and studied several forms individually.

Finally, he tossed one down in front of Marianne saying, "We want that sheep off the ANWR."

Although I pretended not to notice, the hunt report was mine. And although Howe may have thought he was speaking in code, I knew that ANWR was the acronym for the Arctic National Wildlife Refuge.

"It is off the ANWR," replied Marianne.

"No it ain't. Put it at Lupine River."

"Are you sure? I don't want problems."

"There won't be."

Howe put at least four more forms in front of Marianne and told her to make changes. The changes would cover up hunting on the Arctic National Wildlife Refuge and other places Bowman and his hunters were not supposed to be. This would definitely go into my notes along with the fact that Marianne and Billy Howe conspired to cover up the illegal hunting.

Marianne told me that Larry got a sheep with a very long shot, but "Ted" aka Jerry Warner couldn't get close enough to one to get a shot. Danny had been their guide and apparently was furious because Larry shot his sheep on a high and precarious rocky ledge and Danny had to pack the sheep out. He almost couldn't get to it. It was odd that as much as I'd worried about the California hunters, I never saw them again. Watson had flown them back to camp and they were soon picked up by Duane from Prudhoe Bay. As far as I knew they were headed back home. If they were wardens, they'd done a terrible job of documenting crime.

Darkness edged over the camp when a Super Cub came in for a landing. Howe said it was Jack Watson. *Pedro was back.* I shot up from my chair and trotted down to the riverbed. I wanted to be the first to talk to Pedro about his hunt. Marianne and Howe were behind me, and I saw Junior running down from his Quonset hut. The scene was like a Fantasy Island TV rerun where everyone ran to the incoming plane to see what kind of adventure it brought.

We stood silent while the prop came to a stop. Finally, the door popped open and the pilot leaned forward to let Pedro squeeze his way out of the backseat and onto a step mounted on the side of the plane. He was wearing a blue stocking cap and had a two-day-old beard that had turned his face nearly black.

"You look like an escaped convict," I teased in Spanish. *"Como te fue?"* (How did you do?)

Pedro was beaming. "Beeg greesly," was all he said. This was the first time I'd ever heard Pedro attempt English.

"Dónde está?" I asked. (Where is it?)

Watson hopped to the ground on the other side of the plane and went straight to Howe where they huddled to one side and began talking in low voices. I would have killed to have heard what they were saying.

Meanwhile, Pedro crawled back into the plane and reached into the back storage compartment where he yanked on a bulky bear hide. Grunting, he hauled the hide over the seat and out of the plane onto the ground. Junior stretched out the four legs of the bear so everyone could appreciate its full size.

"Es enorme," he exclaimed.

Measured from head to toe, it had to be about a six-foot bear. Although this was a big bear, I'd heard of ten-foot bear being killed on the same tundra.

Pedro pointed to his watch and said, "Ate-tirty."

Apparently Bowman or Gordon had been coaching Pedro on what to say in English.

"You shot it at eight-thirty this morning?" I asked in Spanish.

"Si . . . ate-tirty," Pedro repeated.

Marianne nudged me. "What's he saying?"

"He shot the bear at eight-thirty this morning. He seems adamant about it."

"Good," she said.

I figured Marianne knew the timing of the kill was made up to make it appear as if there had been no flying and hunting on the same day.

Pedro was eager to talk about his hunt. In Spanish he told Junior and me that he had gotten up at five that morning and that he and Gordon had stalked the bear for several hours before finding it in a thicket. Every few seconds, Pedro stopped talking to give me time to translate his story to the others. Then he crouched low and reenacted the long quiet strides he took while he pushed through the brush in pursuit of his ferocious prey. He circled the bear hide and stopped in front of it with an imaginary rifle raised at eye level.

"I fought my way through the thick brush but I wasn't sure where the bear was. I thought he might jump me from behind." He grabbed his chest for dramatic effect and said, "All of a sudden he raised out of the bushes on his hind legs right in front of me. I said a thousand Hail Marys and fired my rifle as fast as I could. *Zas-zas-zas!* The bear was so close I thought it was going to fall on me. He could have easily attacked me before I even saw him. I tell you, it was a very close call."

My translation didn't include all the drama Pedro intended for his audience. Most poachers I'd talked to claimed that the bear they'd shot had risen up on his hind legs, clawing at the air with intentions of eating them alive. Bears, however, rarely do this in the wild. Pedro was lying and his story of a roaring, bloodthirsty bear was all Hollywood.

When the theatrics were over, Pedro leaned over to me. "Everything I said is bullshit," he admitted. "Mr. Bob found the bear yesterday from the plane and ran it into the thicket so it wouldn't go anywhere. He put Gordon and me out by the thicket and we went in and got it. It was easy. The hunt took two hours and the bear never saw us coming."

"That's great," I said. "Did you shoot the bear?"

"Of course. But don't tell anyone about the plane."

"Oh no. *Todo es un secreto!*"

Junior and Pedro laughed. I asked Pedro where Bowman was during the hunt.

"He was flying over us. If the bear got out of the thicket, he was going to herd it back to us. That bear was dead the minute Bob laid eyes on it."

While Pedro was confessing to me exactly what happened, Billy Howe and the others were within easy earshot, not understanding a word. I felt like I was part of a secret enclave of crime where Spanish was the code language. For an undercover agent, this was heaven.

Junior had turned wide-eyed over Pedro's tales of poaching. He seemed fascinated with the lawlessness of it all and how "daring" Pedro had been. As if not to be outdone, he told Pedro that he had almost been arrested for poaching caribou.

"Es verdad?" Pedro asked. (Is that true?)

"Yes, but Jayne saved me. Otherwise I'd be in jail right now."

Pedro laughed and slapped Junior on the back. "Way to go! Your father will be proud."

Lenny loaded the bear hide onto the ATV while Junior and Pedro hopped on for the ride to the skinning tent. Meanwhile, a conspicuously silent Bowman continued to unpack his plane and get it ready to fly back out to help with El Doctor's hunt. While most poachers I'd known loved to brag about their hunting exploits, Bowman seemed to realize that talking increased his chances of getting caught. The silent treatment had worked for many years — until now.

CHAPTER 17

Culpability and Arrogance

SEPTEMBER 2, 1992, MAIN CAMP, IVISHAK RIVER. After the last breakfast dishes had been cleaned, Marianne asked, "What's wrong with Roy? He spends all his time in his tent."

"He's been a little under the weather and he's trying to rest up until Bob is ready to take him out on a bear hunt. That should be any time now."

"I still can't see anyone coming to Alaska and spending the whole time in a tent. Something's not right."

"No, he's fine."

It bothered me that Marianne was noticing Roy's behavior. To escape her probing, I cut the conversation short and walked down to the skinning tent where I found Lenny and Pedro. While Lenny deftly sliced the flesh from Pedro's bear hide, I struck up a conversation with Pedro.

"Your bear isn't the only illegal critter around here."

"Good," grunted Pedro. "Every hunter should get what they want, no matter what it takes."

"This place could get raided by the authorities. If it does, we could all end up in jail."

"Don't be ridiculous. No one pays attention to the law," he laughed. "This is the best camp I've ever been in. Here the hunter comes first, and with the airplanes the trophies are guaranteed."

"Is that why you chose to come here, because of the planes?"

"Absolutely. My booking agent told me what was going to happen here. And violating the law is no big deal because we'll never get caught. Look around, we're in the middle of nowhere."

My conversation with Pedro had a purpose. The U.S. Attorney would want to know if the Spaniards knew they were breaking the law. Now I could say that Pedro had full knowledge. Pedro had also confirmed that Bowman had assured his clients that hunting with airplanes would guarantee them their trophies. With a guarantee like that, his client list would continue to grow, unless this investigation cut it short.

That evening, as I shoved moose meat through a hand grinder to make burritos, Marianne asked me about my family.

"How long have you been divorced?"

"A little over a year. Mentally, a lot longer than that."

"Are you glad that you did it?"

"Oh yes. I enjoy the freedom. I wouldn't be here now if I was still married."

Marianne told me that both she and Bowman had been married before and had children from previous marriages. They had met in New York where they both worked in a restaurant and left there to pursue Bowman's dream of opening a wild-game restaurant in Alaska. The restaurant did well and Bowman took up flying. He became friends with Billy Howe, who taught him the big-game guiding and hunting business. After a few years, Marianne grew tired of Alaskan winters, so Bowman sold the restaurant and bought another one in Arizona. He also bought the remnants of an old hunting camp on the Ivishak River and invested heavily in modernizing the kitchen and building new sleeping quarters. Marianne agreed to spend the spring and fall hunting seasons with Bowman at the camp if he would build her a shower, which he did.

"How old is your daughter?" asked Rhoda.

"Seven. She's in the second grade." I hadn't intended to discuss Megan, but suddenly I felt the urge.

"Who's taking care of her while you're gone?"

"Her father."

"Is he good to her?"

"Yes, he's the best."

A slip-up: no woman would speak so fondly of her ex-husband. I checked the faces of the two women to see if they exchanged glances. Thank goodness there was nothing.

"I bet you really miss her," said Marianne.

Even though I was on guard, Marianne's words made me realize that I missed Megan more than I could bear. I called her my "wild child," a tribute to her free spirit and undying curiosity. I thought of us singing our favorite silly song about the big fat whale with the polka-dot tail. I longed to curl her golden hair and dress her in her purple cotton dress and straw hat decorated with a huge yellow sunflower. I wished I could be with her at that very moment.

Through tearing eyes, I watched ground meat ooze out of the grinder and said, "How much more of this do you want, Marianne?"

"That's enough. Give it to Rhoda and she'll cook it up with onions."

Marianne put her hand on my shoulder. "It's natural to miss your daughter, Jayne. That's the way we mothers are."

"I don't have any kids," said Rhoda. "But I can imagine. It must be hard. You'll be home soon."

As the moose meat sizzled in her frying pan, the onions overtook the gamey smell and I imagined that the meat was plain, good ol' beef.

Rhoda put down her spatula and turned to me, wiping her hands on her yellowing white apron. "Marianne and I were talking the other day about how much we admire you. You're up here hunting just like the men and you don't make a big deal over it. You're a role model for women and someday your daughter will be proud. In fact, I wish I could be more like you."

This validation from Rhoda came as a total shock. I'd never been called a role model by another woman before, even though I probably was one in my job as an agent. Yet, Rhoda saw me as a role model as a woman hunter who was able to withstand the challenges of the wilderness and remain humble about it. Her comments genuinely touched me.

"Your little daughter will be fine," added Marianne. "We mothers fret endlessly about stuff that usually amounts to nothing. And, Rhoda's right. She'll be proud of you someday."

"Thanks, you two," I said gratefully. For a brief moment I accepted the friendship of the two women, knowing full well of my betrayal that had to come.

* * *

In honor of my mother I picked wildflowers and placed them in the center of the table. The moose burritos were a culinary success and what took hours to prepare was consumed in minutes by Roy, Wilhelm, Lenny, Pedro, Junior, and Wild Bill. After finishing dinner they all vanished from the table. While Marianne retreated to her bedroom with a headache, Rhoda and I cleaned up. I wondered how many other federal agents had such dishpan hands.

Later that night in our tent I explained to Roy that I thought there were at least five illegal animals in the camp. Animals that would have been impossible to document had we not been inside the camp, thus confirming the old game warden adage, "You gotta be there to catch 'em."

An airplane buzzing overhead interrupted our conversation. Roy and I hurried down to the riverbed to find Bowman's plane just landing. Pedro, Junior, Lenny, and Wilhelm had already formed a greeting section. I noticed a set of moose antlers strapped to the struts of the plane.

El Doctor emerged from the plane with a shadowed face from not shaving, slick hair that stuck out from under a stocking cap, and glasses that looked like they had been cleaned with sandpaper. Despite his disheveled appearance, his face cracked with a deep, satisfied smile.

"*Tenias exito?*" I asked. (Were you successful?)

"*Si. Un alce americana y un oso. Bien caza,*" he replied. (Yes, a moose and a bear. Good hunt.)

"Tell us what happened," pleaded Junior.

El Doctor motioned to me to translate and began his story. "I shot the bear first, but almost didn't get him. He ran on me, but came back around in a big circle. I caught him coming back and shot him at about ninety meters broadside. I got two clean shots. Most fantastic hunt I've ever been on. I'm very happy."

"What about the moose?" asked Pedro.

"I got him around nine this morning. We got up very early and hiked a riverbed where some moose had been feeding in the willows." He glanced over at the rack Lenny had just untied from the wing struts and said, "The one I got is very good. I'm happy."

I translated El Doctor's words knowing full well that his brief rendition of his hunts meant there was more to the story. Just as soon as El Doctor, Pedro, Junior, and I walked off to one side, his voice changed to one of a kid with a juicy secret to tell.

"Of course that's not exactly what happened."

The four of us laughed and shook our heads, acknowledging the unspoken camp motto. Huddled together, El Doctor began the real story of his hunt.

"Mr. Bob dropped me off and flew off to find a bear. He was gone so long I thought he'd crashed or something. I started to get really worried. But then I saw that he got one."

"What do you mean he got one?" asked Junior who hung on to every one of his father's words.

"Well," said El Doctor, shrugging his shoulders, "he had the bear in front of his plane. He herded it right to me." Then he laughed, "The plane was so low I thought it was going to land on the damn thing." He went on, "I tell you that bear was scared out of his skin. He kept looking up at the plane and trying to run faster, but it was no use." He mimicked the terrified bear by opening his eyes wide and taking quick glances over his shoulder. "He was so close I could see his tongue hanging out of his mouth. But he never saw me because he was too busy looking at the plane, trying to get away from it." He pounded his chest with a balled fist. "My shots hit him here three times— *zas-zas-zas!* The surprise of his life."

"Increíble," said Junior, whose eyes were wide with wonderment over his father's self-described prowess.

Pedro slapped El Doctor on the back. "Good man. Let's take some wine over to the kitchen and celebrate. Want to come, Jayne?"

"Como no?" I answered. (Why not?) I knew that further conversation with the Spaniards could be very productive.

We all found seats around the table. Pedro poured wine, offering me a glass, but I declined. I asked El Doctor again about his moose hunt.

"Oh, it was completely legal. We didn't fly and hunt the same day. The moose was in a patch of willows and Gordon guided me in to shoot it."

Junior jumped in and described his caribou hunt and how he'd shot two animals.

El Doctor howled. "For your first hunt, that's fantastic!"

"Yes, but Marianne wanted to have me arrested. Jayne convinced her not to. If it weren't for her, I'd be in jail right now."

El Doctor looked at me gratefully. "You are a great friend. Thank you for saving my son."

"No problem," I said, smiling. "After all, I didn't want to go down to the jailhouse to be his interpreter."

More wine flowed, and Pedro and El Doctor dazzled me with their hunting exploits in the Congo, Bulgaria, and Spain. Pedro boasted that he had killed more than a hundred ibex—a European horned sheep. He seemed to have a special fascination with sheep. He bragged on about hunting on La Doñana, a wildlife refuge in Spain.

"Only the king of Spain gets to hunt there, but that's bullshit. Any man should be able to hunt there, so I pulled some strings and went. In fact, I go wherever I want."

I had no idea if Pedro's tales were true, but they'd go in my notes.

"Why do you like to hunt so much?" I asked.

"Because hunting is the only thing that gives me a *zing*. And it's a manly thing to do. I'm also a collector: I want one of everything. And I like the idea of immortalizing what I hunt."

"And you like to bullshit about it," added Junior.

"Well, we all do," El Doctor conceded.

I asked Pedro and El Doctor, "So you both must be interested in getting all four subspecies of North American sheep."

Pedro took another drag from his Cuban cigar. "Very much so, if we can find outfitters like Mr. Bob. We want easy, sure hunts. I can't exhaust myself. I'm crazy about sheep because they are the most difficult to hunt. I may go to Afghanistan and hunt the Marco Polo sheep. I've heard they shoot them right out of helicopters."

Pedro was right. I'd read reports of hunters seeking record-book trophies who spent more than a hundred thousand dollars hunting Marco Polos from helicopters.

El Doctor jumped to his feet and demonstrated how he stalked a lion in Sudan and ended up killing an endangered leopard. "I didn't intend on killing a leopard, but it was right there. How many hunters get that chance?"

"I can't believe the exciting stories you have," I said with enthusiasm. "But, whatever you do, don't talk about your illegal hunting in Alaska. We've all violated federal wildlife laws and could go to jail, even after we leave here. I've heard of it happening."

"*Sheeet,*" hissed Pedro. "We've never been caught poaching anywhere in the world. We're not going to get caught in Alaska."

It was nearing midnight and the party was winding down. Pedro turned to me and asked, "What about this man you're here with? He's never with you. I wouldn't leave a pretty woman like you alone for a minute."

"*Si*," agreed El Doctor. "It's like you're here alone."

Not only did I feel totally abandoned, I was also upset that Roy was attracting negative attention. On top of that, he wasn't doing his job as a witness, and I had no idea what the repercussions of that would be.

CHAPTER 18

Evidence of Crimes

SEPTEMBER 3, 1992, I LAY IN BED WIDE AWAKE as daylight crept into the tent. The dim outline of my socks and purple shirt hanging from the clothesline reminded me of a Girl Scout camp I attended in southern Spain. But this wasn't scout camp. It was a poacher's paradise where the count of illegal animals was rising every day. Some of the animals had been hunted fairly, but others had been chased by Bowman's plane to hunters waiting with high-powered rifles. Later I'd have to be able to identify the illegally killed trophies.

I walked over to Roy and poked him in the ribs. "Wake up," I hissed.

"What . . . what the hell?"

"We need to get into the skinning tent before anyone wakes up."

Roy sat up and threw his heavy legs over one side of the bed. He looked at me over his shoulder. "What for?"

"I want to mark everything in the skinning tent that's illegal."

"Are you nuts?"

"Put your shoes on and follow me."

As we left the tent, I silently eased the door shut. Daylight was fast approaching so we'd have to hurry. We saw no one as we hustled down the rocky slope toward the kitchen cabin, turned left at its corner, and headed for the skinning tent. When we reached it, I noticed that a canvas flap to the tent was tied shut. I pulled on the strings and slipped inside; Roy followed behind me and retied the strings from the inside. The putrid smell of decomposing flesh walloped me like a physical blow and I began breathing through my mouth to keep from gagging.

Turning to Roy I put my finger to my lips to signal silence. I handed my mini-flashlight to him and motioned him toward Pedro's bear hide that was stretched out on the ground. I picked up the right rear foot and fingered the middle claw while Roy held the light to it. With a pocketknife already opened in my hand I quickly etched a symbol along the inside of a claw. Roy followed me to Wilhelm's moose antlers, Junior's caribou antlers, and El Doctor's bear. The knife squirmed in my sweaty palm as I marked each illegal kill with an indelible symbol.

We'd been in the tent about twelve minutes when I glanced around at the remaining carnage to see what else had to be marked. I caught Roy cupping his hand to his ear as he rolled his eyes upwards. Voices. Lenny and Gordon were talking outside. I motioned to Roy to hurry toward the back of the tent where we crouched behind a bear hide that was draped inside-out over a sawhorse—the best cover available. My heartbeat quickened as I grasped my knees and lowered my face. Roy crouched next to me but he was too big to conceal himself behind the hide. If Lenny walked in, we'd have a hell of time explaining why we were in the tent. My mind raced to come up with an excuse—just in case.

As the voices outside faded, I looked at Roy and pointed to my watch and held up three fingers. That meant we would wait three minutes—an eternity when you felt like you were inside a sewer.

After three minutes, I lifted one edge of the canvas and peeked outside. There was no one in sight. Roy and I slipped out of the tent that faced the river and welcomed the relief of fresh air. We appeared from behind the skinning tent as if we'd been out for an early morning stroll, and walked back to our tent without seeing a soul.

At breakfast, a lighthearted conversation with the Spaniards eased the tension I'd felt that morning, but now I felt uneasy because Lenny wasn't at breakfast. He never missed breakfast, and I hoped that Roy's and my visit to the skinning tent didn't have anything to do with his absence. At the end of the meal Roy retreated to our tent with another excuse of being tired. I headed straight back down to the skinning tent to see what Lenny was up to and found him on his knees pawing over Pedro's bear hide. Did he know it was marked?

"What are you doing?" I asked.

He didn't look up. "I'm trying to get this humongous fur ball to where I can tie it up."

"Why? I thought it had to dry out some more."

"It does, but Pedro and the boys are leaving today. Bob told me to pack everything up so they can take their stuff with them to Spain. I guess they got a taxidermist there. All I know is that this is a shit pile of work to do on a moment's notice."

I felt a jolt of panic. If the Spaniards took their trophies back to Spain, most of my case would go with them. The evidence I had against them and Bowman would be outside U.S. jurisdiction and couldn't be used against them. The trophies could not leave the country: I had to think of something fast. Desperate for an idea, I decided to talk to Roy.

"Catch you later," I said.

I broke into a jog back to my tent, but was stopped short by Bowman who was standing outside the kitchen pantomiming something to the Spaniards. When he saw me, he called me over.

"What's up, Bob?" I said.

"Tell these guys to be ready to go at one this afternoon, sharp. Their trophies are being packed now, and a plane will be here to pick them up."

"I didn't know they were even leaving today," I said, buying a few seconds to think.

"Well, they are. So tell 'em, would ya?"

"Sure."

My heart felt like it was going to beat straight out of my chest. I couldn't let the best evidence slip out of my control—it was time to play on the trust I'd developed with my *tres amigos*.

"Mr. Bob says you'll leave at one this afternoon, but unfortunately you can't take your trophies with you. You don't have the right paperwork and you might have trouble with the authorities. You must leave them and have them mounted in Alaska. He'll get the paperwork and ship your animals to you in a few months."

El Doctor responded first. *"Que diablos es eso?"* (What the devil is this about?)

"I wish I had better news. But the *papaleo*, the paperwork, is very complicated and he doesn't want you to have any trouble. Everything will be fine if
he ships your trophies to you. No problem."

Pedro eyed me carefully. "Are you sure?"

"Yes, that's what he was trying to tell you when I walked up."

Pedro and El Doctor hesitated momentarily. Finally Pedro said, "We'll do
what Mr. Bob suggests and especially if you say this is the situation. We don't
want any trouble with the American authorities."

"What are they sayin'?" asked Bowman.

"Uh, they want to leave their trophies here to get mounted."

"What on earth for?"

"According to them, European taxidermists don't have the big forms to
mount grizzly bear."

I had no idea if this was true, but before Bowman could respond, I added,
"They want to know if you can recommend a good taxidermist in Alaska."

"Sure. He's a friend of mine in Anchorage. In fact, you can call him right
now yourself and tell him to pick up the animals at the Anchorage airport."

This was perfect. Eicher could seize the trophies from the taxidermist
later. I explained to the Spaniards what Bowman had said and they were satisfied. We all went to the kitchen where Bowman phoned the Anchorage
taxidermist and let me talk to him. I made the arrangements for him to meet
the Spaniards at the airport. Bowman was happy that he didn't have to ship
trophies to Spain. The Spaniards were grateful to me for saving them from
any trouble with the law. And I was almost light-headed as I walked away
from my ruse.

An hour later, at 12:55 P.M., Bowman and Lenny were at the landing strip
with the trophies. Lenny made sure that the "harvest tags" were clearly visible
on the outside, so that everything would appear legal. I knew, however, that
there were three illegal animals being loaded: a bear killed by Pedro, a bear
killed by El Doctor, and one of Junior's caribou. I still didn't know the details
of Pedro's sheep hunt even though he'd told me it was a completely legal hunt.

As Duane's Cessna approached the landing strip, Pedro, El Doctor, and
Junior emerged from their Quonset hut lugging their gear.

At the landing strip Pedro exclaimed, "I want to always remember this
extraordinary American woman."

As I smiled at the departing Spaniards I thought, *These are my real
Alaskan trophies.*

Pedro presented me with a half-eaten box of chocolates and a T-shirt from the 1992 Barcelona Olympics in gratitude of my friendship. All three of them kissed me on both cheeks, hugged me, and invited me to visit them in Spain. I told them that perhaps I would. As my three amigos climbed into the Cessna I felt no guilt over my forthcoming betrayal of them. Considering all the wild animals they'd poached over the years, it was now their time to become the prey.

The Cessna started up, climbed into the air, and within a minute it was gone.

Abruptly, Bowman turned to Roy and barked, "Get your gear—we're leaving for your bear hunt in fifteen minutes."

"But, I thought you said we'd go after dinner," stammered Roy.

"I changed my mind. So get going, would you."

After Bowman was gone, Roy grumbled, "Shit, after all this time of sittin' around, now I gotta rush."

I grabbed Roy's arm and said sternly, "Things are going to happen out there, so keep your eyes open."

I went back to the tent with him and helped him gather his gear. Back down at the landing strip Bowman was packing the plane.

"I'm ready to go whenever you say," said Roy.

"Well, I say I'm ready. Jump in."

Gordon walked up from behind us, slapped Roy on the back and said, "It's time to kill something."

"You going, too? It's sure gonna be a tight squeeze."

"I'm only making one trip. This ain't a taxi service," spouted Bowman. Then he turned to Gordon. "We're going back out to the Colville where we were with the Spaniards."

"You got it."

Gordon threw Roy's gear in the back and motioned for him to get in first. Roy launched one leg on the step, grabbed the frame of the opened door, and hauled himself into the backseat. Next Gordon hoisted himself up and squeezed in on top of Roy. With Bowman in the pilot's seat, the three men looked like sardines stuffed in a tin can. Meanwhile, Wilhelm was already in the backseat of Jack Watson's Piper.

Bowman and Watson started their engines and taxied to the end of the runway for takeoff. According to the plan, they'd all be back the next day with two dead bear. After the planes were out of sight, I turned back to the skinning shed where I saw Lenny's red Honda ATV parked outside. I walked over to it pretending to look at it and making sure no one was looking, took out a pencil and a piece of scrap paper from my pocket and quickly recorded the serial number. Lenny had used the ATV to transport illegal wildlife and it would be seized later as evidence.

As I headed back to my tent all I could think about was Roy alone with Bowman and Gordon. They were both as cagey as coyotes and if Roy slipped up in any way, he could blow our cover or he could be killed in a staged hunting accident. Then they'd come after me. I felt I could take care of myself reasonably well, but the thought of having my welfare in Roy's hands was chewing me up. But all I could hope for was that the hunts would be short and sweet, and they'd be back without any problems.

CHAPTER 19

Knee Deep

SEPTEMBER 4, 1992, MAIN CAMP, IVISHAK RIVER. At breakfast I stopped a bite of pancakes halfway to my mouth when a call came in on the radiophone.

"Hi, Marianne, this is Jerry Hoff, from South Dakota. Remember me?"

"Sure do. What's up?"

"I've been huntin' moose around Anchorage for days and I can't find nothin' worth taking home. Does Bob have room for another hunter? I know you've got a season opening up tomorrow."

"Sure," said Marianne. "We have plenty of room and the hunting is great. How soon can you get here?"

"I'll take the next flight out of here to Prudhoe Bay where I'll overnight. I should be able to catch a charter out to the camp early tomorrow morning."

I struggled not to let the shock of this news show on my face. Hoff was coming back. If he saw me, he'd surely finger me. I'd written him up for over-bagging on geese. As I recalled, he had shot a total of eight. The day I caught him I'd stood in the field dressed as a hunter and had watched him shoot all eight of them himself.

What would I do when he showed up? I would just have to avoid him and keep a cap and sunglasses on whenever he was around. If he happened to recognize me and confront me, I'd deny everything. My jaw ground. Everything had been going pretty smoothly, now this pain in the butt was about to come back. *Dammit anyway.*

Howe came into the kitchen and said that Bowman had instructed him to fly me over an area close to the camp to find a good moose to shoot the next day. This wasn't illegal; the prohibition was against flying and hunting on the same day.

A few minutes later, I walked outside to Howe's Super Cub and got in. He was already strapped in the pilot's seat doing a preflight check on the instrument panel. I said nothing to him. Even though Howe's attitude toward me seemed to have warmed to a tolerance level, conversation was still strained.

Howe gunned the engine and the plane bumped across the rocks and took off. He leveled it at about eight hundred feet and flew directly south for a few minutes. Almost immediately we spotted the swaying antlers of moose feeding in willows.

After flying over six of them, he shouted over the engine noise, "There's a good one. About a sixty-five incher, I think."

He was right. It was a huge moose with perfectly arched antlers.

"Want him?"

I nodded "yes."

"He's yours. Tomorrow morning," he shouted as he veered the plane back toward the camp.

"Great!"

We landed close to the same spot from where we had taken off. After we got out of the plane, Lenny walked toward the plane hollering, "Did you find one?"

"Yeah," said Howe, pointing toward the willows. "He's out there about two miles south and slightly east. Here, I got him marked on the map." He handed the map to Lenny who studied it briefly.

"Good deal. I'll take Jayne out in the morning. He'll still be hanging out there, or nearby."

"I can't wait," I said, hoping I sounded like an eager moose hunter.

Howe left Lenny and me standing with the open map. I studied the circle drawn with a black pen on the spot where we had seen the moose. "Suppose we'll be able to find him in the morning? Things can look a lot different on the ground."

"No problem," said Lenny. "I know those willows better than my own backyard in the Lower 48."

Carefully considering my next question, I hedged slightly, "Uh, maybe if Howe went back up in the plane in the morning it would save us a lot of time."

Lenny quickly turned his head toward me. "You mean spot the moose from the air while we're in the field. He can't do that, it's illegal."

"Well, it isn't *that* illegal is it?"

"Yeah it is, and you shouldn't be asking about stuff like that. You're starting to sound like a plant."

"What's that?"

"A plant's a person the government puts in hunting camps to find out what's going on. Plants always ask about doin' illegal stuff."

Was I that obvious? I pulled my overshirt closed so he wouldn't notice that my breathing rate had increased.

Lenny went on. "For all I know, you could be a government plant sent out here to spy on us."

I forced a laugh. "Ha! Don't be ridiculous. I've never even heard of such a thing."

"Well, you never know. You could be one or any one of the hunters here."

"Even Pedro?" I asked, seeking any diversion.

"Well, maybe not him, 'cause he's from Europe, but I put my money on anyone from the Lower 48, including those two guys from California."

"Oh yes," I quickly agreed. "I could see them working for the government. One of them didn't even know his own name."

Lenny rolled his eyes. "That's 'cause he was huntin' on someone else's license."

"Really? Is that legal?"

"Nope."

"Maybe you should have been watching him," I said.

Lenny grunted. "I was. I watch everybody. We don't need no trouble around here."

Finally I felt some relief. Lenny wasn't focused on me, so maybe I'd dodged his wary bullet. My objective had been to find out through Lenny if Howe would violate the law but doing so was a serious mistake on my part. I wanted to eat my words.

Later that afternoon I ran into Howe as he came out of the kitchen. From the look on his face he seemed more contemptuous than ever.

He grabbed my arm and snapped, "Go grab your gear."

"Let go of me," I said, jerking my arm away from his grip. At the same time I put a hand in my pants pocket and fingered my knife.

He dropped his hand and bit out, "I'm flying you to a spike camp tonight."

"What? I thought I was hunting moose with Lenny in the morning."

"Plans have changed. We need to fly in fifteen, so get your shit."

Howe's resentment of me seemed to have found a new level, but I thought I knew what had happened. Lenny told Howe that I'd suggested he do something illegal and Howe was mad about it. As punishment he was making me spend the night in a spike camp where I'd have to sleep on the ground and eat dehydrated food. My first reaction was to argue with Howe, but then I remembered that Hoff was coming back in. Maybe this was a blessing in disguise. It would be smart to get out of the main camp.

I ran to my tent and stuffed my boots, hunting jacket, stocking cap, socks, and long underwear into a duffel. When I got to the plane, Howe was waiting for me. The sun was still high in the sky and sweat broke out under my flannel shirt as I handed my gear to Howe and climbed into the backseat. He climbed in, snapped the door shut, and started the engine.

We bounced down the rocky runway, lifted into the air, and soared over the camp like a giant bird. Soon Howe banked the plane among breathtaking snowcapped mountains that surrounded us on all sides. The plane twisted and turned so quickly that I felt tipsy. Suddenly I realized that I had no idea which spike camp we were going to, and I had to push aside the fear that he might dump me somewhere for good.

We flew for about a half hour, north and away from the sun. After we dropped to a lower elevation, we followed a wide creek where I counted fifteen moose feeding calmly in the willows. Finally, I spotted Jake's orange-domed tent perched on a bald spot near the creek bed. Relieved, I knew I'd be safe. After circling the tent once, we landed on a slight incline.

Jake met us as we got out of the plane. "Hey, Jayne. I'm sure glad they sent you out to me instead of one of them stinky Spaniards."

"Hi, it's good to see you. Is Danny here, too?" I asked, hoping that he was since he had the film I wanted.

"Naw, he's at another camp miles from here. It's just you and me."

Groaning inside, I wondered if I'd ever get my hands on the film that held the photo of me bound for Bowman's hunting brochures.

Howe barked instructions at Jake. "We spotted plenty of good moose flying in. See if you can get her one tomorrow and I'll come back just before nightfall. If I don't, it'll be the next morning. Tomorrow's gonna be busy with the opening and all."

A grin spread across Jake's face. "No problem. We'll do fine."

I was sure Jake was pleased. Compared to most hunters Jake had to deal with, I was probably easy duty. Howe hurried back to his plane, and within a minute he was in the air and headed back to the main camp.

As Jake and I walked back to his spike camp I noticed he was limping. There was something wrong with his right hip joint, he told me. "Don't worry, I'll be good to go in the morning."

Jake had some canned chili cooking in a pot on his single-burner cookstove and handed me a bowlful.

"Where's the beer?" I joked.

"You were supposed to bring it."

"I would have if I'd had enough time to pack. Howe wouldn't tell me a thing. That's guy's a little spooky."

"He's okay. He just don't like you."

"I noticed that."

Jake laughed. "He don't like women hunters. But I do. We'll get you a huge moose; that'll shut him up forever. He was pretty mad that a woman shot that nice ram."

I smiled as we chowed down our meager meal. When we finished, I said, "Hand me your dish and the chili pot and I'll wash them down at the creek."

As I walked to the creek in silence I suddenly realized the depths of my exhaustion. I wanted to lie down and sleep right there at creekside. Energy seemed to flow out of me like water down a drain. *Undercover stress,* I thought. It's hard being someone else, and the incident with Lenny and Howe had sent my nerves into overdrive. When I got back to the camp I decided to turn in even though it was only nine o'clock and still light. Jake agreed.

I spread my sleeping bag in Jake's tent, removed my boots, and decided to sleep in my clothes. Jake crawled in behind me and after taking off his boots began layering on shirts and gloves like he was settling in for a full winter's hibernation.

"What are you doing?"

"It's gonna be cold tonight, you watch."

"It's only August. How cold can it get?"

"The cap is the most important part. Put on a cap if you have one."

Taking Jake's advice, I pulled my wool cap over my ears and buried myself in my sleeping bag. After wrestling off my clothes I put on my long underwear and then struggled back into my clothes. If anything, I figured I'd be too hot.

Jake rolled over, turning his back to me. "Good night. We'll have a good hunt in the morning."

"Good night."

I woke up hours later, so cold my bones seemed to creak. I was shivering uncontrollably and I couldn't even think about sleeping. The wind had picked up and the nylon tent snapped and popped as the night wore on. I tried every mental trick I knew to ignore my shivering and to fall asleep, but nothing worked. I stared at the ceiling of the tent and watched it snap viciously in the wind. The noise sounded like the roar of a jet engine. At times I thought the tent might take off like a hot air balloon. Hollywood couldn't have created a more tumultuous night. I looked over at Jake, sleeping like a baby.

The tent was driving me crazy; I had to get out. I got up and put on my boots, insulated jacket, and Thinsulate gloves. I then pulled my hood over my head and cinched it tightly around my face, leaving only a small breathing hole. When I crawled outside I could see my frosty breath as the first rays of morning light struck the tent.

A covey of white ptarmigan startled me as they whistled across the tundra to my left. In the distance they twirled in the misty, silvery light, just like the magical rabbits that danced in *The Velveteen Rabbit*, a story that I had read often to Megan. I shook my head several times to make sure the scene was real. Even though it was, my part in it wasn't. I was only acting. My real life was at home, with Lonnie, Megan, and our dog, Trapper. The only reason I was standing outside in the arctic wind, freezing, exhausted, and at the end of my wits was because I wanted to make a difference for wild creatures. But would all of this ever matter?

The farther I got away from the snapping nylon on the tent, the quieter it became. I found a boulder and curled up next to its flat vertical surface. Silence engulfed me as I finally drifted off to sleep—until I felt the sharp rays of the arctic sun on my face.

I eased myself from behind the rock and slowly stood up. Fuzzy-headed from lack of sleep, I made my way to Jake's tent and crawled inside just as he sat up in his sleeping bag.

"Time to hunt," he said with a groan.

He rolled over and crawled out of his bag on all fours and then stood stooped over with his back to me. He pulled on brown field pants and slipped his arms into a plaid flannel shirt before he went outside.

The sun shone brightly in a cloudless blue sky and a slight breeze brushed across my face. The temperature was crisp and cool, and the mountains in the distance shimmered. I couldn't believe this was the same place where I had just spent such a long and miserable night.

Jake had the water boiling; instant coffee and oatmeal were on the menu again. As I gulped down breakfast I noticed that Jake's limp was more pronounced than yesterday.

"Is your hip worse today?"

He grabbed it with his right hand and bent over as if he was giving in to the pain. "Yeah. I don't know what the heck it is."

I ducked into the tent and came out with some anti-inflammatory pills from my backpack.

"Here take these. They'll fix you right up."

"Thanks, Jayne, you're great."

Jake gulped down the tablets with hot coffee. I slung my rifle over my back and followed him out of camp. He carried a rifle, too, and it was the first time I'd seen him with one.

"You gonna hunt?"

"No, it's for protection. Bears, ya know."

I was thinking about how to ease into a conversation with Jake about his knowledge of the illegal hunting activity in Bowman's camp. I had to approach the subject casually to avoid sounding like the interrogator I could be at times.

As we hiked briskly through the light brush, Jake's injury made it easier for me to keep up with him. We talked about the weather and the ease of hunting on flat ground compared to the mountains. Jake told me that the sheep I'd shot was the largest one he had seen in three hunting seasons. I feigned ignorance as he told me about his hometown in Wisconsin, a town I had driven through dozens of times on my way to the Horicon National Wildlife Refuge.

Then I tried to sound convincing as I answered questions about the Illinois town I claimed to be from, but in reality had only visited once. Finally, I made my move.

"Did you hear about Pedro's bear?"

"No, what about it?"

"Pedro told me Bob spotted it from the air and then herded it to him. Pedro said he shot the bear while it was on a dead run."

"Pedro told you that?"

"Yeah. He told me the whole story. He said the bear's illegal as hell."

Out of the corner of my eye I saw the change in Jake's expression. He pursed his lips as if to keep words from escaping and dropped his head slightly. As he walked in silence I could almost sense his loyalty to Bowman, and his hunter's integrity banging against his conscience.

Finally he spoke. "I wouldn't doubt it. Sometimes I don't know about Bob. He can be a real bastard."

"What do you mean?"

"Sometimes he pushes things to keep his clients happy. That's not what huntin' is about. Sometimes you hit, and sometimes you don't. These critters out here aren't pop-ups in a carnival shooting gallery. When they're gone, they're gone."

I pushed a little more. "Has Bowman ever herded an animal to one of your clients?"

Jake turned his head away from me, and looked over his left shoulder as if to avoid me. Clearly, he was uncomfortable. Another thirty seconds passed before I got an answer.

"Bowman, Gordon, and the rest of them know I don't like that shit. They keep it away from me, but it makes me sick when I hear that it's happened."

"I'm sure it does. Have you ever seen it happen?"

His voice dropped and became softer. "Not really."

He was holding back, but his response left me nowhere to steer the conversation.

Frustration seized me and I imagined myself grabbing him by the throat and saying, *Come on buddy spit it out! Quit playing choir boy and tell me about the dozens of bear you've seen running for their lives under the nose of a Super Cub. Tell me about the gunshots and asshole hunters who killed, and then acted like they had accomplished something heroic. Tell me!*

I kept quiet because I might have pushed him too far already. My little inquisitions were adding up. Eventually someone might put them all together. But they didn't have much time, Roy and I were supposed to be back in the main camp the next morning and we were scheduled to fly out that afternoon. Meanwhile Jake picked up his pace and pulled ahead of me, walking briskly alongside a stream moving deeper into what he called "moose country."

After about an hour, Jake raised his finger to his cracked lips and motioned to me to get down. Apparently he'd spotted a moose nearby. He gestured straight ahead. Stiff willow stems brushed into my eyes and I pushed them away to see. Only twenty yards ahead, I could see the arching antlers of a medium-sized bull moose. His body was mostly concealed in the willows, but he was so close I could see the condensation from his breath. I was amazed he hadn't seen or heard us.

Jake leaned close to my ear and whispered, "He's not that great, we can keep looking."

"He's fine. I'll take him."

"Are you sure? There are bigger ones out here."

"Tell me when I should shoot."

I assumed that because his hip was in such bad shape that he'd be glad to get this hunt over with.

Jake turned and bent over to walk slowly back through the willows to gain distance from the moose and to give me a better shot. I, too, bent over and walked behind him with my rifle over my back. After a minute or two we turned to glance back at the moose. A split-second later, a huge, dark mass of hide and muscle, resembling a whale breaching from the deep, topped the willows.

"RUN!" shouted Jake.

I sprinted out of the moose's path. When I turned and looked again, the moose had stopped in his tracks only fifteen yards away from me.

"Shoot! Now!" barked Jake.

I snapped off the safety on my rifle and "snap-shot" a round by looking over the scope and pointing the rifle at the heart area. *Bam!* The moose recoiled. I had hit it. Was it a fatal shot? I worked the action and fired again. *Bam!*

Got to place these shots better.

Quickly, I chambered a third round and tried to use my scope, but the moose was still too close. When I brought my rifle down, the moose was still standing, and had lowered his head. He was going to charge.

Frantically, I glanced at Jake. His face was struck with terror. "Run like hell," he yelled.

Sweat erupted on my brow as I turned and crashed through the willows. I could taste blood as the willows sliced across my mouth. My heart hammered in my chest as I imagined the moose right on my tail. My left boot caught a rock, but I quickly recovered. Otherwise, the moose would have trampled me like a bull on a rodeo clown.

Suddenly, I heard shots to my left and looked as Jake walked backwards firing rounds from his hip into the charging moose. I counted six shots.

After what seemed like an eternity, the moose's head swayed and his body teetered. When he finally collapsed, Jake eased up to the animal.

Shaking, I made my way back through the willows while trying to catch my breath. "That was close."

"Yeah," said Jake. "Too damn close."

His face was sweaty and twitching nervously. As he stood with his gun still aimed at the moose, he waited to see if it might charge again. It was another minute before he lowered the muzzle.

I moved in nearer to the moose, watched his chest heave, and heard the sound of blood gurgling in his lungs.

"This is the worst part," Jake said. "These critters are so damn big it takes them forever to die."

The sounds of the moose's agony rattled in my ears and pulled at my heart. *Please hurry up and die.*

I walked away to gather my wits. Even though I held tight rein on my emotions, a headache had begun and it was pounding like a hammer. After a few minutes, I walked back as Jake said, "Well, he's dead now but he almost got us." Jake leaned on his rifle as if it was a crutch. His twisted mouth revealed the pain that he seemed to be having from his hip.

"Thank God you had your rifle. If it weren't for you I'd be on the ground eating dirt right now, if not dead. You saved my butt, Jake."

"Maybe, but the whole thing was my fault. I shouldn't have let us get so close." Jake gave me a pleading look. "Don't tell Bob about this. Okay?"

"Not a chance."

Jake pointed out that the moose's uneven, folded antlers didn't make him a prized trophy. He said its mangy hide was a sign of that he was decrepit and old— a deep contrast to the spectacular Dall sheep trophy I had taken just days before.

"Get your camera," said Jake. "I'll take your picture."

Pictures were the last thing on my mind, but I knew it was part of the hunt. I handed my camera to him and he snapped a couple of pictures of me behind the moose, with a weak smile on my face, the best I could manage.

There were no congratulations. Our close call had changed everything— we were just glad to be alive and uninjured.

Jake reached into his backpack, pulled out his knife, and went to work cutting through the moose's abdominal wall. A few minutes later the guts, steaming and hot, spilled out in one, perfect sac. I had never seen anyone do this so expertly. Devoid of internal organs, the cavity was large enough for someone to crawl inside, making me fully appreciate the immense size of moose—even a medium-sized one.

Obviously Jake and I had several hours of butchering ahead of us. Except for bear meat, leaving game meat in the field was strictly illegal. I asked Jake how long it would take the two of us to pack several hundred pounds of meat back to the spike camp, which was at least five miles away.

"Five, maybe six trips."

More like five, maybe six days, I thought.

By mid-morning we had an Indian summer day, allowing us to shed our hunting coats. Working as a team, we moved systematically around the carcass. After skinning one entire side of the moose, Jake instructed me to pull on each of the moose's legs while he skinned under them and severed them just below the joints. He severed the thigh meat by cutting the meat from the hip all the way around. After cutting through all the ligaments, I stood up and leaned my body into the leg forcing it away from the carcass, exposing the hip joint. Then Jake cut through the cartilage within the joint and detached the hindquarter. After that, he went to work removing the shank meat and we used the same procedure to get the shoulder meat off.

After two hours, Jake and I were dripping with sweat.

Taking a short break, I stood up and looked to the sky. "When do you suppose someone from the main camp will be checking on us?"

"Don't expect anyone until tomorrow. The pilots are super busy with the moose season opening today."

Tomorrow? I thought with an internal groan. *Tomorrow I'd hoped to be on my way home.* But there was nothing I could do, so I reluctantly went back to work butchering.

By 2:00 P.M., Jake and I were ready to start packing the meat back to the spike camp. Jake was limping heavily and in obvious pain.

"Jake, why don't you rest and I'll make the first trip alone. It isn't going to do any good aggravating what might be an injury. I'll bring back some more anti-inflammatory pills."

"Naw, I've never had a client do that and I ain't going to start now. Maybe I'll keep my first load a little light."

As he began to stuff his backpack with plastic-wrapped meat, a plane appeared over a mountain top.

Jake looked to the sky and smiled, "Good news, it's Howe. Now we won't have to pack anything outta here."

As much as I disliked Howe, at that moment I was thrilled to see him.

Jake and I stood and watched the plane as it circled over us six times.

"Shit," grumbled Jake. "He can't find a spot to land. We may end up packing this shit out anyway."

"Give him a minute," I said, "He'll find a place. He may be a jerk, but he's a hell of a pilot."

Finally, Howe lowered the plane and brought it down on a spot about one hundred yards from where Jake and I stood. As soon as the plane's tires touched the ground, it bounced back into the air and slammed to the ground a second time before stopping so suddenly that the tail swerved and created a small dust storm.

"Now that was close," gasped Jake.

"They're all close in my opinion."

"We got a little bit of a hike so let's get started."

Jake took off toward the plane and handed his pack to Howe while I ran and gave Jake my load. Then I ran back to the kill site for more meat. With our little relay system in place, it didn't take long to get all the meat and the antlers to the plane. Howe tied the antlers to the struts of the plane.

"We gotta hustle out of here," Howe said gruffly. "There's fog moving in at the main camp. If we don't get back now, we may be stuck out here for days."

"What about my pack? It's still at the spike tent."

Howe said he'd fly me over to get it but added that he didn't have room for Jake. He would have to walk back to the spike camp and remain there until Howe could come for him, which could be the next day or the next week. Fog was that unpredictable.

Although I hated to leave Jake he assured me that he was used to being alone in the bush and actually looked forward to resting his hip for a few days.

"C'mon," urged Howe. "We don't have much time."

We took off without incident, and a minute later landed at the spike camp. I jumped out of the plane and ran to the tent to gather my gear. Inside, I threw a hundred dollars tip money on Jake's bag along with a four-day supply of anti-inflammatory pills.

Both Howe and I were silent as we lifted off and headed over the mountains. Howe's focus was on flying and his face was etched with concern. Perhaps the situation with fog was more serious than I thought.

When we broke into the Ivishak River Valley a dense blanket of fog was rolling in from the south, its leading edge having already reached the camp. We were lucky that the visibility was still sufficient for us to land.

As Howe and I unloaded the plane, his first words to me were cutting. "How come you killed a deformed moose?"

"There's nothing wrong with this moose."

"Look at him. He's deformed. Couldn't you find one with a decent set of antlers? These mangled things weren't worth the effort to bring back."

Asshole.

"I think the antler formations are unusual. I happen to like them."

"Yeah, well I hope the meat tastes better than these damn things look."

I changed the subject. "Are Bob and Roy back?"

"Nope. And if they don't make it back in the next half hour, they won't until this fog clears."

Not only was the density of the fog increasing by the minute, it was getting dark. A landing looked increasingly more unlikely. I hoped Roy would make it in by the morning so we could leave. Howe also told me that Hoff hadn't made it in because of the fog. That of course was good news.

That night at the main camp we feasted on moose burgers with Lenny, Wilhelm, and Howe. The rest of the meal consisted of greasy French fries and a salad. Meals were less elaborate when Bowman was gone.

During dinner I learned that Jack Watson flew Wilhelm into camp the night before with a bear that he'd supposedly shot along the Colville River. Given Wilhelm's shooting skills, I wasn't convinced of this and wanted to get the details. Lenny said Wilhelm had also killed a big moose just outside of camp that morning. Even though it was entirely possible that he shot his own moose, I still wanted to know more.

Outside, the visibility was nearly zero. Marianne told us stories about the many times the camp had been fogged in and hunters had been stranded in the field for days. This made me worry that Roy might be forced to spend more time alone with Bowman and Gordon, which increased his chances of slipping up. I also happened to know that Roy talked in his sleep.

On top of everything, if Roy and I weren't in Prudhoe Bay by tomorrow, September 6, Eicher and a team of agents would be checking out the camp.

___

CHAPTER 20

The Day Time Stopped

"THERE'S COFFEE IF YOU WANT IT," Marianne said absentmindedly as she focused her gaze out the kitchen window.

The first cup of coffee hadn't been poured that morning, even though the pot had sat full for more than an hour. Breakfast pastries sat on a tray with their tops glistening with days-old oil. The table was set. Every hair on Marianne's head was in place, her eyelashes fixed perfectly, her makeup flawless. She didn't move from the window, her arms folded across her chest, the reflection in the window revealed the worried look of a sailor's wife staring out to sea. That was how the first day began with the densest fog I'd ever seen.

It was September 6, the day Eicher expected me to call him announcing that Roy and I were safely out of camp. But Roy was still with Bowman and Gordon in a spike camp somewhere in the bush and I was stuck in the main camp that had turned into a prison with no way in and no way out. Unless I got word to Eicher that we were okay, I could expect an untimely visit from him as soon as the fog lifted. That was the plan. This weighed heavily on my mind when Billy Howe, Lenny, and Wilhelm filed in for breakfast, each taking his regular seat.

"Breakfast is served," I announced cheerily as I carried steaming plates of eggs, bacon, biscuits, and gravy from the stove to the table.

Rhoda remained at the stove, with her back to the rest of us, apparently in no mood for conversation. I assumed she was worried about Gordon and I wondered what scenarios were going through her mind. While the rest of us ate, Marianne sat at the table nervously sipping coffee, constantly glancing out the window.

Except for a few pleasantries, no one spoke much. In the silence I became acutely aware of the sound of utensils clanging on plates. The persistent fog was chewing at everyone's nerves. There were only so many times you could stare out into it, pierce it with your eyes, and wish it away so that the familiar would reappear. After breakfast, Howe and Lenny shoved their plates to the center of the table, got up, and walked out the door.

"I go to bed," pronounced Wilhelm with a bored yawn.

After the door slammed shut behind him, Rhoda muttered, "Good riddance."

"Don't you like our genteel German hunter?" I joked.

"He's a lazy SOB," said Rhoda.

"He's only living in the manner to which he's accustomed."

"Hummph!"

"Say, did he get a good moose yesterday?" I asked.

"Yeah," Rhoda answered with her hands deep in soapy dish water. "He got the one you were supposed to get. Pissed me off. That was a good one."

"Yes, it was," I said slowly. Rhoda had just given me some valuable information. Then she said Howe had spotted it for Lenny from his plane because the moose had moved. Another violation. All I had to do was piece it together.

Because Rhoda had already washed the pots and pans, it was only a matter of minutes before the three of us had the table cleared and the kitchen spotless again.

Marianne put her arm around my shoulder and said, "Jayne, you're the only hunter we've ever had who helped us with anything. Are you sure you don't want to stay?"

"I would, but it's far too exciting. Especially when the fog rolls in."

"I'd like to get out of here and hunt fossils for a while but I'm afraid of missing Bob's call," said Marianne.

"Go ahead," I said. "I'll stay here and answer the phone."

"That would be great," said Rhoda, grabbing her fossil-collecting bag.

"Are you sure?" asked Marianne. "We don't want to leave you alone."

"I'm happy. I've got a book," I assured them.

"You're the best," said Marianne, smiling. "Holler at us if Bob calls in."

"You got it."

From the kitchen window I watched them stroll out onto the tundra until they disappeared into the foggy soup. Relieved to be alone, I sat down at the table and tried to rub the tension from my eyes. When I looked out the window, the fog made my mind drift right along with it. All I could do was wonder. Had Bowman's plane crashed? Had Roy been found out and was he in trouble? Or were they just sitting out the fog? I had no idea. No one did.

I imagined that Eicher had worn out the floor pacing with worry and had already developed a strategy to rescue Roy and me. Eyeing the radiophone, I decided to try to make contact with him but couldn't remember his office phone number. I'd have to risk a short call to Lonnie so he could call Eicher and let him know what the situation was. I looked at my watch: it was noon in Wisconsin. Lonnie would be home for lunch. I had to call him now—or never.

I knew the radiophone procedure from watching Marianne. I pushed a button and turned a dial to make contact with a repeater tower. I listened as the radio crackled; it sounded just like the police radio installed in the glove box of my Explorer, reminding me of who I really was.

When contact was made I dialed an operator who would place the call over a land line. As I gave my home number in a low voice, I glanced outside the kitchen windows and around the room. My heartbeat picked up. Anyone nearby could hear both sides of the conversation. Getting caught was not an option. There were fifteen seconds of agonizing silence as I waited for the phone to ring. Then I jumped at a noise inside the kitchen, only to discover it was the refrigerator kicking in.

Shit!

Finally, there were four rings and Lonnie's voice. "Hello."

"Hi, this is Jayne."

I'd never used my undercover name around Lonnie and wasn't sure how he'd respond. Silently, I begged him to recognize my voice and go along.

"Oh yeah. How are you?"

Thank God.

"I'm fine, but the camp is fogged in and it may be a few more days before we can get out. Don't worry, okay?"

"Okay. Everything's fine?"

"Yes. But this is important. Call Tim in Fairbanks for me. Tell him all is okay but we'll be a few days late getting out of camp due to fog."

"Yeah, I'll call him."

"Thanks. Hugs and kisses."

"You, too. Bye."

"Bye."

Perfect. Now Lonnie knew I was okay and he'd call Eicher so that he wouldn't send a team of agents to the camp. I poured a glass of cold water and sat down to consider my next move. Rhoda had told me about the moose Wilhelm had shot. Not only was it useful information, it was good ammunition and I knew exactly how to use it. I finished my water and made my way down to the skinning shed where I found Lenny rearranging hides on sawhorses.

I let him know right away that I was furious. "I just found out that you let that idiot German shoot the big moose that was supposed to be mine."

Lenny looked at me, dumbstruck. "Who told you that?"

"He did."

"Well, yeah, we knew where the moose was and . . ."

"And you kicked me out of camp and let that lazy old coot shoot my moose. Did you see what I came back with? Pure crap compared to what I could have had."

"I had no idea you'd be so upset."

"Of course I'm upset. First you accuse me of being a spy, then you cheat me out of a great trophy with a sixty-eight-inch spread. I'm so mad I could spit."

"Jayne, what I said about you being a plant, I didn't really mean . . ."

"You must have meant it. You and Billy Howe kicked me out of camp so Wilhelm could shoot *my* moose."

"It wasn't that way—"

"Then what was it?"

"Jake needed a client."

"Yeah, right. Send me to a guide who can barely walk. He was so lame I had to shoot the first thing we spotted. You guys are good, real good. Wait till Bob hears this story."

Lenny removed his stocking cap and twisted it in his hands. "I really wish you wouldn't mention this to Bob. He gets awful mad when clients complain."

"I'll think about it. Just lay off me over this spy crap, and I expect exceptional treatment around here from now on. Understand?"

Lenny dropped his head. "Yes, ma'am."

I stalked off leaving Lenny to wonder whether I was going to rat him out to Bowman. More important, I was now in the driver's seat, and if Lenny had ever really suspected me it was unlikely that he still did.

Nonetheless, although my own safety seemed ensured, I was deeply concerned about Roy's. He was somewhere on the tundra with Bowman and Gordon, who were two very unpredictable men. Both of them had a lot to lose if they were caught violating wildlife laws and it was difficult to predict how far they'd go to protect the hunting operation. Bowman was known to have made statements that if he ever found an undercover cop in his camp, he'd kill him. This kind of talk is usually nothing more than bravado, but the more I got to know these characters the more ominous it sounded. If Roy mumbled something in his sleep or slipped up revealing who he really was, I knew there could be a "hunting accident." Then they'd come back to the main camp and deal with me. They'd have no choice.

This reality hit me hard as I poked slowly through the fog back to the kitchen to be near the radiophone. If Bob and Gordon penetrated Roy's cover, my life would be in jeopardy and I wouldn't know anything was wrong until it was too late.

I glanced toward the riverbed, where the outlines of the parked planes were barely visible. Out of the corner of my eye I caught a ghostly image of Howe lurking around the Quonset hut the Spaniards had used. Bending over, walking back and forth, and fading in and out of the fog like an apparition. I could feel his presence. *How long had that bastard been watching me?* I had to admit that the fog and boredom had an irrational grip on me and my mind was working overtime.

Should I try to get out of the camp without Roy? I could tell Marianne that my daughter was having a medical treatment done in a couple of days and I had to be home. Yes. Marianne would understand and I'd make her my ally in getting me out. Once I got out of the camp, I'd call Eicher from Prudhoe Bay. I'd wait one day for Roy, until Eicher and I organized a rescue effort. If he was dead, there would at least be one of us to tell what had happened.

That night I went back to my tent where I waited hour after hour for Roy's return. His shirt hung in the tent refusing to let go of its dampness and his book remained tossed in a corner. Nothing moved, not the clocks, not the worry, not the fear.

———

CHAPTER 21

Please Say No

THE NEXT MORNING, SEPTEMBER 7, my sheets were damp with sweat after another night of dreaming that I was slogging through thick marsh muck trying unsuccessfully to get to the other side. I was thoroughly convinced that with so much time alone with Bowman, Roy had caved in and revealed our true identities. I was anxious to get out of the camp. I got up and put on the purple shirt with a fuchsia overshirt that had become my uniform and went to the kitchen. Bowman still hadn't called in. Since his radio wouldn't transmit to the main camp unless he was in the air, this meant he was still grounded. Of course, no one knew where.

For the rest of the day I waited within earshot of the radiophone, waiting for it to crackle. At 7:00 P.M., it finally came to life. Marianne ran over to it and cranked up the volume. A voice came through. It was Jerry Hoff.

"I'm in a hotel in Prudhoe Bay, they say the fog's gonna lift tonight. I'm getting ready to fly in."

Silently I begged, *Marianne, say no. Please say no.*

"Come on in. We're ready," said Marianne.

"Good, see you tomorrow."

My face twitched nervously. There was no question now. I had to get out of the camp before he flew in.

Marianne hung up the radiophone and smiled sweetly. "It's a shame for him to come all this way and not get a decent moose."

I looked outside. The fog still had the camp in a lockdown. Even if the fog lifted in Prudhoe Bay, Hoff couldn't fly in until it was clear at the camp. But then I couldn't fly out, either.

The following morning, September 8, Marianne was at the table sipping coffee and thumbing through a decorating magazine. The sun was trying to break through and according to weather reports the fog was on its way out.

I sat down at the table and asked, "Would you call Duane and ask him to pick me up just as soon as he can?"

At first Marianne questioned my leaving before Roy, but then I explained that Megan had a doctor's appointment I had to attend.

"I'd feel like a total heel not being there. It's time for me to be a mother again."

"I understand and I'll be glad to help you out. You've been so good to us around here; it's the least I could do for you."

She placed the call to Duane who agreed to pick me up within an hour. Apparently it was completely clear in Prudhoe Bay and the camp would be clearing soon. My gear was packed and all I had to do was hope that I'd get out before Hoff came buzzing in. The stars were lining up and I thought surely I'd make it.

Forty agonizing minutes later, I heard the buzz of a plane. I raced outside thinking it was Duane's Cessna. Unbelievably, it was Bob's red-and-white tail-dragger. Was Roy with him? Was he okay? Was our cover still in place?

—————

CHAPTER 22

Some Trouble Never Stops

I TURNED TO MARIANNE. "Here comes Bob."

"Thank God," she gasped, throwing down her magazine.

We bolted out the door and jogged down to the riverbank, passing Rhoda's Quonset hut.

"Come on, Rhoda," shouted Marianne, "The boys are back!"

Rhoda hurried out of the hut throwing a sweater around her shoulders. Huddled together on the river rocks, we watched anxiously as Bowman's plane rocked from side to side and hit the ground, sending a small explosion of dirt behind the wheels.

Another controlled crash landing.

As the plane drew closer, I caught a glimpse of Roy and Gordon crammed in the backseat of the cub. *Roy was okay.*

My breathing turned shallow as the plane turned and parked. A split-second after the prop stopped, Bowman jumped out of the plane followed by Roy and Gordon. Roy walked with a heavy limp toward me. His hunting clothes were smeared with dirt and blood, his beard was snarled, and had turned white from dust. Heavy bags hung under his bloodshot eyes. He looked like a prisoner from a gulag.

Bowman's hair was matted and dirty, his blond beard had grown in irregular patches on his face, and his clothes looked worse than Roy's. I studied him carefully. Was his jaw tight? His eyes narrow? Were his motions jerky?

These would be signs that something was very wrong. But all I could detect was exhaustion and a sense of relief to be back.

I watched Gordon as he yanked a grizzly bear hide from the rear of the plane. "Looky here, Jayne, your man got a big one."

"Wow, I'll have to drool over it later."

I walked briskly up to Roy and pulled him close to me. He leaned on me to take weight off the leg that was bothering him.

"Hey, bud, everything okay?"

"Yeah, but I've never been through nothing more miserable. Hell and bullshit is what it was."

"I want to hear all about it," I said, checking behind us to make sure the others weren't within earshot. Fortunately, Marianne and Rhoda were greeting their men as if they were war heroes. "Is everything cool?"

"I think so, but them guys acted so crazy and weird all the time, I didn't know what to think. Bob threatened to kill me if he ever found out I was a game warden. Then those two bastards made me sleep between them in the tent. I was too scared to even close my eyes at night."

There was no doubt Roy had been though hell, but the real point was that he hadn't been burned, which was a tremendous relief to me. "I'm just glad you're okay. I've been worried sick. Listen, we've got to get out of here. The guy from South Dakota is coming back in today. I can't let him see me. Marianne called Duane and he's on his way to get us."

Roy shot me an anxious look. "Shit! This could get real bad. Yeah, I'm ready to get the hell out of here. Good work."

I felt guilty that Roy had given me so much credit. Little did he know, the plane was originally just for me. As we made our way across the river rocks and up the riverbank, I took one of his bags and slung it over my shoulder. It was heavy and I kept shifting its weight to keep it from digging into my shoulder. Only when we were inside the tent and I had shut the door behind us did I dare talk about his hunt.

"I see you got a bear."

Roy sat on the bed and spoke softly. "Yeah, but the first bear we went after was for Wilhelm."

"Where were you?"

"All Bob would say is that we were about 230 miles west of Happy Valley. That's where he stashed several cans of gas near an old radio tower. Anyway, Bob said we were huntin' the Grayling and Colville areas. While we were flying Bob showed me how he relocated good bear and moose from the air by pushing the 'go to' button on his GPS navigational device and it would display bear and moose locations he had logged in from previous sightings."

Roy handed me a piece of paper with the latitude and longitude coordinates from the GPS and said, "These are the locations for Wilhelm's bear and my bear."

"Good job, Roy. This is good evidence. Tell me about Wilhelm's bear hunt first."

"Yeah, it was killed on Friday."

"September fourth?"

"I guess so. We had camped near the first coordinates because Bob knew there was a decent bear nearby. Around noon Bowman, Gordon, Wilhelm, and Jack Watson all took off on foot to hunt it. Bowman told me to stay in camp and be ready to shoot a bear or wolf if I saw one. I told him I didn't have a wolf tag, but he told me to shoot one anyway.

"These guys walked out of sight around the corner of this little bluff. About fifty minutes later I heard three shots and then a few minutes later I saw Jack Watson come running back to the camp to get his airplane. He said that Wilhelm had shot a bear but it was just wounded. Anyway, Watson took off and at some point he must have landed because he came back to the camp with Bowman. Bowman was super pissed that there was a wounded bear running around and I guess they couldn't find it. He told me to get my gun and go with him up on the bluff south of camp. We hiked up the bluff while Watson went back up into the air. Bowman kept waving a handkerchief to let Watson know where we were."

"Did you have any idea what was going on?" I asked.

"No, and I asked, but Bowman told me to be quiet and follow instructions."

"So then what happened?"

"I could see Watson circling at a real low altitude and I could see Gordon lying prone with a rifle by the riverbank. I had no idea where the German was. Finally I saw a bear about three hundred yards off. Bowman kept sayin' to me 'shoot, stupid, shoot!' I gotta tell you, I didn't want to shoot him. I honestly couldn't get a decent shot off because even though the bear was supposedly wounded, it was still able to move pretty fast. But to keep Bowman happy I fired a few rounds that I knew were too short because Watson's plane was so low and close to this bear, I thought I was going to hit the plane."

"Sounds like a disaster," I said, biting my lips.

"It was horrible. Watson drove the bear into the Colville River and I could see Gordon through my scope shooting at it. Finally, as the bear was climbing out of the river on the west side one of Gordon's shots took the bear down."

"Some hunt."

"Yeah. I saw the hide later, and it turns out that the German only hit it in the left hind paw. Crappy shots like that shouldn't be allowed to leave home."

"So Gordon killed it."

"Yeah, but still the German acted like he is such a big-man hunter. What a fake. Bowman made me swear not to talk about using the plane to help kill it. He came up with some bullshit about how it was technically okay because the bear was wounded."

"We'll straighten him out on that later. So tell me about your bear hunt, was it equally as exciting?"

"Sickening is the word. The next day, Saturday I think, Bowman was on me right away not to talk about how a plane was used to hunt Wilhelm's bear. I kept telling him that I didn't give a shit about the planes. By now Watson had flown the German back to main camp, which was fine with me, I was sick of him."

"You're not alone."

"It was around two in the afternoon when Bowman announced we were going to break camp. I think we were moving to the location of the second GPS coordinates. Once again I was crammed in the backseat with that stinking three-hundred-pound Gordon on top of me. We ended up near a riverbed at a Quonset hut with a bunch of fifty-five-gallon barrels of diesel fuel around it. That night Bowman tried to start a Coleman stove and due to a fuel leak part of the cabin caught on fire. If it weren't for me, the whole place would have burned down."

"Roy to the rescue!" I said, smiling.

"We didn't go out bear hunting until the next day. Bowman said he'd seen a good one while we were flying in the day before, but it was too far to hunt on foot. He took off in his plane to try and find it again and came back all excited because he'd found two more that looked pretty good. Then he and Gordon took off again to check them out. When Bowman came back, he was alone and had come to pick me up. I asked him where we were going and he told me to just get ready to kill a bear."

"Bowman's communication skills aren't the most stellar," I said.

"No kidding. I never knew exactly what was going on and it was spooky as hell. Anyway, we hooked up with Gordon who was staked out on the east side of the riverbed. I think we were still on the Colville—just a different section of it. Gordon and Bowman set up a system that if Gordon saw any planes in the area he was supposed to wave a game bag.

"There was blowing snow and the wind was coming out of the north. I saw Bowman flying in and out of sight behind a bluff and the airplane engine was making a sound like it was diving at something. Then I saw the plane circling a bunch of times and finally I saw this grizzly running from the north to the south in the river bottom. Gordon started laughing about how much bears hate airplanes. That bastard acted like this was an everyday thing."

"It probably was."

"Every time the bear tried to run one way, Bowman was on his tail making it run the other way. When the bear finally got within gun range I just sorta stood there. I didn't want to shoot it. I couldn't believe that 'cause I'm a bear hunter. But this was so cruel. Gordon kept screaming, 'Shoot you idiot, shoot!' I thought about missing it, but I knew Bowman would just get pissed off and then he'd be off chasing another one down. So I shot the critter when he was in a full run. Twice. I felt like shit."

I didn't say anything for a few minutes. I imagined an immense animal using every reserve it had to escape Bowman's air assault. I saw his muscles rippling, his mouth open as streams of saliva streamed out. I imagined the sheer terror in his eyes as he tore across the tundra. In my mind I heard the rifle blast and saw the bear recoil from the force of the bullets and then crash to the ground, his whole body sliding from the momentum of his run. I could hear Gordon's boisterous laugh, and Bowman veering away in his plane as if to give Gordon an aerial high-five, signaling another "valiant" bear hunt.

I put my hand on Roy's shoulder. "We'll get those bastards, I promise."

"God, I hope so."

"What happened to your leg?"

"It's my ankle. Just after I shot the bear Bowman landed the plane and Gordon made me run down the hill so we could get to the bear in a hurry. I twisted it then. Those guys went into this big frenzy. Bowman was screaming and cussing at me to hurry so he could take pictures. Gordon was hollering like an Indian in one of them old movies."

"Will the pictures give us a location?"

"No, Bowman made a point of taking pictures real low so there weren't any landmarks. We could have been on Mars. But there's a GPS unit in Bowman's plane and I seen him punch in the latitudes and longitudes so we'll have that."

"That's great. Then what happened?"

"Gordon and Bob skinned the bear. Bob made me get some brush and erase the tire tracks the plane made. It was real obvious they were trying to cover everything up."

"Did they hide the carcass?"

"Yeah. In what little brush there was. But the wolves have got it by now."

"Did you get any pictures?"

"One. I took it by the wing of the plane. It shows Gordon and Bowman hiding the carcass. I was in a hurry and scared shitless, so it might not have come out."

"That's okay. You did a fantastic job, Roy. I think he'll see prison over this. Gordon's probably looking at a new address, too, and Watson will at least lose his plane."

"I hope so. Those guys ought to be chased with a plane and gunned down just like they did with those bears."

Roy put his face in his hands. He had his faults, and I'd been plenty mad at him, but now he'd come through with flying colors. Roy had exceeded my expectations and had done a fantastic job. I was proud of him.

I stepped outside to make doubly sure there was no one around and went back inside the tent.

"Meanwhile, Bowman's laughing all the way to the bank. Every bear means seven thousand dollars in his pocket," I said, snapping my fingers. "A legal bear hunt takes three to five days of hard-ass scouting and hunting. These guys have got it down to three to five hours."

"Or less. Except this time the fog screwed them up."

"What did you guys do for all that time in the fog?"

"We just sat around and bullshitted. We weren't that far from here, but Bowman couldn't see a hundred feet to fly. The problem was I had to be extremely careful about what I said." He gave me a straight-from-the-heart look. "I gotta tell you, I almost blew it a couple of times."

"Like how?"

"I ain't sayin'. It was just really hard not to slip up. Finally I just kept my mouth shut and listened. They talked constantly about how other hunting guides have been busted over the years. One pilot in particular, Ron Somebody."

"Ron Hayes. He was an airborne hunter the feds busted in the 1980s."

"Yeah. Bob ranted on and on about how that was never going to happen to him. He's totally paranoid about undercover agents. I can't believe we ever got into this place."

"We may have had some luck, but luck can't last forever. We're getting the hell out of here today."

"Man, am I glad. Oh, there's one thing I forgot. Gordon cut the gall bladders out of both bears."

This didn't surprise me. Bear gall bladders went for a thousand dollars each in the illicit Chinese medicinal market. These guys didn't miss a thing.

Roy began reorganizing his gear for our exodus when he cocked his head. "Is that a plane I hear?"

I opened the door and looked outside. "It's probably Duane."

I recognized Duane's Cessna as it popped through layers of thin clouds into the clear. But as it came in for a landing I could see more than one head in the front seats. *Who's with him?* I wondered. My answer came a few seconds later. It was Jerry Hoff.

—————

CHAPTER 23

Good-Bye, Jayne

I SLAMMED THE DOOR SHUT, rushed to the window, covering most of my face with the curtain, and watched Jerry Hoff.

"He just went to the kitchen. There goes lunch," I muttered.

"What! No lunch?"

"You can go eat, but not me. Bring me back something."

"Yeah, I'll do that. I'll tell Marianne you're busy packing."

"She knows I'm packed. Tell her I have a headache."

Roy ambled out the door and while I sat alone in the tent and thought about how I had come full circle. The same threat I faced the minute I had arrived in camp was back. But it would soon be over. After lunch Roy and I would jump in Duane's plane without letting Hoff get a good look at me.

Thirty minutes later Roy came back. "What'd you bring me?" I asked anticipating another one of Marianne's delicacies.

"Uh, I forgot. Want me to go back?"

"No, forget it." My stomach was growling, but eating would have to wait.

Peering out the window, I spotted Bowman across the camp. I motioned to Roy, "C'mon, Let's tell Bob we're leaving."

Just as he approached our tent I stepped outside. "Hey, Bob, Roy and I are going back to Prudhoe with Duane in a few minutes. We wanted to say good-bye now." I extended my hand. "It's been great, really."

"I gotta get the German outta here first. He's pitching a fit."

"Wait a minute," I demanded. "I called Duane. That plane is ours."

"Not if I say it ain't. Wilhelm goes first. You can leave tomorrow."

I could feel my face getting hot. "Tomorrow!"

"This is bullshit," interjected Roy.

"Too damn bad you don't like it, but I say what goes on around here." Bob jabbed his index finger into Roy's chest. "Not you."

"Is there someone else who can fly us out?" I asked.

"Not that I know of. This ain't Los Angeles International you know."

"What about Dave Knowles? He's flown in here twice just to drink coffee."

Bowman's eyes narrowed as he considered my idea. "He might do it, but he's not licensed to fly passengers."

"Is that a problem?" asked Roy.

"No, except you'd have to pay him plenty."

"We've already paid Duane for a round trip," I countered. "You mean we'd have to pay again?"

"Yeah. If you want to fly with Knowles you have to pay again. Or else wait until tomorrow. What's the big rush?"

Roy looked to me for an answer.

"I need to get back home. My daughter has a doctor's appointment."

"We're inside the Arctic Circle for God's sake. You can't just come and go whenever you want. Sometimes you have to wait."

"We can't wait. C'mon, Bob, call Dave or any other pilot you know. Just get us out of here today."

"I don't understand what the big deal is."

"The big deal is that my daughter needs me. I've been sitting around here in this fog for days and I can't take it anymore. Tell Dave we'll pay him whatever he wants."

"I know he'll want four hundred dollars. Give it to me and I'll pay him."

"Why can't I just pay the pilot directly?"

"'Cause he ain't suppose to fly passengers. It'll look better if he takes the money from me."

Bowman was probably skimming off the top but I was in no position to argue further. I took some money out of my pocket, counted it, and stuffed it into Bowman's hand. "When can he be here?"

"In an hour and fifteen."

As Bowman marched off, I felt a mixture of rage and relief. I was furious with him for putting the German ahead of us, but glad to be escaping from Camp Hell. From the tent's window Roy and I watched Bowman escort Wilhelm to Duane's plane. Lenny had already loaded his illegal trophies. As the Cessna lifted into the sky, I felt totally defeated. Not only had the seemingly harmless old German taken our plane, he was escaping with valuable evidence, and there was nothing I could do about it.

A half hour later, Lenny came by in his ATV loaded with our trophies. They were wrapped and taped together with yards of duct tape. He flung them on the rocky runway and drove away. Fifteen minutes later, Dave Knowles touched down in his Cessna Skywagon.

"Let's git," said Roy.

Lugging our gear over our shoulders, we hiked out to Dave's plane as quickly as we could. I asked Roy to walk closely behind me so Hoff couldn't see me from the kitchen window.

As the prop shut down, Dave cracked his window open. "Do I got time for cookies and coffee?"

"Nope," responded Roy. "She wants a shower and I want a drink."

"Okay, let's load up and get going."

By chance, I glanced toward the kitchen and saw Marianne and Rhoda running toward us. Bowman was right behind them. I hoped that Hoff wouldn't follow, and to my relief he didn't.

When Marianne reached me she was half-scolding when she said, "You weren't going to run off and not say good-bye were you?"

"I'm sorry, Marianne. I avoid good-byes at all costs."

"You'll come back won't you? It was great having another woman around," said Rhoda.

I had intended to tell them that I'd be back the next hunting season with great recipes, new card games, and a fossil chart—all blatant lies, of course. But these women had taken me in like a sister, consoled me when I struggled with my emotions, and cheered me on when I had a successful hunt. They had offered me friendship that I didn't even have at home. I couldn't lie to them anymore. "I don't know if I'll be back," was all I could say.

"I'll make you a deal," interrupted Bowman, "A free grizzly bear hunt for two weeks' translation for another group of Spanish hunters. I don't know what I would have done with the Barcelona boys without you."

I gave him a wry smile. My translations may have seemed convenient to him at the time, but they would likely contribute to the demise of his hunting operation.

"You might have a deal, Bob. I'll let you know."

"What about me?" asked Roy.

"Maybe I'll give you a discount," grunted Bowman.

"Better than nothing," said Roy as he opened the passenger door of the plane and climbed inside.

Marianne and Rhoda gave me hugs and said they'd miss me.

"Thanks. But sometimes things change."

Rhoda looked at me completely dumbfounded. "What on earth do you mean by that?"

I turned and put my foot on the plane's small metal step, grabbed onto the door frame, and pulled myself into the back of the plane.

"Things just change, that's all. Okay, Dave, I'm ready."

I hoped that Rhoda and Marianne would remember my last words. It was a subtle message that even though my friendship may have seemed genuine, and to some degree it was, it also was part of an agenda—an agenda to gather intelligence and snare their outlaw husbands. Rhoda and Marianne would be the civilian casualties in this war for wildlife. They would never completely understand my betrayal of them, of course. As for me, it wouldn't bother me that much. Betrayal was one of the brutal realities of undercover work. Those who couldn't do it didn't belong undercover.

The back of Dave's plane looked like a military cargo plane compared to the Pipers I'd become used to. There was plenty of room for all of our trophies. I sat in the back on a plastic bag stuffed with the hide from my sheep while Roy sat up front in first class.

As the plane bounced down the riverbed, I glanced out the window and waved to Bowman, Marianne, and Rhoda. When the camp finally disappeared from sight, I felt like a caged bird that had been released. As we flew across the flat tundra of the north slope I took a last look at a herd of caribou, a few meandering moose along a creek bed, and a single grizzly bear feeding in the lingering light. My throat tightened. Maybe this case would save them, or critters like them, from Bowman's marauding planes, guns, and renegade hunters. Mixed in with the exhaustion I felt, pride swelled in my chest. I was satisfied that Roy and I had completed some damn hard and stressful work. I hoped that our efforts would help the wild creatures in this beautifully wild place.

Dave Knowles landed his plane on the concrete runway at Prudhoe Bay and pulled across the tarmac and parked at his hangar. Roy and I jumped out and faced the chore of hauling our gear and trophies to the terminal some distance away. Knowles wasn't about to help, since he didn't want to be spotted with passengers he wasn't legally allowed to transport.

As we dragged our bags across the slick tile floor of the Prudhoe Bay airport headed toward the Alaska Airlines ticket counter, Roy commented that he was glad we weren't around "those pukes" anymore. Just then we spotted none other than Wilhelm.

"This can't be happenin'," he said, clearly annoyed.

"Stay in character."

"What?"

"He's walking over here. Stay in character."

"I've about had enough of this shit."

Wilhelm was smiling and his eyes were shining at the sight of familiar faces. He shook our hands like we were old, lost friends.

"Wilhelm. I thought you would be gone by now," I said.

"Vaat?"

I pulled my ticket out of my bag and pointed to it.

"Ticket?"

"Ja," he said as he handed me his Alaska Airlines ticket.

I examined the ticket. "He's on the same flight we are to Anchorage."

"I can't believe this shit," muttered Roy, barely under his breath.

I handed the ticket back to Wilhelm and pointed to the three of us. "All together to Anchorage."

"Ja, ja!"

Roy and I waved good-bye and continued on to the Alaska Airlines desk to check in. Obviously we weren't out of the woods yet. But seeing Wilhelm reminded me of how much I wanted his illegal trophies, which I assumed he had already checked in as baggage. I considered suggesting to Eicher that we seize his trophies out of baggage in Anchorage. But the airlines would have to advise Wilhelm about the seizure and then he'd immediately complain to Bowman. Alerting Bowman about the investigation would jeopardize the rest of the case. We were still months away from serving search warrants and arresting suspects and Bowman had to be kept in the dark until we were ready to make our move.

At the Alaska Airlines counter, we weren't the only passengers with duct-taped trophies to check in. A dozen other hunters were in line with piles of raw antlers, hides, and meat. How were these animals killed? How many were poached? Questions impossible to answer in the Prudhoe Bay airport terminal.

After we'd checked in I said, "I've got to call Eicher. Let's find a phone as far away from that goofy German as we can."

We found a public phone just outside the terminal door. Even then, I hesitated to talk openly. When Eicher answered I kept it short, "Hi, Tim, we're out. Everything went fine and we'll be in Anchorage at seven tonight. Can you pick us up? Good. You're gonna be happy with what we have for you. See ya later."

As Roy and I sank into our seats for the flight to Anchorage, we commented that the airplane-seat gods had smiled upon us. Wilhelm was seated five rows behind us. Even better, this was the first flight for this particular aircraft, so the flight attendants were pouring complimentary champagne to celebrate. Roy and I, however, were celebrating a much different occasion. As the drink warmed my blood, I leaned back and fell into a sleep more peaceful than any I had had in a long time.

At the baggage claim area in the Anchorage airport I spotted Wilhelm's trophies spinning around the baggage carrousel. It grated on my nerves to be so close to such compelling evidence and not be able to touch it. On the other side of the carrousel Wilhelm stood looking lost and disoriented in a sea of people. He probably needed a cab and a hotel and didn't know how to go about getting either. His eyes caught mine and seemed to beg for help from his old camp buddy Jayne but I was in no mood to help this indolent, self-important German crook who had just ripped off America's wildlife. I turned my back on Wilhelm's silent plea. While Roy loaded our gear on a cart, I walked outside to find Eicher.

I first caught a slight glimpse of the quintessential Marlboro Man at the end of a sidewalk that was crammed with people toting luggage. A sense of urgency gripped me as I shoved past hunters, oil men, and regular folks to get to Eicher. When I got closer I was surprised at just how relieved I was to see him.

"Am I ever glad to see you," I said with a grin.

"It's good to see you, too."

As we walked toward the baggage claim area Eicher added, "I'm damn glad to see you out of there. I gotta be honest: I've been plenty worried."

Seeing Eicher was tangible proof that I had survived and was safe. I wouldn't have to go to sleep at night memorizing the lies I had told that day. There would be no more watching my back and fighting the delusional demons that had me convinced Roy and I were going to be found out and silenced. There would be no more choking on my words and playing a part in a badly written play. I was finally free to be me. Someone I had missed dearly.

———

CHAPTER 24

Yellow Ribbons

ON SEPTEMBER 11, 1992, Roy and I arrived at Chicago's O'Hare Airport at four in the morning. As we trudged, dirty and exhausted, through the nearly empty terminal, I was barely conscious of the stares that we drew from the few other passengers.

The short-term parking fee for my Explorer was $225, and I groused at Roy as I paid it. "If I have to pay this out of my pocket, I'm sending you half the bill."

"Don't waste a good stamp," he grumbled.

We spoke very little during our three-hour drive to my house in Madison. After the last of Roy's gear was loaded into his car, our good-bye seemed anticlimactic after what we'd been through.

"Take it easy. I'll call you in a few days," I said.

"It's been real. Keep in touch."

After Roy pulled out my driveway, I checked the time. It was 7:30 A.M., and Lonnie had probably just dropped Megan off at school. Waiting until the end of the day to see her seemed liked an eternity. Since her classes had not yet begun, I jumped into the Audi and headed to her school. I walked inside as I've done a hundred times, but this time I felt unusually anxious. *Where is she?* I studied the faces of the first- and second-graders who lined the hallway, but I still didn't see her. Smiling, I asked one of her schoolmates, who I knew well, if she had seen Megan. The little girl stared at me and remained speech-less. It never dawned on me that my reeking hunting clothes and blood-covered boots might frighten her.

From behind me I heard a woman's voice. "Hey, Mrs. Schroeder!"

I froze. Even though I was out of the camp, my real name still sounded forbidden. My feet may have been in Madison, but part of my mind was still in Alaska. Swallowing against a dry throat, I turned to see Megan's teacher, Mrs. Hanson.

"Megan's in here," she said, pointing to a classroom.

I walked quickly into the room and saw Megan standing near the front. She was wearing her blue jumper with a butterfly embroidered on the shoulder over a white turtleneck shirt. Lonnie had curled her blond hair so it framed her beautiful little face that was sprinkled with reddish brown freckles. When Megan saw me she shrieked with delight and ran into my arms. We hugged and kissed each other on both cheeks. Her arms were so tight around my neck that it hurt—in a good way. I didn't want to ever let her go.

"Lubber," she said, referring to her earliest attempts to say "love you."

Tears blurred my vision. "I lubber, too."

"Did you have fun?" she asked.

I laughed. "It was fine, honey. I missed you like crazy, but I'm home now and we're going to ride bikes just as soon as you get home."

I felt like Megan and I were the only two people in world, but the magic moment was broken by a doe-eyed doctor's wife with the makeup and nails of a woman with plenty of leisure time. She stood looking at me critically. "Where on earth have you been?" she sniffed.

I stood up, but held on to Megan's hand. "I was in Alaska, working."

"Oh," she said with cocked eyebrows. "Can't you possibly find a better job?"

That evening Lonnie's tired face indicated that he'd been under stress during my absence. Although he didn't say much about it, I knew that he'd been getting up at six every morning to get Megan ready for school so that he could get to work on time. After working in the field all day, he'd done the grocery shopping, the cooking, taken Megan to ice skating lessons, piano lessons, and had bought her new clothes for school. On top of everything, he'd been burdened with the constant worry that something might go wrong at the camp. Since there had been essentially no communication between us, I was sure that at times he'd imagined the worst. I was touched by the yellow ribbons he had tied to the lamps in the living room.

That night after Megan was tucked into bed, Lonnie and I sat on the couch while I chattered nonstop about my hunts, the Spaniards I'd met, and the evidence Roy and I had collected against Bowman. I was running on pure adrenaline. As I talked, I sensed that Lonnie was simply relieved that I was home and was safe. It was impossible for him to feel the same gratification I did over the case. Finally, I shut up and cuddled in his arms, thanking him for being such a wonderful dad and husband. It was time to restore our family life.

———

CHAPTER 25

Operation Brooks Range

FOR THE NEXT THREE WEEKS I worked ten hours a day in my office on the case report for what was called "Operation Brooks Range." The notes I had taken during my undercover work proved invaluable. In its final form, my investigative report, which detailed every violation of federal wildlife laws and incriminating statements made by Bowman, his hunters, guides, pilots, and cooks, added up to more than fifty pages.

In late September 1992, Special Agent Eicher presented my report of the investigation to Steven Cooper, an Assistant United States Attorney (AUSA) serving in Fairbanks. AUSA Cooper, born in the eastern United States, moved to Alaska in 1958, when it was still a territory. He attended college at the University of Alaska and then went on to law school at Berkeley, California. Drawn by the adventurous spirit of the last frontier and vastness of the far northern wilderness, he returned to Alaska to work as a prosecutor. In his job, AUSA Cooper, a slender, athletically built man, was a hard-liner. He always said in a low gravely voice, "Lawbreakers don't get any sympathy from me."

Although AUSA Cooper had a caseload that included felony drug violations, contraband smuggling, and bank robbery, he particularly liked wildlife cases. He believed that due to the availability of wild game in Alaska and the isolation that hunters and guides found themselves in, the temptation to violate the law was doubly enticing. He understood the extremely difficult job the

U.S. Fish and Wildlife agents had in apprehending subjects in the wilderness and supported them wholeheartedly.

AUSA Cooper readily accepted the Brooks Range case for prosecution. Although he appreciated the quality of my documented observations, he was concerned that most of the case hinged on my observations. Roy had not been a witness to my conversations with suspects, and except for my sheep hunt, Roy's bear hunt, and the German's bear hunt, there were no federal witnesses on any of the other illegal hunts.

One day, Eicher called me to talk about Roy. "Where the hell was Roy when all this illegal stuff was going on? How come he's not in the reports?"

"To be honest, he claimed he was sick and stayed in the tent most of the time. I couldn't get him out for love or money. Only food."

"Was he really sick?"

"I think so. He was sweaty and shaky; it looked real to me."

"If I'd known Roy was going to pull that, I'd have gone with you," grunted Eicher.

"Hey, Roy pulled through in the end. We're in a bind now, but we'll figure a way out."

To substantiate the case further, AUSA Cooper asked that the violations I'd developed through conversations with hunters at the camp be further corroborated through official interviews with guides and hunters. Eicher and I were confident that with the help of some of the other fine special agents in the U.S. Fish and Wildlife Service, we'd be able to put together an airtight case.

Over the next two months Eicher and I developed a plan for when we would simultaneously make arrests, seize the three airplanes used in committing violations, serve search warrants, and conduct interviews. All of this had to be done on the same day at approximately the same time, or we'd lose the element of surprise. Also, since bad news travels fast, we'd run the risk of losing evidence that might be destroyed or defendants who might flee.

We agreed that November 20, 1992, would be the takedown date. We immediately contacted agents so that they could begin preparing affidavits for search warrants at Bowman's Arizona residence and his camp on the Ivishak River. Eicher notified other agents to prepare seizure warrants for the three planes used at the camp.

We then identified the guides to be interviewed: Jake, Danny, Wild Bill, and Ben Snyder, who was Pedro's second sheep guide. Eventually all of Bowman's guides would be interviewed, including those from past years. Lenny was also on the list.

Under The Speedy Trial Act, anyone arrested for a federal crime is entitled to a trial within thirty days. For this reason, federal prosecutors like to keep arrest lists short so that they don't become overloaded. Also, unlike what's seen on TV, agents have to articulate to a judge a good reason to arrest a suspect. Consequently, our arrest list only consisted of Bowman, Gordon, and Danny because they were considered flight risks. Because Bowman had an airplane and had much to lose, we argued that he might flee the country. Gordon was a Canadian citizen and would surely return to Canada, where the United States had no extradition agreement for wildlife crimes. In Danny's case, we'd learned that he lacked strong family ties and a steady job. We argued that due to his instability he was likely to leave Alaska for points unknown.

At this stage, our biggest challenge was to get Gordon back into the United States so that we could arrest him. I told Eicher that Roy and I had claimed that we belonged to an exclusive hunting club in Chicago.

"Maybe I could invite Gordon to speak at our club about his bear hunting guide service in Canada. I'll set the date for November 20. He'd jump at the chance, especially if 'the club' offered to pay his way."

Eicher liked the idea immediately and told me to give it a try.

The next day, I hooked up the tape recorder to my office phone and installed a fresh tape. The idea of luring Gordon into the United States only to have a set of silver bracelets slapped on his wrists tickled me. Gordon's killing days needed to end.

I dialed the phone number to Gordon's cabin, located somewhere in the woods of British Columbia. There was no guarantee that he'd be there, but since the hunting seasons were over and it was deep into the winter, I thought the chances were good that he'd be around. As usual, I took a piece of paper and wrote "JAYNE" on the top so I wouldn't slip up and use my own name. Then I took a deep breath as the phone rang.

"Hello," said a voice I recognized as Gordon's.

"Hey, Gordon, this is Jayne. Remember me?"

"No kidd'n'? How ya doin'?"

"Good, good. You got snow up there?"

"Yeah. I can't even see out no more."

"Can you dig out?"

"Maybe. Why?"

"Roy and I want you to come to Chicago. Some of the guys in our hunting club want to hear about your bear-hunting operation in Canada. Roy's been bragging up a storm about you. You might even be able to pick up some clients."

"Hey, I'd like that."

"The club would even pay your way."

"That sounds even better."

I smiled to myself. The hook was set. All I had to do was reel old Gordon in.

"Are you available during the next couple of months?"

"Anytime except December fifth."

"Why not December fifth?"

"I got to be in Anchorage to take my big-game hunting guide's test."

I scribbled on my pad: "Dec. 5th!!"

"Uh, no problem. How about late December?"

"That works for me. Your stuff get back to Chicago okay?"

"Oh yeah. Roy's bear is still at the taxidermist. That thing's a monster."

"Only the best when you hunt with me," said Gordon, laughing.

"No kidding. I'll call you mid-December to set everything up. Chicago's a great town and I'm sure Roy will take you to a couple of his favorite joints."

"I'm already looking forward to it. Tell him I said hi."

"I will. Hi to Rhoda."

I hung up the phone and clicked off the tape recorder at the same time. I removed the tape, labeled it as evidence, and immediately called Eicher.

"We need to change our takedown date to December fifth. That way we won't risk spooking Gordon about making a trip to Chicago. You never know what might go through his mind that might make him back out. But he'll definitely go to Anchorage to take his guide's test."

"This is great," said Eicher. "It's also better if he appears before a magistrate in Alaska rather than Illinois, since the crimes were committed here."

With that, the countdown began to December 5, 1992.

On the morning of December 5, I woke up early and made coffee. Sitting in the kitchen I thought about the day ahead. Except for the Europeans, everyone I had come into contact with at Bowman's camp would learn my true identity. I sure wouldn't be getting Christmas cards from them this year.

Dozens of U.S. Fish and Wildlife Service special agents would be serving search warrants, seizing airplanes and evidence, and would be making arrests based on what I had witnessed. All agents had been told to be on the lookout for any brochures with my photograph on them.

I worked from home that day, wanting the seclusion to field the phone calls from agents who would need my undivided attention. No one knew the case like I did, and there would be many questions. I would also work with Eicher tracking the progress of the takedown, which we would both report to our supervisors. A takedown like this one involved a high level of coordination and professionalism and I was thankful that today's was in the hands of several seasoned U.S. Fish and Wildlife Service special agents.

I made breakfast for Lonnie and Megan. Megan was excited because she was going to play the flute at school. Lonnie offered to drive Megan and just before leaving he kissed me good-bye and wished me luck with the day ahead.

The first phone call came in around 8:00 A.M. from Special Agent Bonnie Bell. She and Special Agent Mike Luekino had arrested Bowman without incident at his luxury home in Flagstaff, Arizona. They awakened him at approximately 6:30 A.M. and allowed him to change into a sweat suit. I had seen Bowman minutes after crawling out of bed myself and had no trouble imagining his hair looking like a tumbleweed, his eyes puffy, and, most of all, his curmudgeonly scowl—although it was probably worse than usual this particular morning. According to Agent Bell, Marianne stood speechless and bewildered in the doorway as Agent Luekino and an Arizona conservation officer transported Bowman out of his driveway to a federal lockup in Phoenix.

Agent Bell's search of the home turned up hundreds of photographs of Bowman's clients, including Roy and me, with big-game animals killed under his direction. She also seized videotapes, client records, and several hundred glossy colored brochures. The brochures were intended as advertisement for the 1993 hunting season and were ready to be sent out. My picture with the sheep I had killed on the Arctic National Wildlife Refuge appeared prominently on the top left.

When Bonnie told me about the brochures, I said, "Send them directly to me. Find the negatives, too. I don't want them out. Not anywhere."

"You bet," she replied.

I trusted Bonnie to do this. She understood that I needed to protect my identity in order to conduct future undercover operations.

Briefly, Bonnie described Bowman's home as a ranch-style house with an enormous glass window in the front to allow for an expansive view of the mountains. It was expensively decorated with original Southwest oil paintings and handmade Indian pots. She described a full-body mount of a trophy mule deer with a fully mounted cougar ambushing it from a thick tree branch. The cougar's teeth were embedded in the deer's neck. This rare sight in nature, captured in a twenty-thousand-dollar taxidermy scene, reminded me of a different kind of ambush the U.S. Fish and Wildlife Service had accomplished that morning.

At the federal lockup, Bowman was booked and incarcerated. He refused to give a statement and demanded an attorney. I was sure he was wondering how he'd been caught, and his imagination was driving him mad.

The next call came from Eicher, informing me that agents had just arrested Gordon in his motel room in Anchorage. Special Agent Wally Soroka and two conservation officers from the Alaska Department of Fish and Wildlife banged on his door just after 6:30 A.M. Gordon answered the door wearing a white T-shirt and blue jeans. He'd apparently been up for an hour studying for his big-game hunting guide's test. Before he had any time to react, Agent Soroka pushed through the door and announced that he had a federal warrant for his arrest. Gordon tried to force his way past the agents and escape. But Agent Soroka slammed the door shut, while the other two officers wrestled him to the floor. Soroka then moved in and cuffed his wrists behind his back. According to Eicher, Gordon let out a string of obscenities but gave up when he realized he was outnumbered and overpowered.

"He's in the federal lockup in Anchorage right now, but he's not talking," said Eicher. "When he hears what we have on him, he will."

"Great," I said. "What about Danny? Has he been picked up yet?"

"They can't find him. Apparently he went to Iowa to visit a brother."

"A brother in Iowa?"

"Did he ever talk to you about this?"

"Never."

"I've already put a call in to agent Walt Kocal in Des Moines. Walt will find Danny; he's pure bird dog."

Bowman's and Billy Howe's planes were seized at the Anchorage airport and Jack Watson's plane had been picked up in Idaho. Watson gave the agents a statement saying that if there was anything illegal going on in Bowman's camp, he didn't know about it. I told Eicher we'd just have to remind him of the German's bear hunt.

Around midday, Special Agent Mark Webb from Fairbanks, along with a ranger with the Bureau of Land Management and two Alaskan wildlife conservation officers, drove pickup trucks pulling snowmobiles to a cabin on Gabriel's Lake some thirty miles north of Bowman's camp. Agent Webb had a search warrant for hunting records and photographs believed to have been left there. He would also put a seizure tag on the ATV that Lenny used to transport illegal animals and to haul Wilhelm out to the site where he killed his illegal moose. The actual seizure would take place during the spring or summer.

The agents set out on their trip in brutal weather. The temperature was minus-forty degrees and there was no daylight. Less than an hour into the trip the wind started to blow and one of the snowmobiles ground to a halt from an engine too cold to run. Two of the men then shared one until it, too, broke down. The men partnered up on the remaining snowmobiles, which were all beginning to run sluggishly. Fearing that they'd be left without transportation on the bitterly cold tundra, Webb had no choice but to abandon serving the warrant. The lives and safety of the other officers were in his hands and clearly whatever evidence was at the Bowman camp was not worth their lives.

By the time the group arrived back at the parking lot, they were near hypothermia. They climbed into their trucks and sat with the heaters running for nearly an hour before they were warm enough to drive down the road. Fortunately no one suffered serious injuries, except for one officer who was treated at the hospital for frostbitten corneas.

Later in the day Special Agent Jim Klett from Wyoming called. He had just interviewed Ben Snyder, who was Pedro's guide on his second sheep hunt. Klett, one of the best interviewers in the Service, had procured a sworn statement from Snyder in which he insisted that Pedro had hunted his sheep the day after he had flown with Watson. My suspicion that Pedro's sheep was illegal wasn't enough, so unless we developed more evidentiary information, Pedro was home free with his sheep.

Agent Dick Dickenson interviewed Jake at his home in Wisconsin. Jake provided a detailed and truthful statement about everything that occurred in my presence, but he didn't provide additional information about other violations. His statement was a mere reiteration of what we already knew. I felt that Jake knew more, but he wasn't talking. All we had against him was that he helped Danny with my sheep hunt on the refuge, although it was doubtful that he'd be charged with this because the case was getting too big.

By the end of the day, U.S. Fish and Wildlife special agents had arrested Bowman and Gordon, seized three airplanes, eleven illegal trophy animals, a dozen crates of financial and business records, and had interviewed thirteen guides and hunters. The case had been cracked wide open, exposing everything that had once been a closely held secret.

Two days later, Special Agent Walt Kocal located Danny's brother who lived just south of Des Moines, Iowa. Kocal went to his house and learned that Danny was traveling in a motor home with his father and brother, headed toward Minnesota. Kocal contacted Deputy U.S. Marshal Jon Anderson who put out a BOLO (be on the lookout) notice for the motor home. The next day a police officer radioed Kocal; he'd spotted the vehicle near Ankeny, Iowa, headed southbound on I-35 just north of Des Moines. Since Kocal had an arrest warrant, he asked the Ankeny police officer to follow the vehicle until he and Deputy Anderson could get there.

Agent Kocal and Deputy Anderson caught up with the motor home and the Ankeny police cruiser, and with lights flashing and sirens blaring the cruiser signaled it to the side of the road for a felony stop. After the stop, Kocal and Anderson quickly approached the driver, flashed their credentials, and ordered Danny, his father, and his brother out of the motor home. Kocal informed Danny that he was under arrest for violating federal wildlife laws in Alaska. Stunned, Danny glanced at a nearby open field as if he was going to make a run for it. Deputy Anderson grabbed him and forced him onto the pavement and stretched him out in a prone position while Agent Kocal snapped a pair of handcuffs on him. Meanwhile, the squirming suspect screamed his undying innocence.

Agent Kocal and Deputy Anderson transported Danny to a federal lockup in Des Moines, where Danny was arraigned before a federal magistrate and later released to his brother on a twenty-five-thousand-dollar bond. After the arrest, Deputy Anderson, who was more accustomed to arresting murderers and bank robbers, commented on the deep satisfaction he felt arresting a wildlife poacher.

* * *

Over the next few weeks, Eicher and I reviewed the reports from the interviews conducted with hunters who had hunted in Bowman's camp over the past few years. Several of the interviews produced information that later resulted in the confiscation of several more illegal animals. One was a huge moose that Eric Shepard, a taxidermist in northern Wisconsin, had shot after Bowman spotted the animal from the air. Shepard had bragged to another hunter at the camp that he'd shot his moose five minutes after jumping out of Bowman's plane.

I had a photograph of Eric and his moose that had been found during the search of Bowman's house. On a cold day in February when the ground was still packed with snow, a conservation officer and I walked into Shepard's taxidermy studio that, except for one set of moose antlers, was full of deer heads and fish mounts.

Shepard came out of a back room where he'd been working on a mount. He was a thin, bearded man, wearing blue jeans with a denim shirt and a rubber bib apron. After the conservation officer and I identified ourselves, I asked him about his moose hunt in Alaska during the fall of 1992.

Shepard, who was twenty-eight years old, looked at the moose antlers on the wall and then broke his glance to the floor. "There wasn't much to it. I had to wait in the main camp for a few days until Bowman could take me out. We stayed one night in a spike camp so we wouldn't be flyin' and huntin' the same day. The next morning I got up and hunted for a few hours and got this big one."

I showed Shepard a photograph of himself with the moose shortly after he'd killed it.

"Where did you get this picture?" he asked.

"We seized it from Bowman." Shepard's eyebrows twitched when I revealed that a hunter told an agent that Bowman spotted this animal from the air, landed, and that Shepard had jumped out and shot it. "Apparently you bragged about your hunt to the wrong guy."

I went on to explain that Bowman had been arrested and his operation had been shut down. I pointed to the moose antlers on the wall and said it had been identified as one of the illegal animals taken in Bowman's camp.

"It's over," I said.

"Will I lose the antlers?"

"Yes, they're illegal."

"Shit!" he said, slamming his fist on the counter. "This was a dream hunt that cost me five thousand dollars."

"Then why did you blow it?"

"Bowman was busy taking his big-shot European hunters out and made me wait. By the time he got to me I didn't have time to spend all day huntin' and had to get a moose as quick as I could."

I looked at him squarely in the eyes. "You're making excuses. I think you knew that Bowman's hunts were guaranteed—and knew exactly why they were guaranteed."

Eric leaned against the counter and dropped his head. "I'd heard some stuff. But I didn't know for sure."

I didn't tell Eric this, but from the interviews we'd conducted, many of the hunters knew exactly how the hunts would be conducted. I surmised that Eric thought he'd be safe with Bowman, where the chances of being caught were slim to none.

I pulled out a blank U.S. Fish and Wildlife Service statement form and wrote Shepard's full confession as he dictated it to me. He was too upset to sit down and write anything on his own.

As the conservation officer and I carried away Shepard's trophy moose antlers, I looked back at him. The look on his face told me that this was one of the worst days of his life.

A few days later special agents seized the black timber wolf from Thomas Sage, a pharmacist in Hudson, Wisconsin, who had shot it after Bowman spotted it with his plane. This was the same one Danny Bridges ran down on a snowmobile to finish off. The animal had been mounted and was still at the taxidermist drying before going on display with dozens of other wildlife mounts at the pharmacist's drug store.

On the same day, Special Agents Mark Johnson and Scott Heard seized the mounted grizzly bear on display at The Bear's Den that I'd seen on my first visit there. Gordon admitted to Eicher that he was guiding the hunt when Bowman used his plane to herd the bear to Moose's father for the kill on a fifteen-minute hunt. Moose was along on this hunt as well. As the agents left the bar with the bear, they took the GRIZZLY BEAR INSIDE sign with them.

Finally, Eicher, along with several other agents, went to McMurphy's Taxidermy in Anchorage and seized all of the Spaniards' trophies, with the exception of two bears that were still at a tannery in Montana. Special Agent Branzell would seize these later.

After his visit to McMurphy's, Eicher called me with some surprising news. "When we got to the taxidermist, we found Wilhelm's trophies there, too."

"You're kidding."

"Nope. McMurphy said that Bowman called him from the camp and said that he'd found out that European taxidermists don't have big enough molds to mount grizzlies, so he wanted the German's bear mounted in the U.S. There was some sort of confusion at the airport and McMurphy ended up picking up all of Wilhelm's trophies before the old fart took off for Germany."

"So we have everything?"

"You bet."

I smiled as I remembered seeing Wilhelm's trophies at the Anchorage airport and how desperate I had been to get my hands on them. They were ours, and we now had something to hold over Mr. Leisure Hunter.

"Where did Bowman get this ridiculous idea about European taxidermists?" asked Eicher.

"I told him," I admitted, barely able to contain my laughter.

"Why'd you do that?"

"It was baloney I fed him to keep the Spaniards' trophies within U.S. jurisdiction. It was all I could think of."

The evidence against Bowman and his cronies was piling up and I spent Christmas of 1992 confident that things would continue to go well. But in early February 1993, Eicher called. Bowman still refused to cooperate and many of the crimes alleged in my investigation remained uncorroborated. In spite of everything I'd done, AUSA Cooper was not confident that he had enough evidence to file the number of charges needed to put Bowman in jail or shut him down. I couldn't believe my ears.

———

CHAPTER 26

Wounded

"THIS CAN'T BE," I wailed into the phone.

"Right now, it don't look good. Right now, we've only got enough evidence to file charges against Bowman for the violations he committed on Roy's bear hunt, the German's bear hunt, and your sheep hunt."

"I don't understand. Pedro and El Doctor told me all about their illegal bear hunts and that old German coot told me about his illegal sheep. Rhoda spilled the beans on the German's so-called moose hunt. And don't forget about Junior's illegal caribou. It's all in my report."

"It's all good stuff, but it's still stuff they *told* you—you weren't there. You can't testify as an eyewitness and the German and Spaniards aren't around to confess."

"That's true, and as noncitizens we can't force them to come to the U.S. and testify."

"Sworn statements from them would sure help this case."

I groaned. Getting statements from the German and the Spaniards were out of the question. Although Gordon's confessions of shooting Wilhelm's bear and sheep and his role in Pedro's and El Doctor's hunts were valuable, they pitted him against Bowman's denials. Statements from the Europeans would definitely tip the scales in favor of the prosecution.

"Look, Tim, let's be honest, those guys won't give us truthful statements. When they find out who I really am, they'll be fighting mad and any notions of cooperation will go right out the window."

"I know. But we really need those statements."

I felt sick. This was exactly what Bowman had counted on. By catering to European clients, he knew if he ever got caught a case against him, or them, would be nearly impossible to make.

Eicher and I discussed sending out formal requests called Letters of Rogatory in which Wilhelm and the Spaniards would be interviewed by law enforcement in their own countries. We'd write the questions and the police would fill in the answers. This sort of thing worked best for interviewing cooperating witnesses, not violators like these. They'd lie like crazy and the police wouldn't know the difference.

The case against Bowman seemed in serious jeopardy and, as it stood, he could be convicted of federal wildlife crimes, pay a fine, and still walk free. It was even possible that he could continue his guiding operation in the Brooks Range. I couldn't let this happen. Bowman needed to go to jail for what he'd done. The image of the bloodied ram lying dead on the shale and the bear and wolves running for their lives under the roar of a plane ran through my numbed mind. Somehow, there had to be justice for the wildlife that had died to line the pockets of the greedy men I had come to know.

As Eicher and I continued to discuss the case, I glanced out my office window at the grove of oak trees that graced the property. I spotted a badger persistently digging near the roots of the trees. The badger—a varmint to some—in Indian lore represents aggressiveness, single-mindedness, and passion. Suddenly, the badger's spirit had new meaning to me.

"Tim, I'm going after them," I blurted out.

"You can't do—"

"They can't lie to *me*. I know exactly what they did—and they know it. I'll get the biggest, meanest cops they've got in Germany and Spain and go banging on their doors. Somehow, I'll make those killers confess to everything."

"You're talking a real long shot."

"I've taken long shots before. And hit."

"And if you miss this one?"

"We won't be worse off than we are now."

"Shit, we'll never be worse off than we are now. I gotta admit I don't think it'll work, but I'll back you up. Porter's going to be a real hard sell."

"You do your job, and I'll do mine."

"Sometimes I think you're nothing but a crazy little bulldog."

Over the next several weeks Eicher made several visits to Porter's Anchorage office trying to convince him that sending me to Europe was critical to the successful prosecution of Operation Brooks Range. Since the case was in Porter's district, the funds for the trip would have to come out of his budget. Eicher never completely leveled with Porter about the extreme difficulty of getting Wilhelm and the Spaniards to confess and led Porter to believe that the chances were actually good that they'd cooperate.

One day Porter called me to discuss an alternative. "Why don't you call these guys and interview them over the phone?"

How could a supervisor at his level suggest something so ineffective? I held the phone to one ear and rested my forehead in my other hand as I slowly explained Interview Techniques 101.

"Well, for one thing, a face-to-face contact is more effective when you're trying for a confession. You can apply more pressure."

"I just don't see why you can't just call 'em. It'd be a lot cheaper."

"They won't tell me a thing over the phone. I've got to surprise them, confront them with the fact that they've been caught, and then convince them that it is in their best interests to cooperate."

"I see. You gonna do this by yourself? I'm not sending anyone with you."

"You don't have to send anyone with me. I plan on recruiting some local law enforcement help, just like I do here."

"Like who?"

"The Guardia Civil—that's the Spanish National Police. In Germany it's called the ZKA."

"And you think they'll help you?"

"No question about it," I said with my eyes squeezed tightly shut. *Please buy this.*

"Can you *guarantee* that these guys will confess?"

"They'll confess. Especially with the local police breathing down their necks." *Just let me go. I can make this happen.*

"It doesn't seem to me like there's much of a chance that this will work."

"It'll work. The police mean business over there. Together we'll get this done."

I was stretching my argument considerably, but Porter had never worked an international investigation and was having trouble with a counterargument. There was a long silence on the phone, which meant Porter was thinking.

"I got a call from the U.S. Attorney's office about this. They want us to at least try for these statements, so I guess they can take the blame if everything goes to hell. I don't like it though."

I leaned back in my chair, rubbed the muscles at the back of my neck, and took a deep breath. Porter was going to send me to Europe.

"Call Washington," said Porter, "and make your travel arrangements, but don't expect any great sympathy from me if this thing collapses on you. Understand?"

"Yes, sir. Everything will be fine."

After I hung up the phone I realized that I had dug myself into a huge hole. The truth was I had no idea if my grand plan would work. All I could do was take one step at a time and feel my way through this uncharted territory.

I called a desk agent in the Washington, D.C., office who filed the required paperwork with the Spanish and German governments through their embassies in Washington. All proposed official travel had to be submitted in writing, stating its purpose and duration. Approval usually came within two weeks.

The Spanish government cleared my travel within days, but the German government held back. The desk agent in charge of my travel was confident that the German government would clear my travel within a few days and advised me to fly to Spain and begin my work there.

Many of my agent colleagues were surprised that management would send me to Europe alone to work such a difficult case. Steve Hamilton, a colleague from Texas, put it succinctly, "We don't let agents go to Muskogee, Oklahoma, alone. Maybe they don't want you to come back."

BOOK III

CHAPTER 27

A Bullfight

ON THE COLD BUT SUNNY MORNING OF MARCH 16, 1993, I strode onto the glassy marble floor in the huge lobby of the American Embassy in Madrid, Spain, and confidently flashed my badge to a young Marine. Even though I'd only been on foreign soil for less than twenty-four hours, it felt good to see another American.

"State your business," he commanded with no emotion.

"I have a nine o'clock appointment with Mr. Alfonso Ruiz."

"Take the elevator to the second floor, Room 204. Have a good day."

I was dressed neatly in a navy blue skirt and gray blazer, with a blue striped blouse. I looked good and my confidence was sky high.

I poked my head into Mr. Ruiz's office only to find that he hadn't arrived yet. I went down the hall and spoke with Scott Rearson, a thirty-something regional security officer who allowed me to wait in the reception area of his office.

When I explained to Rearson that my investigation involved wildlife he stopped what he was doing and said, "Wildlife crimes aren't a high priority matter with this embassy. So don't expect much help. Mr. Ruiz can't give you much of his time."

My confidence took a sharp jab, but I recovered quickly. "All I want is a reference for the Guardia. Can Mr. Ruiz give me that?"

"Maybe."

An hour ticked by and Mr. Ruiz still had not reported to work. Rearson offered no explanation for Ruiz's tardiness. He went about his busy day making phone calls and running to other offices while I sat thumbing through magazines and looking nervously out the window down onto the busy Madrid streets. Everyone seemed to know where they were going, except me.

Every twenty minutes or so, I'd walk down the hall and exchange casual greetings with other office workers. One in particular was Gregorio Trampal, a heavy-set man who I estimated to be in his mid-thirties. He was as neat as a pin with short black hair and pale skin, and was dressed in a well-worn dark suit, white shirt, and navy blue tie. He sat behind a fastidiously neat desk, shuffling papers from one side to the other, sometimes initialing one in its corner. He had an especially bright face and always smiled when I walked by.

At one point I told him I was waiting for Mr. Ruiz, at which he nodded in acknowledgment as if to say I wasn't the first person to pace these halls for the same reason. By 11:30 A.M., it was obvious that Mr. Ruiz had stood me up. I was confused. This was an American Embassy. Why was I being ignored? With my head pounding and my stomach growling I decided to get something to eat.

At the elevator I met two other American federal agents. One was from U.S. Customs, and the other from the U.S. Drug Enforcement Administration. Things were looking up. Maybe they'd tell me something about Mr. Ruiz and the inner politics of the embassy. Better yet, maybe they'd invite me to lunch.

"What agency are you with?" asked the Customs agent.

"U.S. Fish and Wildlife Service."

"Ha! Are you here on a butterfly investigation or something?"

"Oh no," said the DEA agent, looking down at his loafers, "she's gonna take my alligator boots."

"Are you with the wildlife or nightlife department?" howled Mr. Customs.

"Exactly how wild are you?" questioned Mr. DEA.

The elevator door opened and we all got on. I stood speechless and stunned at the verbal bashing from two agents I had assumed would offer me camaraderie in a foreign country.

As we stepped out of the elevator, I struck back. "It scares me to think that you two are actually law enforcement officers."

But my words had no impact. The good ol' boys had each other as they whirled out the revolving glass doors cracking more wildlife jokes.

"Sexist, arrogant, jerks," I sputtered. "To hell with them."

I went out onto the chilly street and sought out a small restaurant that was warm with the smell of olive oil. In Spain, the midday meal wasn't eaten until 2:00 P.M., so by Spanish custom I was too early for lunch, too late for breakfast. Nearly alone in the restaurant, I ordered huevos rancheros, which was a childhood favorite. I'd ordered it dozens of times when I lived in Madrid with my parents and looked to it now to comfort me during my rising despair.

While savoring my food, my resolve came back and I decided that I couldn't wait on Ruiz. I had to move on. I paid my bill and went back to the embassy and ran into Scott Rearson just as he was leaving his office.

"Look, it's obvious that Mr. Ruiz isn't coming in. Is there anyone else I can meet with today?"

Rearson gave me an impatient look. "You can't come over here and expect us to hold your hand. Go about your business however you want. Just don't get into trouble."

"Thanks," I said flatly as Rearson brushed by me. *I should have gone to the Russian Embassy.*

I turned and walked directly into Gregorio's office. "I need a favor," I said.

He set his papers down and smiled.

Twenty minutes later, Gregorio and I walked up the steps of a nondescript gray five-story building that bore the sword, sheath, and crown emblem of La Guardia Civil. On the way, I briefed Gregorio on the case and he was eager to be a part of something other than his daily routine.

On the first floor we entered a large room with twenty or so young male officers in olive green short-sleeved uniform shirts, as they sat at gray metal desks lined up in rows. These men didn't look at all like the elaborately uniformed Guardia Civil officers I had seen on the streets armed with assault rifles. I surmised that they were either clerks or cadets-in-training. I smiled to myself as I caught some of them trying to steal inconspicuous glances at Gregorio and the American woman who had just walked in.

The office was covered in peeling beige paint. There were a few pictures of officials hanging on the walls, nothing more. I couldn't tell if the lack of decoration was by design or due to severe austerity. Either way, it seemed like a dispiriting office atmosphere.

I knew something about La Guardia Civil from my years in Spain. They were known for their courage and loyalty, which was exemplified in the trademark hats worn during ceremonies. Rounded in the front, the back was flat symbolizing the wall that many died against during the Spanish Civil War. Generalismo Francisco Franco's army won the war, securing Franco's iron grip over Spain for more than thirty years. During those times, officers of La Guardia Civil were his henchmen and were greatly feared.

But these were gentler times.

Even though Gregorio had called ahead asking for an appointment with some of the *comandantes*, our arrival caused a minor stir. Chairs were being shoved into a separate office, while officers wearing uniforms scurried inside carrying pads of paper.

Finally, Colonel Manuel Labandira, who was dressed in an olive-green military-style uniform loaded with medals, came out of the room, shook Gregorio's hand, and then mine. He led us into the room and introduced us to three other officials who I presumed were high ranking. La Guardia Civil was a paramilitary organization where protocol was very important. For this reason I kept quiet while Gregorio explained why we were there. Since he was a fellow countryman, he had far more clout than I did.

Gregorio's short presentation explained that three Spanish citizens had violated U.S. wildlife laws while hunting in Alaska. As if on cue I brought out the photographs of Pedro with his sheep and grizzly bear, El Doctor with his moose and grizzly bear, and Junior's two caribou. The officers passed the pictures around, chattering enthusiastically, appearing fascinated with the case. Relief flowed through me like a cool breeze. Finally, I was in the right place.

Gregorio asked if the Guardia could locate the three hunters who were believed to be living in Barcelona.

Two of the officers said, *"No hay problema,"* while the others nodded in agreement. A restaurateur and medical doctor would be easy to locate.

Carefully choosing my words, I said I wanted to interview the three hunters for the purpose of getting sworn statements for a federal prosecutor.

Once again, my small audience nodded their heads.

I turned to Colonel Labandira. "Would it be possible for a member of La Guardia Civil to accompany me on the interviews? I feel the results of my interviews would be more successful if an official from your agency was present."

The room turned oddly quiet. Gregorio shifted in his chair, while Colonel Labandira folded his arms across his chest. I worried I had said something wrong, maybe even offensive. No one spoke a word for a minute until Colonel Labandira finally broke the silence.

"*Especial agente* Lucinda, we are very interested in your investigation and would like very much to help you, but it would be detrimental to your case if we were present during your inquisitions. You see, the Spanish people still fear La Guardia from the old days. If one of our officers was present during any questioning, you wouldn't get the answers you need and your investigation would fail."

I hardly knew how to respond. I had counted on La Guardia's help. I looked into the Colonel's eyes for a better answer, but nothing came.

Another one of the officers talked about a murder case in which he received no cooperation because he was with La Guardia, but when he brought in a local police officer, that officer was able to break the case. I heard about every other word. My head spun as I envisioned my grand plan swirling down the drain.

Gregorio kept the conversation going on my behalf, reiterating the crimes committed by the Spanish hunters. Heads continued to nod in agreement, concerned faces turned to one another and spoke of the serious nature of the situation, while tiny beads of sweat covered me like a veil.

My work in Spain seemed doomed on the first day.

That night in my hotel room I called Eicher in Fairbanks.

"Hey, how's it going on the continent?"

"Not good, Tim. La Guardia can't help me with the interviews. It's a political thing, too long to explain. All I can say is that this thing is going to hell in a handbasket."

Eicher took a deep breath. "Well, we knew it was a long shot. Don't be too hard on yourself. Are you going to head on to Germany?"

"I'll call Berlin in the morning and find out if my travel has been cleared. I called Washington this afternoon but they hadn't heard anything yet."

"They're always the last to know."

"That's what I figured."

"I hate to tell you this, but you're running out of time. Bowman's court date was moved up and he's to appear before Judge Stewart in four days. You need to get as much as you can or he'll plead not guilty and we'll be in for a hell of a fight and might lose."

"Four days!"

"Yep. This just happened today. The defense probably knows what you're up to. Maybe you should head on to Germany and forget the Spaniards. The idea is to get as much as you can."

By now, my nerves were in shambles. How much could I possibly get done in four days?

"I gotta think about this, Tim. I'll call you tomorrow. You just turned an already bad day into pure crap."

The next morning I woke up after a restless night. I ordered a continental breakfast, which was brought to my room. Sipping strong coffee I called the U.S. Embassy in Berlin and spoke with a rather curt-sounding regional security officer. He informed me that my travel to Germany had not yet been cleared. "Call back tomorrow," he said.

I plopped down on the spongy hotel bed with its ornate, crimson bedspread and stared at my image in a mirror propped on a mahogany dresser. My hair hung lifeless around my bloodshot eyes. Anxiety had brought on a hollow thudding in my chest. Somehow I had to get these confessions and I had to get them damn quick. My hunt for the Spanish hunters wasn't over. Taking a deep breath, I took stock of my situation.

La Guardia Civil had shut me down, the RSO wasn't going to give me the time of day, and Mr. Ruiz was obviously out. That left Gregorio—my only ally in Spain. I took a shower and tried to rehabilitate my appearance by spending more time on my hair and makeup.

Outside the Hotel Occidental Miguel Ángel on the busy Paseo del la Castellana, I waited for a cab. It was only 10:00 A.M., and the smell of diesel was already thick in the air. Women in high heels and miniskirts perched precariously on the back of motor scooters, clinging to their men as they sped past me. For a moment I took in the fabulous Iberian architecture of the tall and ornate buildings around me. There was so much to see here, dating back to pre-Roman history. But I had business to do and sightseeing wasn't even a consideration. After a few minutes a cab pulled over to pick me up.

"La embajda Americana, Calle de Seranno, por favor."

"Si, señorita."

At the American Embassy the same Marine commanded, "State your business."

"Gregorio Trampal."

He waved me through.

I found Gregorio in the same position behind his desk, shuffling papers. He smiled when he saw me. *This guy likes me,* I thought.

"Mr. Ruiz is here today. Would you like to see him?"

Since I didn't know how to say "hell no" in Spanish, I just handed Gregorio a piece of paper with Caza Todo, Jose Abascal, 55, written on it.

"Can you take me there?"

"Caza Todo is a big-game booking agency. Why do you want to go there?"

"I know the guy who runs it. His name is Luís. He can get me in contact with the Barcelona hunters."

Gregorio laughed as he tossed the piece of paper across the desk. "*Señorita* Lucinda, you are so naive. This guy isn't going to tell you anything. Why should he?"

"Do you have a car?"

"The embassy does, yes."

"Then let's go. I just want company. You don't have to say anything, and if he won't talk, we'll come right back."

He picked up the paper again. As his eyes scanned the address a stern expression crept across his face.

"Is it far?" I asked.

"No, not at all."

"Then what's wrong?"

Gregorio shook his head. "This man Luís, it's not a good idea to talk to him."

I realized that Gregorio didn't want to get into a confrontational situation. I had to downplay my intentions. "Listen, I just want to visit with the guy. After all, I already know him."

"You do?"

"Sure, I talked with him on the phone when I was at the camp in Alaska. We became quite friendly."

"So all you want is to say hello?"

"Yes. Can we go?"

Gregorio seemed hesitant to leave the security of his desk, but eventually he retrieved a set of car keys from his desk drawer, got up, and lifted his suit jacket off a coat rack. As we walked down the hall he muttered something about Americans being impossible to understand.

Gregorio and I got into a white, four-door Chevy and left the embassy parking lot, driving south on Calle de Serrano. Gregorio spun around La Plaza de Independencia onto Calle de Alcalá and around the spectacular Fountain de la Cibeles — an eighteenth-century sculpted fountain depicting Cybele, the Roman Mother Earth goddess who ruled over wild beasts. She was sitting in her chariot drawn by a pair of lions, and I knew her well. When I was thirteen, I'd circled her many times in a taxi while going downtown. The feelings of exhilaration and independence touched me again as I remembered navigating not only the roads of Madrid, but also the untried trails of my adolescence. The goddess Cybele was still there and I had come back to Spain to champion her cause.

The traffic was fast and furious and I hoped that Gregorio had enough eyes in his head to keep up with it. An instant later he dumped the car off into the traffic on Calle de Marqués de Cubas, and then made several more turns onto very narrow streets. Occasionally he'd steer the car sharply onto the sidewalk on one side to avoid an oncoming car. An old woman dressed in black jumped inside her doorway to keep from getting hit by us. These streets had been in place long before the automobile had been around.

After stopping twice to look at a map, we ended up outside a centuries-old town house with a set of huge wooden doors decorated with brass medallions and heavy brass rings for handles. The doors appeared to be locked tight. Oddly, there were no signs anywhere to identify the address as Caza Todo.

"Is this it?" I asked.

"I'm not sure. This is the address you gave me. Are you sure it's right?"

It had never occurred to me that I might have a bad address, or that Caza Todo might have moved, or that Caza Todo never even existed. My nerves prickled. I didn't have time for dead leads. This was day one of the three days I had to find the Spaniards.

"Would you please go knock on the door and see if someone answers?"

"Me?"

"It would look better."

Gregorio eased out of the car and slowly ascended the steps to the town house and found a doorbell. A few seconds later the door creaked opened and a dark-haired man appeared and spoke to Gregorio. Gregorio then turned and waved his arm for me to come in.

When I arrived at the door, Gregorio muttered that this was the right place. The man at the door, who was neatly dressed in a white shirt and dark slacks, led us into a room with a burgundy tapestry-style carpet and a dark, Mediterranean-style wooden table with eight leather chairs. Our greeter offered us seats at the table under a gaudy chandelier with electric candles.

There were no desks, no computers, no phones, no office people walking back and forth. One fax machine on a small table made me wonder if this was a front for a Mafia-like operation. Only two African travel posters, with elephants and lions, hinted of any connection with a travel agency for big-game hunters.

Gregorio nervously adjusted his suit jacket, and cranked his neck as if to loosen it. "We're here to speak to Luís. Is he here?"

"He's on the phone in the other room. I'll tell him you're here. You said you're from the American Embassy?"

"Ahem, yes, that's right," said Gregorio his voice cracking.

I smiled and set my purse in my lap. My weapon would have made me feel more secure in this place, but I wasn't allowed to bring it into the country.

Our greeter retreated to a back room and a few minutes later came back with a decidedly slender man in his early thirties wearing skin-tight pants, a white shirt, and a vest.

"I'm pleased to present Mr. Luís Arroz."

Both Gregorio and I stood, shook Luís's hand, and quickly rattled off our names. Our greeter retreated and Luís settled into a seat across the table from us looking very much in charge. His ink-black hair was slicked back away from his forehead, highlighting a prominent nose in an angular face. His thin lips seem pursed and curled at the same time, and although he looked a little odd, his confident demeanor made him appear better looking than he really was.

"What brings visitors from the American Embassy? Potential clients, I hope."

"Past clients," I said. "Do you know Pedro Montros, El Doctor Casio, and his son, Junior?"

Luís's eyes widened to hear these names roll off my tongue so easily.

"Of course I do. But the question is, how do you know them?" he asked, glancing nervously at Gregorio, then at me.

I stood up and walked around the table with my badge and credentials open and showed them to Luís. "I'm an investigator with the U.S. wildlife department. It seems your clients violated the law while they were hunting in Alaska."

Luís's face went rigid. "Impossible. My clients are law-abiding citizens."

I took a seat next to Luís and turned the chair to face him. I didn't want any barriers between us. I wanted to watch every twitch in his face as I introduced him to a new reality.

"Actually, your clients are poachers. Pedro and El Doctor both killed grizzly bears illegally, and Junior gunned down an illegal caribou. They're in a lot of trouble. So much trouble that the United States government has sent me all the way to Spain to talk to them."

"Ha! You've wasted your time coming here. You can't touch them. Besides, you don't have anything on them. You're all talk."

I leaned forward and locked eyes with him. "Don't you recognize my voice?"

Luís thought for a minute. "No, should I?"

"Yes. I'm Jayne. The translator at Bob Bowman's camp. Remember?"

Luís turned as white as his shirt. He stood up and marched across the room, his boots pounding through the thick carpet. He turned abruptly and stood like a statue, with his hands parked on his hips, and his eyes piercing as he sized up his new adversary.

Dealing with Luís was going to be a dogfight. No, a bullfight. It was Hemingway who had said that a bullfight was a tragedy in three acts, where every detail was determined in advance and the outcome was inevitable. I already had Luís in the throes of the first stage. He was mad, tormented—ready to charge. Now I had to bring out the picadillos and inflict some pain.

"Your clients confided in me every detail of their crimes. Consequently, the United States government has indicted them for felony violations."

"I don't believe you," scoffed Luís. He then moved to the window and stared outside. He was trying to avoid me, but I could tell his chest was heaving. I was getting to him.

"But you should," I said calmly. "The United States wouldn't send me to Spain unless it was important."

"My clients only did what they were told; they did nothing wrong on their own."

"Well, if that's true there is a way to prevent your clients from facing criminal charges in the United States."

Luís turned. Clearly, he was interested. "How is that?"

"Mr. Bowman is the primary target of the investigation. The government wants to put him in prison. If your clients will give me statements confessing their crimes, while implicating Bowman, then I could possibly convince the federal prosecutor to leave them alone."

"Why are you coming to me for this?"

"Because you know where your clients are and can arrange for a meeting. I want a meeting with them. Tomorrow."

The picadillos were in.

Suddenly Luís exploded. "This is ridiculous! Outrageous! You can't expect me to do that. I won't!"

I glanced at Gregorio, who had slid down in his chair in a vain attempt to disappear. I couldn't expect any backup or support from him. In fact, if things got nasty, it would be my job to protect him.

I had trained myself to stay calm in the face of an irate subject, even though my heart pounded. The stakes were high and I had to stay in control. "I'm very surprised at your reaction, Luís. I thought you'd want to help your clients out. You're the one who booked them with a flagrant violator. You bear some responsibility here."

"Bullshit!" he spat.

"All you have to do is call Pedro and tell him to have El Doctor and his son meet me in Barcelona for an hour or so. It won't take long. They give me the statements, and I'll ensure that the charges are dropped. You understand, Luís, that with outstanding felony charges your clients will be arrested if they ever try to enter the United States. That means no more hunting anywhere in the United States."

I detected a sickening shade of green in Luís's face. He slid into another chair that was positioned against a wall—still keeping as far away from me as possible.

"You seem to be a woman with a lot of power," he muttered.

"I am."

As the room grew hotter and the air stuffier, Gregorio asked for water and removed his jacket. For the moment, he seemed content to sit back and watch the fight, which was good because my strategy was to wear Luís down and I didn't want to be interrupted by Gregorio.

Finally, Luís said abruptly, "You can leave now."

From the corner of my eye, I caught Gregorio easing out of his chair. I held my palm toward Gregorio, signaling him to hold off. It was time for stage three of the bullfight—the time when the matador pulls the sword and aims for the triangular shaped area between the shoulder blades that leads directly to the bull's heart. In this case, Luís's pocketbook.

"Luís," I said. "Is it true that you've booked your clients for hunts all over the world?"

"Yes, they are my best clients."

"Do you know that I still have your clients' trophies?"

"No, I wasn't fully aware of that."

"Well, I do."

"What are your intentions?" he asked cautiously.

"To keep the trophies. Unless of course, you arrange for a meeting and convince your clients to give me the statements I want for my case."

"Just because you come from a big country you think you can do this?"

"I assure you I can."

"What American law allows such a thing?"

"The law of possession. I have the trophies and you don't."

"This is totally unjust!"

"Maybe. But it gets worse. If you don't do as I ask, I'll make sure that Pedro and El Doctor know that when they don't get their legal trophies back, it was your fault. You see, Luís, this is in your hands. You can either make everyone happy or I'll make your best clients so mad, they'll probably fire you."

"You . . . you are a . . . a devious, malicious woman. This is blackmail," he stammered.

"I'm seeking justice for the wild animals in my country. I suggest you call Pedro and arrange for a meeting."

"But what if Pedro refuses to meet with you? I have no control over him."

"Pedro is fanatical about sheep. He wants his Dall trophy more than anything. I'm not accepting any excuses from you. Do your part of the bargain, Pedro will get his sheep trophy, El Doctor will get his moose trophy, and Junior gets his legal caribou."

"This makes me sick," he groaned.

"That's my offer."

Luís staggered over to the chair by the wall and collapsed into it. The bull was weakening. His face was flushed, and his carotid artery pressed against the no longer crisp collar of his white shirt. Resting his elbows on the heavily padded armrests of the chair, he held his head in his hands with his eyes closed as if he was carefully weighing his options. Then he looked up, glanced at his watch, stood up, and walked to an adjoining room that I assumed was an office with a phone. Breathing easier, I knew I was close to getting what I came for.

"Do you think we can leave soon?" whispered Gregorio across the table.

"I hope so. I think he went to call our boys."

"Of course," nodded Gregorio.

Exactly eight minutes later, Luís came back into the room his face looking tighter than when he'd left.

"Were you able to contact anyone?" I asked.

Sneering at me he said, "I'm still thinking about your proposition. I'll call you later at your hotel."

This delay tactic set me back. I didn't want to leave without a commitment from Luís that he'd cooperate. I didn't have time for delays but he wasn't giving me a choice.

"I'm at the Hotel Miguel Ángel. I expect to hear from you very soon. I must have this meeting by tomorrow."

"I'm aware of your time constraints," said Luís, still not giving any hints of what his intentions were. The bull wasn't down yet.

Reluctantly, I walked to the door as Luís escorted Gregorio and me outside. I smiled politely; otherwise, there were no pleasantries. Even though I was leaving empty-handed, Luís was in a very tight spot. Pedro especially was a belligerent, arrogant man who would have Luís for lunch when he heard the bad news.

At the car, Gregorio threw his jacket in the backseat and got into the driver's seat while I slid in on the other side. His white shirt hung limp over his shoulders and he seemed exhausted by the long afternoon.

"Whew, you are a very stubborn American woman."

I sunk into the seat. "I'm doing this for a ram."

"For a what?"

"Never mind. Luís better come through, or I'm done."

Gregorio winked at me and smiled. "He will. You've given him no choice."

"I hope you're right."

Gregorio started the car and roared down the narrow Calle Jose Abascal, taking an even more circuitous route than before out to a main street. He seemed very anxious to get back to the safe haven of the embassy.

It was 4:00 P.M., stores were reopening and traffic was increasing after the two-hour siesta. Soon we were back on the Paseo del la Castellana where Gregorio dropped me off at the Hotel Miguel Ángel.

"Let me know how it turns out," he said as I got out of the car.

"I will. Thanks for everything."

Inside the hotel I went straight to my room to wait for Luís's call. As I sank into an overstuffed chair, I tried to relax, but relaxing was an activity I had no talent for. I looked at my watch and realized there was just enough time to call the U.S. Embassy in Berlin.

When I got through to the regional security officer he informed me quite bluntly that the German government didn't want any U.S. officials interviewing Wilhelm. My travel to Germany had been denied. I knew right away what had happened. Wilhelm had used his wealth and influence to pull political strings and prevent my appearance.

The RSO had more news. "If you show up at the border, orders have been given to have you arrested. My advice is to stay away."

After all the disappointments I'd experienced in this case, this one burned more than any other. I slammed the phone down and shouted, "That jerk just got away with poaching our wildlife and we can't touch him!"

I thought of the animals he'd killed in Alaska with his money and how he'd thought nothing of it. We still had his trophies though, and I took some satisfaction in knowing that he'd never get them. Reluctantly I faced the fact that I had to give up on Wilhelm. In terms of making the case stick against Bowman, everything now hinged on the Spaniards. I hoped it was enough.

At around 6:00 P.M., I went to the hotel restaurant for tapas, traditional Spanish appetizers. I was too hungry to wait until 10:00 P.M. which was the normal Spanish dinner hour. I chose *patatas bravas*, which was a fried potato in a delectable sauce. I also had pork in olive oil and meatballs, but stayed away from the tripe and snails in hot sauce. There were at least thirty varieties of tapas to choose from so it took me nearly an hour of grazing until I was full.

Back in my room I sat by the phone. By 9:00 P.M., I was becoming increasingly worried that Luís was going to blow me off. Exhausted, I put the phone next to me on the bed and collapsed.

In the middle of a sound sleep, I heard a faint ringing near me on the bed. Raising my head, I looked at a nearby digital clock. It read 11:15 P.M.

I answered the phone. *"Diga."*

It was Luís. He was in the lobby bar and wanted to meet with me.

"I'll be there in five minutes," I replied, enormously relieved. I stood up and looked in the mirror as I quickly brushed my hair and applied a bit of makeup. Thanks to my nap I felt sufficiently rested for another round with *el toro.*

Downstairs, I found Luís standing nervously near the entrance to the bar. I was surprised to see that he wasn't alone. With him was a strikingly handsome man, with large black eyes and thick black hair. Luís introduced me to his friend Hugo, who took my right hand and held it sensuously in both of his hands for a few seconds.

He looked into my eyes and murmured, "It's a pleasure to meet you, *Señorita* Lucinda. *Que mujercita más linda!"* (What a beautiful woman you are!)

Hugo was the best-looking man who had ever paid attention to me. I was so caught off guard, I couldn't respond.

Then Luís spoke. "I talked to Pedro and he's outraged at your betrayal of him and at your outrageous proposition."

"Let him be mad," I said, regaining my composure.

"Let's go sit and talk some more," said Luís as he led the way into the dark, smoked-filled bar. He arranged three chairs and squeezed me in between him and Hugo. A whiff of Hugo's cologne made me swallow hard. This guy was too much.

Hugo leaned toward me, studying my face as if it was a fine Spanish sculpture and said, *"Las estrellas están llorando gatas de azul y su refugio es tu cara."*

Hugo was saying that the stars were raining blue and had taken refuge in my face, which I assumed was a compliment. Just then a waiter happened by to take drink orders.

"What would you like to drink?" asked Luís. "Wine, whiskey, a nice sherry?"

"Agua mineral," I told the waiter.

Ignoring Hugo the best I could, I turned to Luís. "Will your clients meet with me tomorrow?"

He lit a cigarette and blew smoke away from my face. "Pedro's lawyer says you have no basis for keeping his sheep. It's a legal sheep."

"I know it's legal, but I can still keep it."

"Why?"

"Because I have it."

"This is blackmail."

"No, it's the manner in which I choose to get Pedro and his friends to cooperate. They violated laws in the United States. Remember?"

Scotch and waters arrived for Hugo and Luís. Luís tapped ashes into an ashtray. "Perhaps there is a sum of money you would accept?"

His ludicrous suggestion made me laugh so loud I covered my mouth. "You've got to be joking. Forget it, Luís—the only way out of this is for you to make your clients give me what I want. Full confessions."

Then Hugo leaned over and whispered softly, "Let's forget this and go dancing."

Dancing? It became obvious that Hugo was there in a feeble attempt to woo me into forgetting about this whole thing. I couldn't let it go on another minute.

I stood up, glared at Hugo and spat, *"Suéltame, mujeriego!"* (Leave me alone, you womanizer.)

Hugo leaned back as if he'd been slapped. Then I turned sharply toward Luís. "You've got until noon tomorrow to arrange a meeting between me and your clients. If I don't hear from you, I'm leaving for the United States on the five o'clock flight, and your clients can forget about their trophies."

"But . . . but, what will you do with them?"

"Burn them. And it'll be your fault."

Luís reached toward me. "Please sit back down. We can talk some more."

I backed away. "There's no more talking. You know what I want. Arrange for the meeting, or I'm gone."

Quickly, I left the bar, only turning back briefly to see Luís and Hugo looking at each other as if they each had been hit by a wrecking ball. The bull was down for the count.

CHAPTER 28

War of Wits

JUST BEFORE NOON THE FOLLOWING DAY I was nervously pacing the floor of my hotel room when Luís called. "Jayne . . . *Señorita* Lucinda, my clients have agreed to meet with you with their lawyer. There's no guarantee that they'll cooperate, but they will talk with you. It's the best I could do. They said to call them when you arrive in Barcelona."

"Good job, Luís. That's all I wanted. Tell them they'll hear from me tomorrow."

I hung up the phone feeling lighter than air—I was finally winning this little war of wits. But I wasn't about to meet my adversaries alone: my first step in Barcelona would be to find allies.

I took a taxi back to the American Embassy where I booked a flight and hotel through their travel agency. Then I popped into Gregorio's office and told him the good news. A grin spilled across his face as he congratulated me for getting the better of Luís.

That evening I boarded a plane for the one-hour flight to Barcelona. Once seated I caught curious glances from other passengers eyeing the American flag pin I wore on the lapel of my blue blazer. At first the glances made me feel uncomfortable and I questioned my judgment for even wearing it. But then I reminded myself that I was an American in Spain on a critical mission for wildlife, and proud of it. The pin would stay.

Barcelona is in the province of Cataluñya, where the Catalán dialect is the official language. I don't understand or speak Catalán, but when I arrived at the hotel I learned that just about everyone in the region was well versed in Castilian, the dialect I knew.

The next morning I grabbed a cab to the Policia-Mossos de d'Esquadra, Bolivia 30–32 in downtown Barcelona. The cab dropped me off outside the police station, which bore a gold and red shield and a sign that read, GENERALITAT DE CATALUNYA, DEPARTMENT DE GOVERNACIÓ DIRECCIÓ GENERAL DE SEGURETAT CIUTADANA POLICIA-MOSSO D'ESQUADRA. Inside, a uniformed male clerk seated behind a counter said something to me in Catalán, which I didn't understand.

I showed my badge, and in Castilian said I was an investigator from the United States and wanted to speak with an investigator in the office regarding a wildlife case. The clerk seemed to understand me and for some reason thought this was a matter of great urgency. He picked up the phone and began speaking frantically in Catalán. Within minutes I heard several pairs of footsteps drumming down three flights of stairs—as if a fire drill was in progress.

Before I knew it there were three men, dressed in sport coats and ties, standing before me. They rattled off their names, shook my hand, and ushered me upstairs to an office with glass walls and a big round table. I set my briefcase on the table and presented my business card, and they gave me theirs. Now I knew who I was talking to.

The tallest of the three was Xavier Creus i Arolas. Xavier didn't look to be quite forty, although a few gray hairs were already creeping into his thick, curly black hair. His gentle face was set off by penetrating blue eyes and a thick mustache that was twisted at the ends. His card read, "*Cap de al Divisió de Serveis Especiales.*" He was the Captain of Special Services. We were in his office, and from the size of his desk and the number of plaques hanging on the wall, it was obvious that he was high ranking.

The second of the three was a short and stout man who appeared to be the oldest, just over forty. Slightly balding, he wore a perpetual smile that broke through a graying mustache. He was Francesc Jimenez i del Olmo, *Cap de l'Area del Medi Ambient.* He was in charge of the environmental department.

Enric Pérez was the youngest of the trio, still in his twenties. His olive complexion was clean shaven and his haircut was a conservative, almost military style. A well-worn tweed jacket hung over a set of narrow shoulders. He was an officer assigned to the environmental department and I could tell from his demeanor that he deferred greatly to Francesc and Xavier, who were his supervisors.

I felt an instant camaraderie with these three men who, like me, were law enforcement officers. Quickly, I explained that I needed their help to locate and interview three suspects who lived in Barcelona and had violated wildlife hunting laws in Alaska. The Spanish officers were immediately interested in the case and locked onto every word I uttered. But the pictures told the real story. When I displayed the photos of Pedro and El Doctor with their illegal grizzly bears, and explained how the animals were killed with the aid of a menacing aircraft, the look of disgust and contempt covered the faces of Francesc and Xavier. Enric was totally wide-eyed—I was sure he'd never heard a story like this one.

Francesc spoke first. *"Estes hombres son sinverquenzas. Como podemos ayudarle?"* (These men are despicable. How can we help you?)

I handed him the phone number for Pedro's lawyer. "They have agreed to meet me with their attorney, but I would like your assistance. I would like you to call Pedro's attorney, arrange a place and time for a meeting, and have someone go with me as a witness. I'll be getting written confessions, so it might take a couple of hours."

"You have already done a lot in this investigation," observed Xavier.

"Yes, but getting the confessions for our court is critical and I need them by tomorrow morning. Otherwise we may lose the case against our primary suspect who was the main pilot and organizer of the camp."

Xavier picked up the phone and called Pedro's lawyer. He said the meeting would take place at Pedro's restaurant at 9:30 the following morning.

I handed out three pages of questions in Spanish that I had prepared to ask Pedro, El Doctor, and Junior. By reading them Xavier, Francesc, and Enric got an even better feel for the case. Xavier decided that he and Francesc would accompany me. I was so relieved at my good fortune I was near disbelief. It was a very professional gesture for these two high-ranking investigators to accompany me.

That afternoon the Spanish officers introduced me to everyone they encountered in the hallways. Apparently I was the first investigator from the United States to ever drop by.

Around 2:00 P.M., a dozen of us went out for a delicious five-course meal, which I assumed was compliments of the police department since Xavier kept saying it was "free." The atmosphere was party-like and I reveled in the thought that not only did Pedro and his friends know I was coming, but that I was also bringing the police with me.

CHAPTER 29

The Sundance Kid

THE NEXT MORNING AT 8:00 SHARP, I arrived via taxi at the Policia-Mosso d'Esquadra station where the same young clerk waved me through. I was excited and energized because it was the day I was going to accomplish my mission in Spain.

I went directly to Xavier's office, where I found Francesc and Enric waiting. Francesc poured me a cup of very strong cappuccino and apologized for not having the weaker *café Americano*. After my first sip of coffee I sensed something was very different. The electricity that had been in the air the day before was gone. Enric's eyes looked almost fearful.

"What's going on?" I asked.

"We've been pulled off your case," explained Xavier.

"What?"

"Pedro called the mayor."

"Pedro knows the mayor of Barcelona?"

"Yes, the mayor eats at his restaurant. Pedro complained about our intervention. He argued that since he wasn't being investigated for violations of Spanish law that the Spanish police had no business being present during the meeting."

Francesc shrugged his shoulders. "In a way, he's right. Although we could have found some reason to question him, we don't have time. The meeting is in less than an hour from now."

"The mayor called the chief of police late last night. The chief called me at midnight. Believe me, this has created a big stir," said Xavier, who looked at me like this was the worst news he'd ever delivered.

I sat stoically, breathing deeply to control the sensation of fight or flight I was feeling. The plaques on the walls blurred and my mind spun, searching for options. But I couldn't find any. Xavier's words swirled around my head like gnats. All I really caught was that as much as they wanted to help me, they couldn't. They were so sorry. Enric looked totally bewildered.

Going at it alone would be extremely tough. I'd be outnumbered and out-maneuvered in a foreign setting. I didn't see how I could win. The Spanish hunters would never give me their confessions. I was at the end of my game, but had to play it out anyway. I couldn't go home without even trying.

Finally, I asked, "Do you have any blank statement forms I can use?"

"*Formas de Declaracion Voluntaria?*" asked Francesc.

"*Si.*"

Francesc left the office momentarily and came back with a short stack of forms that required the affiant to fill in his name, address, and date of birth at the top, and then sign at the bottom affirming that the statement provided was true and correct. It was an official police form, written in Castilian Spanish. Sitting at a computer, Francesc brought up the form and composed a short paragraph to suit my purpose and inserted it at the top of the form.

> *Ante me, LUCINDA D. SCHROEDER, Agente Especial del Ministerio del Interior, Division de Protección de al Naturaleza, perteneciente al Gobierno de Los Estados Unidos de America, comparce el Subdito Español . . .*

He printed off eight copies and handed them to me.

"*Gracias,*" I said as I slid the papers into my briefcase.

"I don't totally recommend that you go through with this. These men could be dangerous," cautioned Xavier.

"They can't kill me. They know that you know where I am."

The three men chuckled at my humor during such a dark moment.

Francesc put a firm arm around me to show his support. "We want you to come back here and tell us what happened."

I gulped. "I'll do that. I should get going though. Xavier, do you have the address for the cabdriver?"

He handed me the address to Pedro's restaurant; it was on the ritzy side of town.

I was at the door and had swallowed a couple of antacids when Enric, who had been virtually silent all morning, spoke up. "Wait!"

I turned. Had I forgotten something?

"I'm going with you."

"What?"

"It's too dangerous for you to go alone. I'm going with you. I'll be undercover."

"Undercover what?"

"I'll say that I'm with the American Consulate."

Francesc and Xavier exchanged surprised glances. I expected them to protest immediately, but they didn't.

Xavier responded first. "The orders were for Francesc and me not to attend the meeting. Nothing was said about Enric."

Francesc, who was Enric's immediate supervisor, had a different approach. "I won't order him not to go. I'm giving him the morning off. He can do what he wants."

Enric had an eager grin on his face, like the Sundance Kid, and seemed ready for action. "Let's go, or we'll be late. We'll take one of our unmarked cars."

I looked at Francesc and Xavier with grateful eyes. "*Mil gracias*. I'll watch him."

"He's supposed to watch you," winked Francesc.

Outside the police station, the wind was blustery and cold. I stopped for a moment and took the American flag pin off my blazer and pinned it onto Enric's lapel. "There. You're official."

He slapped his hands together. *"Vamos!"*

From the police station Enric maneuvered the car down Carrer de Mallorca past the incredible spirals of a cathedral called La Sagrada Família, built by the famous architect Gaudi. Then he veered off through a dozen side streets and finally to the El Restaurante Bodega. He parked the car on the corner of a one-way street, pure police style, so we could make a quick getaway if necessary.

The spotless thick glass doors to the restaurant were locked but when a white-jacketed waiter saw us, he responded immediately and opened it. I took his inhospitable demeanor as an indication that he knew why we were there.

"Follow me," he said with an edge to his voice.

The waiter led us through a large formal dinning room. The tables were covered with white tablecloths and set with crystal glassware and silver dinnerware. Not surprisingly, the walls were lined with Pedro's mounted trophies—all shrines to his ego. I spotted a greater kudu, a wildebeest, a Cape hartebeest, and two Barbary sheep, all from Africa. Another wall was dominated by several Alpine ibex from Europe. Conspicuously missing from his collection were North American sheep—the very reason Pedro had to have his Dall. But he didn't have it. I did.

Enric and I entered a waiting area where I noticed pornographic magazines thrown conspicuously about. This, in the presence of female employees, who were no doubt wives and mothers. *Pedro the pig,* I muttered to myself.

I was the first to enter Pedro's office, where he was leaning back in a large leather chair behind an expensive walnut desk, a picture window at his back. A cigar burned in an ashtray. He nodded in my direction as if to acknowledge me, but his dark eyes exuded pure contempt. His white shirt was wrinkled and perspiration stains showed under his armpits.

An oval conference table positioned in front of Pedro's desk accommodated six chairs. El Doctor, seated to the left of Pedro, stared at the tabletop, refusing to make eye contact with me. Next to him sat Junior, who looked at his former Scrabble partner with how-could-you-do-this eyes. Next to Junior was a paunchy man, wearing gold-rimmed bifocal glasses, a white shirt with a conservative blue tie, and suspenders. His suit jacket hung over the chair. I assumed that he was their lawyer.

As I took a seat in a chair on the opposite side of the table, Enric rattled off a phony name and said he was an associate from the American Consulate. He explained that it was policy that an American citizen be accompanied by someone from the consulate in such matters, although he had nothing to do with the investigation. "I'm just here as a courtesy," he added.

Everyone shook his hand cordially. I was surprised that no one questioned Enric's position nor asked to see a business card. I worried that if Enric's true identity was discovered, he could lose his job.

Pedro's lawyer, whose name I never caught, tried very hard to look important by taking the lead.

"Uh . . . *Agente* Sch . . ." He stumbled, unable to pronounce my name.

"You can call me Lucinda."

"*Si, Agente* Lucinda. We find your proposition totally unacceptable and demand that you release my client's Alaskan trophies immediately."

"I'd be happy to."

"*Si?*" The lawyer beamed with having gained my compliance so quickly.

"If they give me written and signed statements detailing their illegal hunting activities with Bob Bowman on their hunts in Alaska. No statements, no trophies."

The lawyer, Pedro, El Doctor, and Junior all shifted positions in their seats. An obvious sign that they didn't like what I'd said. I was in for a fight.

I glanced over at Enric, who sat quietly and confidently between the lawyer and me. The shiny American flag pin he wore made him look important and official. Enric was turning out to be the best backup I could have asked for. I just hoped that no one would realize that Enric didn't speak a word of English, which would blow his cover as an American Embassy employee.

I pulled out three subpoenas from the United States District Court in Alaska and laid them on the table. "I should first inform you that you've been subpoenaed to testify in a trial against Bob Bowman. Signed statements from each of you would preclude you from this obligation."

The lawyer picked up the subpoenas and looked them over. "I don't read English; I assume what you are telling us is true."

The lawyer looked at Enric who assured the lawyer that I was telling the truth.

"Of course what I say is true," I added. "You can see for yourself that the paperwork is official." In reality, they had been issued as a formality: no one expected the Spaniards actually to appear in court. In this instance I was using them as ammunition.

"Is this civil or criminal?" asked the lawyer.

"Criminal. All the violations I speak of are felony violations of federal law. This is a very serious matter."

The lawyer frowned and continued to review the papers that might as well have been written in Chinese. I sensed he wanted to speak to his clients in Catalán so I wouldn't understand the conversation, but with Enric present he didn't dare.

The lawyer tossed the papers back onto the table. "The American government can't make my clients testify."

"That's true. But you see, your clients have also been indicted by a federal grand jury in the United States for violating federal wildlife laws."

"So what does this mean?" asked Pedro.

"It means that your names have been placed in a U.S. Customs database and all three of you will be arrested if you ever attempt to enter the United States," I replied sternly. "Then you'll be tried, and if you're convicted, you'll serve time in jail."

Pedro looked like he'd been hit with a stun gun and was temporarily paralyzed. El Doctor choked up a cough and clutched his chest. Junior swayed in his chair. His skin was yellow, and his eyes were glazed over like a deer in headlights. I thought he might faint.

The smothering cigar smoke filled the closed room, making the temperature rise. The tension was as suffocating as the smoke.

Then I added calmly, "Of course all this could be cleared up if you cooperate today."

El Doctor looked at me. "You can have the American charges against us dropped?"

"Sure, that's part of the agreement. It's a very good deal for you."

"Are you a prosecutor?" asked the lawyer with an ugly, prim little grin.

"No, but I represent and speak for the American prosecutor. This proposal has already been approved."

"I see."

"Maybe we should consider this," said El Doctor cautiously. "I would like to go back to the United States and hunt someday."

"No way!" shouted Pedro. "This is blackmail. We only did what the professional hunting guides told us to do. We shouldn't be punished for that."

"Pedro," I said slowly, "may I remind you that you knew you were violating the law in Alaska. On the night of September 2, 1992, you told me that the only reason you chose Bowman as an outfitter was because you knew he used airplanes to illegally spot animals from the air and herd them to the hunter. You knew you were hunting in the wrong area, you knew that your grizzly bear was guaranteed, and that you wouldn't have to hunt like a real hunter. You admitted to me that you were a poacher."

"Lies. All lies," growled Pedro.

I pulled out the pictures of the Spaniards with their illegal wildlife, and slammed them on the table.

"All three of these animals are illegal. Gordon and Wild Bill have already confessed to what happened on these hunts. You already told me at the camp what happened. All you have to do is put it in writing. And if you do, Pedro, you'll get your Dall sheep back, Junior will get his legal caribou back, El Doctor will get his moose back, and all three of you will be able to return to the United States any time you want."

Pedro's face was flushed with near madness. "I won't!" He pointed to his lawyer. "Don't just sit there, do something."

The lawyer pulled at his collar. "This is a very complicated matter. I'm no . . ."

"Bullshit on all this!" screamed Pedro. "I'm not writing or signing anything and I want my sheep!"

I held up the picture of Pedro with his sheep. "Pedro, without statements from all three of you, you'll never see this trophy. When I get back to the United States I'm going to burn it." With that, I ripped the picture into two pieces.

Juniors eyes widened in shock, El Doctor dropped his head in defeat, and Pedro reeled back in his chair. He sounded like a screaming lunatic. "You are like the devil."

Then, there was a deathlike silence in the room, which meant I was getting close. I sensed that both El Doctor and Junior wanted to give in, but Pedro's arrogance was getting in the way. Perspiration had drenched the lawyer's shirt and he appeared lost in the swirl of American legalese. He, too, waited for Pedro to make the next move. All I had to do was convince Pedro, and the rest would follow.

Finally, I broke the silence. "Pedro, have you ever heard of Interpol?"

"Yes."

"They track international fugitives all over the world. They're very good at it."

I stood up, giving me the slight tactical advantage of height over my adversaries. "If you don't give me the statements, here, today, all three of you will lose your trophies and you'll be subject to arrest at any American border. On top of that, your names will be entered into the Interpol database as international fugitives."

The lines in Pedro's face deepened with a new level of understanding as he stared at me with a penetrating steely look.

CHAPTER 30

Truth or Consequences

"WHAT WAS MY PROFESSIONAL GUIDE'S NAME?" asked Junior looking up from the *Declaracion Voluntaria* he was writing.

"Bill," I answered. "B-i-l-l."

Pedro looked over at Junior. "Don't ask her any questions," he grumbled. "Just write. I want to get this over with."

I walked around the room like a schoolteacher checking on her students' essay work. Pedro and El Doctor wrote quickly, seemingly without much thought, while Junior was considerably more reflective.

Enric sat monitoring the progress, nodding his head in approval as the confessors wrote their statements. If there was the slightest complaint, he stopped it and firmly suggested that the bellyacher do as the *señorita agente* asked. He was better than a dreaded school principal with a big stick.

El Doctor finished his statement first and handed it to me. Quickly, I read it.

> *I contracted a hunt in Alaska with outfitter Bob Bowman. In Alaska, hunts are conducted under the instruction of the outfitter. On the bear hunt, we left the camp in the two airplanes. After an approximately three hours of flight, we landed and set up camp. On the next morning we saw a moose and a bear. I went with guide Gordon and we went for the moose at about eight in the morning.*

My partner left with another pilot and they went back to the base camp before midday. I remained with Bob and Gordon. Bob went flying and Gordon and I went hiking. After about an hour I saw Bob's airplane that was flying at low altitude. All of the sudden Gordon pointed to a bear that was running right towards us in front of the plane. The bear could not escape the plane. Gordon told me to shoot and I did, killing the bear at about 40 meters.

I knew we were going to use the airplane to hunt bear before going out and the señorita agente *has explained that my bear hunt was illegal and I regret my actions. I ask that in exchange for my statement today that my moose be returned to me.*

"This is very good," I said to El Doctor. "On the basis of this statement I'll be able to release your moose."

El Doctor tossed his pen in the middle of the table and slid back in his chair. The color was back in his face and he was breathing easier.

Junior handed me his short statement next.

In the month of September we contracted a hunt with B. Bowman to hunt caribou.

While hunting we saw a group of caribou. I fired a shot at one in the group. My guide, Bill, told me to shoot again. I picked out another animal and shot at it and saw it fall. When we went out to look, it was a great surprise to me to find two animals dead, because I didn't see the first one fall. Bill was very upset but to me it was an accident. Since my father had a license for caribou Mrs. Bob said we could use that one so that's what we did.

"Thank you, Junior. You did a very nice job."

Junior smiled radiantly for having pleased me.

Junior failed to mention that his father didn't have a caribou license and had purchased one after the fact, to cover the illegal caribou that Junior had shot. But this detail was already confirmed by both Gordon and me, so I let it go.

Finally, Pedro handed me his statement, which was difficult to read due to his hasty handwriting—which I felt was deliberate. After struggling through it once, I handed it back.

"You forgot to mention that you hunted your bear in an area you were not licensed for."

The lawyer spoke up. "Was this area posted with signs?"

"Of course not. That would be like posting the Pyrenees Mountains."

The lawyer shrugged.

Nice try, I thought.

"But I didn't know we were in the wrong area," protested Pedro.

"You did, too." I grabbed my case report and flipped through it. "You told me you knew on September 2, 1992, and again on September 3, 1992. You have to remember, Pedro, I took notes on every word you said."

I handed him a blank form. "Why don't you try again, I'm in no hurry. Also, you have too much stuff in there about how none of this was your fault. That's not the issue. Bowman is the one we're after, not you. Just write about what you did on your hunt with Bowman."

"Would you like to use my pen? It's a Lacrosse," offered Enric.

"No," grunted Pedro.

Fifteen minutes later Pedro produced another statement.

In 1992, I contracted the services of hunting outfitter Bob Bowman through a Spanish agency called "Caza Todo" to hunt the Dall sheep and grizzly bear. When I got to Alaska I was taken to the Bowman base camp. On the same day they took me to another camp to hunt the Dall sheep. I wasn't successful on this hunt because I suffered an accident. To make up for this, he gave me another chance two days later. After I finished this hunt we flew from base camp by plane, to another zone which took about three hours, after which we landed and made camp.

I had to shoot my bear with the help of Bob's plane because of my hurt back. He helped the bear to me. In the zone Bob took me to hunt there were no signs visible stating any prohibitions and at the time I was acting upon the instructions of the expert (Bob) I had contracted. I was surprised at the statement by the señorita agente *that the trophy I got was in an illegal area. The surprise is because of the good faith and confidence I had in the company that should have been competent and I must explain that my innocence is total and that I present this to reclaim the trophies that according to the* señorita agente *have been confiscated.*

Pedro still insisted on proclaiming his innocence, but he did say that Bowman took him hunting in an illegal area, and that Bowman herded a grizzly bear to him with an airplane. That's all I needed.

I looked at my watch. It was 6:00 A.M. in Fairbanks. Bowman was scheduled to appear in court in four hours. Enric and I had to get going. I shot Enric
an anxious glance and pointed to my watch. He nodded and stood up to leave.

"Gentlemen," I said, extending my hand to the lawyer. "We'll be leaving
now. Thank you for your cooperation."

Pedro, El Doctor, and Junior sat looking at me, like crumpled sacks that
had been thrown out after a bad lunch.

"When I get back to the United States I'll order the release of all your
legal trophies."

Enric and I hurried though Pedro's trophy hall and then outside onto
Calle Balboa where a chilly March wind was still blowing dust and newspa-
pers everywhere. The shelter of the car was a welcome relief. Once we had
turned two corners Enric reached under the seat and pulled out a red light
that had a magnet on the bottom and slammed it onto the dashboard. I
plugged it into the cigarette lighter and we had a flashing light that immediately caused the burgeoning traffic to yield to us.

At the Policia-Mosso d'Esquadra station, Enric and I met with Francesc
and Xavier, where Enric excitedly explained to them in Catalán about what
had transpired at the meeting. Meanwhile, I took refuge in a corner and concentrated on translating the three statements into English. Then I faxed the
original signed documents, along with the translated versions, to Fairbanks.
On the cover sheet I asked Eicher to call me the minute court was over. As I
watched the documents roll through the machine, I prayed that these would
end the war against wildlife that Bowman had waged for so many years.

Exhausted, I bid good-bye to my Spanish colleagues and took a cab back
to the hotel where I waited for Eicher to call.

———

CHAPTER 31

Come Home, Girl

AT THE HOTEL THAT NIGHT I laid on the bed watching the TV and the clock at the same time. The phone finally rang around midnight.

"Hey, it's me," said Eicher.

"Hi, Tim, I've been waiting for hours. Did you get my fax? What happened today?"

"Yeah, your fax came through fine. Great job by the way. How did you get those guys to confess?"

"I won't be telling that story for a long time. What happened in court?"

"AUSA Cooper got the statements to Bowman's lawyer right away. Bowman figured that since the Spaniards had written statements against him, they'd probably testify against him, too."

"And . . ."

"And he came into court with his lawyer and agreed to enter into a plea agreement. Guess he didn't think he'd survive a trial after all."

"That's fantastic! That's exactly what we wanted."

"I know. I've been on the phone all day with the Alaska Department of Fish and Wildlife, our Washington office, and the media. This case is making big news up here right now."

"What do you think will happen to Bowman?"

"The AUSA says jail time for sure."

"And a fine?"

"You bet. He's going to ask for fifteen thousand dollars. It all depends on the judge though."

"What about the camp?"

"The camp's history. Alaska Fish and Wildlife made a statement today that he'll be permanently barred from guiding or outfitting in Alaska. He won't even get a hunting license."

"Now that Bowman's pled guilty, the rest of his crew will take the fall, don't you think?"

"You bet. This will make the subsequent prosecutions a lot easier."

"Back to Bowman. Do you think he ever figured out who Roy and I really were?"

"Naw," chuckled Eicher. "He never saw you two comin'."

I sighed deeply, spilling out days of tension. "We won, we finally won. What do you want me to do now?"

"Come home, girl. You earned it."

Slowly, I hung up the phone and closed my eyes and let my mind drift back to the Brooks Range. I'd go back there someday. I'd hike it in new boots and see it through the eyes of a stronger woman. From high on a mountain, I'd watch the caribou move as soundlessly as smoke, while rivers ran around them like silver ribbons. I'd smile at the sky, empty of the tormenting machines that drove wolves and bears to their agonizing and certain deaths. I'd watch the moose and sheep that would no longer be unfairly hunted down. Like innocence, the wildlife lost to Bowman's greed could never be brought back. But the creatures born in their place would roam wild as they were intended.

Operation Brooks Range had been long in the making and although it had taken its toll, I had grown in the process. When I thought I'd exhausted the entirety of my physical and emotional energy, I was able to find more to carry on. When fears I didn't know existed nearly consumed me, I overcame them. When burdens nearly crushed me, I learned that it's not the load you carry, but how you carry it. But most of all, while hunting for justice for wildlife that had no voice of its own, I learned that faith in God has a special power, and that it is only when you give of yourself, that you truly give. And for that I'm eternally grateful.

Epilogue

THE SENTENCES IMPOSED ON THE DEFENDANTS in Operation Brooks Range were the result of plea bargain agreements made between the U.S. Attorney's Office in Fairbanks, Alaska, and the defense attorneys for the indicted individuals. Although each defendant faced numerous charges, many were dropped in exchange for guilty pleas or for information that helped in the prosecution of other defendants.

The laws violated were primarily the Airborne Hunting Act, which prohibits hunting with the aid of an aircraft, and the Lacey Act, which prohibits the transportation of wildlife taken in violation of state or federal laws, the possession of illegally taken wildlife, the export or attempted export of illegally taken wildlife, and "sale" of wildlife taken illegally, which includes money earned by illegal guiding.

Pilot and Outfitter BOB BOWMAN served fifteen months in a federal prison in Arizona and paid a ten-thousand-dollar fine. Upon release from prison he was placed on supervisory probation for a period of two years. He forfeited his Piper Super Cub to the State of Alaska, along with his .300 Winchester magnum rifle, and a Garmin GPS unit.

Pilot BILLY HOWE served ten months in a federal prison in Alaska, and paid a thirty-thousand-dollar fine. Upon release from prison he was placed under one year of supervised probation. He forfeited his Piper Super Cub to the U. S. Fish and Wildlife Service. (Howe faced additional charges from violations that took place in the 1980s.)

Pilot JACK WATSON paid a fine of five thousand dollars and was placed on one-year probation. He forfeited his plane to the U.S. Fish and Wildlife Service.

Guide DANNY BRIDGES served twenty-one days in a federal prison in Alaska. He paid a two-thousand-dollar fine and was placed under supervised probation for two years. He also lost his guide's license.

Guide GORDON MCALPINE served twenty days in a federal prison and was placed under two years probation.

Hunter PEDRO from Spain forfeited an illegal grizzly bear hide.

Hunter EL DOCTOR from Spain forfeited an illegal grizzly bear hide and a set of illegal caribou antlers.

Hunter WILHELM from Germany was later visited by German authorities who presented him with a Letter of Rogatory containing a series of questions regarding his illegal hunting activities in Alaska. Wilhelm returned a false statement indicating that all of his hunting was done legally. Although he was charged by the U.S. Department of Justice, he refused to return to the U.S. and was never tried. His trophies remain in U.S. custody.

Guide MOOSE JAMES paid a twenty-five-hundred-dollar fine and forfeited the life-size grizzly bear mounted and displayed in his place of business, The Bear's Den.

Hunter ERIC SHEPARD forfeited a set of moose antlers from moose he hunted illegally with Bowman.

Hunter THOMAS SAGE forfeited a life-sized mounted "black" timber wolf that he shot while his guide chased it on a snowmobile in the spring of 1992.

Hunter "TED" aka Jerry Warner, was charged by the State of Alaska for hunting with another person's license. The original license holder had suffered a house fire and had sold his license to "Ted."

A dozen other hunters not mentioned in this story were cited for possession of illegal trophies they had hunted while at Bowman's camp during previous years.

* * *

Informant ROY HANSON received an award from the U.S. Fish and Wildlife Service for his valued contribution to this case. He died in October 2003, of organ failure, at age fifty-two.

* * *

For our work in Operation Brooks Range, Special Agent Tim Eicher received a Special Achievement Award from the U.S. Fish and Wildlife Service and I received one of the Service's "Ten Top Employees" awards. A few years later, Tim Eicher transferred to Wyoming, and I transferred to New Mexico to assume a supervisor's position. I left that position and joined an undercover unit, and finished my career working covert investigations that uncovered sophisticated criminal schemes designed to exploit wildlife. I often coordinated my cases with foreign governments and other federal agencies such as the FBI, the IRS, the USDA, and the U.S. Park Service. I retired in 2004, and soon after was invited to Lillehammer, Norway, to speak at the FBI's National Academy Associates conference on International Organized Crime about international cooperation in combating crime.

As with anyone who has worked in a profession for nearly thirty years, I've seen a lot of changes. In the days of Willie J. Parker, special agents spent a lot more time in the field and the office was viewed as a place of last resort. Agents knew that most of the time violators had to be caught red-handed. Too few hunters and informants were willing to report violations, a fact that is even truer today.

Due to the inherent difficulties in apprehending wildlife violators, it takes specialized expertise and a great deal of time to get the job done. Today's U.S. Fish and Wildlife Service special agents are fighting better organized and more sophisticated wildlife criminals than ever before. Supervisors, who in years past carried a small case load, are now burdened with so many mandatory administrative and noninvestigative duties that they can barely keep up. Meanwhile, much of an agent's time is now consumed with time management reports, gas usage reports, travel vouchers, safety reports, business books, surveys, financial disclosure reports, property inventory reports, and the list goes on. These time-robbers don't include the enormous amount of time it takes agents to type their own case reports, and to enter data regarding seized evidence and court dispositions into a notoriously slow computer program.

U.S. Fish and Wildlife Service special agents today are dedicated and hard working, but are desperate for more time to conduct the lengthy and complex investigations that most benefits our natural resources. Keeping the agents in the field is critical to enforcing important conservation laws such as the Endangered Species Act, the Migratory Bird Treaty Act, the Bald and Golden Eagle Protection Act, the Marine Mammal Act, the Airborne Hunting Act, and the Lacey Act. When these laws can't be enforced, wildlife and plants can't be adequately protected, making their measured demise certain.

In stark contrast to other federal agencies, the U.S. Fish and Wildlife agent force has remained a relative constant in the last thirty years. The number of agents has only grown from around 200 to 220 agents nationwide. While agent positions exist, managers are forced to leave them vacant to save funds for their regular operating budgets. In short, more funds and a larger agent force with a stronger support staff are the basic essentials needed to protect what is wild and free about America.